Living Stones of the Himalayas

ADVENTURES OF
AN AMERICAN COUPLE
IN NEPAL

Thomas Hale

ZondervanPublishingHouse
Grand Rapids, Michigan

A Division of HarperCollinsPublishers

Living Stones of the Himalayas
Copyright © 1993 by Thomas Hale

Requests for information should be addressed to:
Zondervan Publishing House
Grand Rapids, Michigan 49530

Home Mission: Interserve (International Service Fellowship),
Box 418, Upper Darby, PA 19802
Field Mission: United Mission to Nepal, Box 126
Kathmandu, Nepal

Library of Congress Cataloging in Publication Data

Hale, Thomas, 1937–
    Living stones of the Himalayas : adventures of a Christian in Nepal / Thomas
Hale.
        p. cm.
    ISBN 0-310-38511-3
    1. Hale, Thomas, 1937–   . 2. Surgeons—United States—Biography. 3.
Missionaries, Medical—Nepal—Biography. 4. Missionaries, Medical—United
States—Biography. 5. Hale, Thomas, 1937–   . I. Title.
    RD27.5.H33A34   1993
    617′.092—dc20
    [B]   93-18398
                                                                        CIP

Edited by Linda Vanderzalm
Cover design by John Lucas
Cover photo by Tom Hale

Printed in the United States of America

93 94 95 96 97 98 99 00 / DH / 10 9 8 7 6 5 4 3 2 1

CONTENTS

ABOUT THE AUTHOR

TOM HALE AND HIS WIFE, CYNTHIA, serve as medical missionaries under the United Mission to Nepal. For the first twelve years they served in a rural mission hospital in the village of Amp Pipal, the setting for most of the events in this book. Subsequently they have moved to Kathmandu, Nepal's capital city, where they have continued their work with the mission. Recently Cynthia has taken a position as associate professor at Nepal's only medical school, and Tom has written a one-volume commentary on the New Testament, first in Nepali and subsequently in English for translation into other languages.

During their high-school years Tom and Cynthia were both called by God to serve as medical missionaries. Though they both grew up in Albany, New York, they did not meet until the first day of medical school, when they were assigned to the same cadaver in the anatomy lab. In such a romantic setting—and in view of their similar calling—marriage was inevitable.

After Tom completed training in general surgery, and Cynthia in pediatrics, they left for Nepal in 1970, with their two sons, Chris and Tom, who now have taken up missionary careers of their own. Chris serves with Operation Mobilization in India, and Tom serves with Interserve in the Central Asian Republics.

Many of the Hale family's adventures have been related in two previous Zondervan books, *Don't Let the Goats Eat the Loquat Trees* and *On the Far Side of Liglig Mountain*.

An Enchanted Land

WHEN PEOPLE in the States hear that Cynthia and I work in Nepal, they conjure up visions of a remote mountain kingdom inhabited by quaintly dressed tribal people dwelling in thatch-roofed villages that are unspoiled by the creeping inroads of the twentieth century. And their picture, as far as it goes, would be correct. Nepal is indeed a unique and intriguing land, a storybook kingdom of royal palaces, exotic temples, breathtaking scenery, fearless Gurkha soldiers, tiger hunts in sweltering jungles, bleak desert highlands, and even, it is said, abominable snowmen. But this romantic picture no more reveals the real Nepal than the skyline of a city reveals the quality of life in its streets. To get a truer picture of Nepal, travel with us through the following chapters and meet some of the people who inhabit this enchanted land.

Nepal, a country the size of Tennessee, is home to twenty million people. Sandwiched between two giant neighbors, India and China, Nepal straddles the mightiest mountains on earth, the Himalayas, which run east and west throughout its entire length. In all the world only two countries are predominantly Hindu: Nepal and India. India regards all faiths equally, but Nepal does not. Until recently Nepal has been a theocracy whose king is regarded as an incarnation of Vishnu, one of the three major Hindu gods. And although technically all people in Nepal are free to practice their own religion, Nepali citizens face severe persecution from society if they forsake their Hindu faith and follow another religion. This is tantamount to betraying both their country and their king.

Of Nepal's many distinctive features, it is the topography that most determines the whole character of life in Nepal, from the weather to the way farmers plant their fields. Many people think of Nepal mainly as a land of ice, snow, and high mountain peaks; but, in fact, most of its people live below 5000 feet. Large parts of the country are barely above sea level, in particular the densely populated southern portion that slopes into the broad Ganges River basin at the same latitude as southern Florida. From there, low-lying valleys run northward, cutting into the very base of the highest mountains and creating an irregular network of deep winding gorges all but lost beneath the steeply rising ridges on either side. To illustrate the extreme variation in altitude, imagine yourself at a point fifteen miles from our home in the village of Amp Pipal. Within the space of only two miles, the elevation changes from a valley floor 2000 feet above sea level right up to 26,000 feet—the sharpest change of elevation found anywhere on earth!

The variation in climate is equally extreme, ranging from torrid heat to biting cold. Indeed, the Nepalis' whole manner of living varies according to the altitude at which they live. Within an hour's walk up or down a mountain, travelers can find groups of Nepalis that dress differently from one another, build their houses differently, plant different crops, and even speak different languages. And all of them to a greater or lesser degree are isolated from each other and from the outside world by the difficult mountainous terrain.

The great majority of Nepal's people are subsistence farmers—illiterate, superstitious, set in their ways, sharing much in common with the poor of all developing countries. However, Nepalis possess several attributes that set them apart from most other people. The first of these is their unaffected frankness and friendliness. Never having lived under colonial rule, Nepalis treat foreigners in a natural and casual manner, with none of the hostility seen so commonly elsewhere. They are engaging to talk to and will agree with anything you say in order to please you. If you are a traveler in their hills, they will make you feel at home, take pains to look after your welfare, and ply you with personal questions, eagerly curious to know all about who you are, what you're doing in their country, whether or not you're married and, if not, why not—all without meaning the slightest offense. You feel that they like you, and it's very hard not to like them back.

Nepalis are also remarkably honest. Porters, who carry loads for trekkers and others, can be consistently trusted with goods of high value, even though at the end of an entire day's journey they will receive a wage amounting to only one or two dollars. Patients coming to a hospital bring whatever money they've saved and even sell their possessions in order to pay their hospital bills. They wear their best clothes to see the doctor even though they know that if they had dressed in rags and pretended to be poor, they could have gotten their treatment free. Deception is not a way of life in the hills of Nepal.

The third distinctive feature of the Nepali people is the degree to which their lives are bound by their religious beliefs. The chief religion of the country, Hinduism, is liberally intermingled with varying elements of Buddhism, animism, spirit worship, and magic. Visitors to Nepal's capital, Kathmandu, find themselves surrounded by temples of all descriptions and by a profusion of gods varying from enormous, grotesque figures to small painted stones set in little shrines along the streets. The pervasive influence of the priests and astrologers affects not only the lives of individuals but also the timing and conduct of important government functions.

Hindus believe that all matter is really of one essence. Thus Nepalis find it perfectly reasonable and acceptable that flowers and bushes should take root in the mortar of their houses, that their walls and floors should be plastered with mud and cow dung, and that their courtyards should function as latrines and the alleys of their cities as sewers. To many Nepalis the whole idea of germs is just another peculiar Western superstition; in their minds, disease is simply a dispensation of the gods. In view of this, it isn't surprising that standards of sanitation and hygiene are low and that diseases spread easily among the people, especially in rural areas where footpaths and village streets all too often serve as public toilets. Indeed, one of the first lessons learned in Nepal is to watch your step and keep to the middle of the road.

Actually, there is much truth to the Nepalis' belief in the unity of all matter, as a walk down any back street in Kathmandu will readily—and graphically—demonstrate. A few years ago while showing Cynthia's brother, Dicran, some of the sights around the Kathmandu valley, we happened on a small boy squatting down to relieve himself in the alley along which we were passing. No sooner had he finished, than two hens arrived and gobbled up his production. Within a minute the street was clean again. It beat any sanitation department we knew of—and it was cheaper besides. In the next block we went by a meat shop where plucked chickens hung in rows outside the door. As Dicran stared at the chickens, the thought of what they must have eaten all their lives gave him such a shudder that he couldn't look at chicken meat for the rest of his time in Nepal. He had taken to heart the idea that all matter is one.

It doesn't do, however, to poke fun at newcomers to the country: We all have been newcomers at one time or other. I well remember one afternoon soon after we had moved to Nepal when I experienced in a very tangible way some of the outworkings of this concept that all matter is one and the same. I had been told that to get anywhere in Kathmandu a bicycle was the most useful and inexpensive method of transportation. So, shortly after our arrival at the United Mission language school, I purchased a fine Indian-made model and immediately rode off into town. I was shaky at first, not having ridden a bicycle in almost twenty years, and I was certainly unfamiliar with the hazards of riding on the streets of Kathmandu. Soon I was pedaling into an intriguing part of the city I hadn't seen before, and lured on by the exhilarating sounds and sights and smells, I eventually found myself on a busy thoroughfare that led down a rather steep incline. The street was cluttered with carts and pedicabs, playing children, piles of garbage here and there, and the ubiquitous droppings of cows and buffalos. Along each side of the uneven pavement ran the open gutters, which I had already learned to avoid with care. Gathering speed, I tested my brakes, only to find they had gone askew somehow and were almost useless. At that moment I spotted a boy squatting to relieve himself on my side of the street. Realizing that the child wouldn't move out of the way, I started to swerve toward the middle of the road. But just then a large bus belching oily black exhaust came bearing down on me from behind, and at the same moment a taxicab ripped around a corner ahead of me and started coming my way. Seeing no room on the street for bus, taxicab, squatting child, and me, I swerved off the pavement and into the gutter.

The first thing I encountered with my left handlebar (we drive on the left in Nepal) was a stringy-haired *sannyasi* (holy man) muttering his incantations, the volume and fervor of which heightened perceptibly as I passed. Immediately in front of me two dogs appeared out of nowhere, then several goats and a quantity of chickens. But they were not the main problem: Two large water buffalos were moving rapidly out of the path of the bus. The only way past them was blocked by an eight-inch stone image protruding up from the gutter. At the crucial instant, as I was about to execute a highly complex maneuver, somebody dumped a large pail of vegetable peelings directly onto my path from an upstairs window. I also remember the manure-saturated tail of one of the buffalos catching me squarely on the neck as I flew past. I had no time for reflection or recrimination.

I hit the little stone image dead on the center and shot into the air. Somehow I landed back on the bicycle and grasped for the handlebars to keep from falling. In fact, the only thing wrong was that the seat had fallen off during the bump, leaving only an upright pipe in its place. I came away from the experience, if not convinced of the unity of all matter, at least impressed with its interrelatedness.

Hinduism embraces a broad spectrum of religious beliefs and practices, from primitive and superstitious idol worship to lofty ethical and philosophical heights. Most popular forms of

Hinduism are, of course, corruptions of the ideal; yet it is these popular forms that are prevalent among the ordinary people of Nepal.

Nepalis are generally far more religious and correspondingly less materialistic than Westerners. They see their gods as real— spiritual powers to be feared and appeased. Nepalis believe that every detail of their lives is ultimately determined by one or more of these gods. The people try hard to influence the outcome of any event by observing appropriate rituals and offering sacrifices, but when that is done, they are quite content to leave the matter with the gods.

The ordinary villagers, then, maintain a general attitude of shrugging resignation to their fate, an attitude that is largely free of the restlessness and discontent so common in the West. This attitude of resignation has both a good and a bad side: On the good side, it has contributed greatly to the stability of Nepali society; on the bad side, it has perpetuated a social system that oppresses not only the lowest castes but also women in general. This social system is the most regrettable legacy of the Hinduism practiced in rural Nepal.

The caste system has been officially outlawed by the government and is uniformly decried by the educated classes, who are doing their best to eliminate it from Nepali society; nevertheless, it persists throughout the land, reinforced by centuries of tradition and by the Hindu doctrine of *karma*, which stipulates that a person's condition in this life is predetermined by his previous life, and that he'd best accept it—a concept altogether guaranteed to kill any inclination toward social progress and reform.

The lives of most Nepalis are still conditioned in one way or another by their caste. A Nepali's house can be defiled if entered by a member of a lower caste (or a foreigner), requiring the costly ministrations of a priest to purify it, as well as a new layer of mud and cow manure for the walls and floors. Low-caste Nepalis are in reality outcasts. They are almost always the poorest people in a community, living apart from the rest of the village and having little or no land of their own. Many low-caste

Nepalis work as porters for our mission, and as a result we have come to know many of them. They often have arrived exhausted, late in the evening, with a heavy load for the hospital, only to be denied both food and lodging at the nearby teashops that serve as hotels. We've seen them forced to sleep in the gutter on a rainy night. When we know about it, we give them lodging ourselves.

Most sobering of all, however, is to behold the people as they worship: To see them kneel before images of great six-armed, sword-wielding gods carrying handfuls of severed heads; to watch them sacrifice thousands of animals during the Hindu festival of *Dasai*; to see the fear, the fatalism, the hopelessness that is written on their faces. Although Nepalis may at times seem cheerful and even carefree, it is in spite of their religion, not because of it.

We have been told by some of our friends how nice it is that we have come to Nepal to practice medicine—as long as we don't tamper with the beliefs and customs of the people. And to a point we would agree: There are many aspects of Nepali culture we admire, and we try to reinforce these every way we can. But as for *religious* beliefs and customs, if our friends could see what a heavy burden these lay on the shoulders of Nepal's people, they would understand that the spiritual affliction here is as grave as the physical illnesses we have come to treat. Our concern extends to those oppressed in spirit as well as body, whether they are outcasts, women, or simply those in bondage to fear, the fear of gods who inspire terror in place of hope.

Aside from three-day sanitized excursions to view Mount Everest or the Annapurnas, or to watch overfed tigers eat their evening ration of fresh meat at a jungle tourist hotel, most visitors to Nepal never get beyond the Kathmandu valley. For most of them, Kathmandu is experience enough. But let them just step out of Kathmandu and into the country, where ninety percent of Nepalis live, and they enter another realm altogether. And the link with civilization, as they knew it, is cut.

The most striking aspect of life in the Himalayan foothills is the sense of remoteness and primitiveness, arising largely from the absence of electric power lines, telephone communications, and roads. The geography of the region in itself accounts for much of the isolation. Except for the Kathmandu valley and a narrow strip of alluvial plain along its southern border, Nepal has almost no flat land. Just visiting a neighboring village may mean descending thousands of feet into a precipitous river gorge and then climbing over steep ridges rising to more than 10,000 feet.

In the rainy season, from June to October, contact even between nearby communities is severely curtailed because the trails, previously thick with the dust of the dry season, are turned to slippery mud, and the little trickling streams become broad and dangerous torrents. Footbridges are frequently washed away by floods, and much of the energy and money that should be expended on new bridges is used up in rebuilding old ones. Far worse is the damage that occurs to Nepal's sparse highway system each monsoon season. Washouts and landslides are commonplace; sometimes many days pass before a road can be opened, and in the meantime all travel and transport comes to a halt. During bad floods hundreds of workers with their baskets and shovels are enlisted to help clear the roads; on occasion the army aids in the effort. One of our mission doctors once found himself caught between two landslides: Having run into one landslide, he turned around to drive back, only to come on a second landslide that had occurred in the meantime. He ended up stranded for three days.

It was into this rural setting that the first Amp Pipal missionaries came, some as agricultural specialists, some as teachers, others as doctors and nurses. In the 1950s, when foreigners were first allowed to work in Nepal, the country had two immediate and desperate needs: education and health. Villages in the hills had virtually no schools or medical facilities. Of slightly less urgency but ultimately crucial for an overpopulated agricultural society was the need for improved farming techniques. Therefore His Majesty's Government gave the newly formed United Mission to Nepal permission to open schools, dispensaries, and agricultural projects in several areas in the interior, one of which was the village of Amp Pipal in Gorkha District, sixty miles—as a crow flies—northwest of Kathmandu.

From the beginning, the undertaking at Amp Pipal was envisioned as a community service project to include education, medical, and agricultural work. First, the mission established a school, which was an immediate success. Then a Saskatchewan wheat farmer started a demonstration farm to introduce villagers to new crops and fertilizers, to provide seeds and fruit-tree seedlings, and to breed the village cows with a high-grade species of bull. And over the years, except for a period when the government shut down the farm, the agricultural work has grown to include reforestation, village water systems, nutrition, and agricultural extension work.

At about the same time the farm was started, the mission opened a small dispensary, staffed by two missionary nurses. Soon they found themselves swamped by multitudes of very sick patients, so they called for the help of a physician who could treat the seriously ill. Dr. Helen Huston, a Canadian who had been working in Kathmandu, responded to the need, and Helen moved out to Amp Pipal to take charge of the dispensary in 1960. However, increasing the staff only increased the workload; and within a few years Dr. Helen and her two nursing colleagues were seeing twenty thousand patients a year, many of whom needed inpatient care. In response Dr. Helen made plans to construct a small hospital, to be located twenty minutes down the mountain from Amp Pipal. Thus was born the Amp Pipal Hospital, which opened in 1970, the same year Cynthia and I arrived in Nepal. And it has been our privilege and joy to share in its growing pains—just as it has shared in ours.

Patients and Patience

Of Cleft Lips and Cataracts

L EPROSY IS a major health concern in the hills of Nepal, as indicated by the patients who come to the Amp Pipal Hospital with their white spots, red bumps, palsied hands and feet, missing fingers, and sores—terrible sores—to name just a few of leprosy's complications. One such patient was an attractive seventeen-year-old young woman who had walked ten days from her village near the Tibetan border to reach the hospital, a journey that would have taken only five days for a healthy person. The reason it took her so long quickly became apparent when we took off her yak-skin boots: Her feet were covered with putrid sores, the flesh eaten away by the secondary infection that often accompanies the primary lesions of leprosy. Her feet were literally rotting inside her boots—which, of course, hadn't been removed for at least the ten days of her journey. Getting those boots off produced an odor that was truly breathtaking—and it did wonders for her feet too. By the end of the month in the hospital they were nearly healed.

The young woman spoke only her Tibetan dialect, so we couldn't communicate with her except through her mother, an unusually alert and intelligent woman who spoke fluent Nepali. We asked the mother if other villagers had the same disease, and she said she thought there were many. But most of them were poor, she added, and could never hope to come to the hospital. Even she hadn't been able to afford porters to carry her daughter for such a long journey. When the mother and daughter finally decided it was time to leave, we tried to persuade them to stay until the daughter's feet were completely healed, knowing that another eight to ten days on the trail in those boots would probably wipe out all benefit gained from her month in the hospital. However, they insisted on going, not for the usual reason that their money had run out, but because the warm weather was approaching, and since they were accustomed to a colder climate, they were afraid of dying on the trail from the heat.

The hospital staff also see lots of broken bones, most of them the result of falls from trees. Such was the story of one middle-aged patient who had been high up in a tree getting leaves for his goats when the branch on which he was sitting suddenly broke. The next thing he knew, he was lying on the ground with a sharp pain in his back and a funny tingling in his legs. He went home and lay down for a few days, but not getting better, he decided to walk to the hospital. He came alone, without a friend or relative, because it was rice-harvesting time and no one was free to accompany him, much less carry him. When I first saw him, I thought he was drunk. He bounded into my office like a puppet on strings, his feet bouncing off the floor as if he had springs in his shoes—except he had no shoes. As he came toward me, I thought he would overshoot his seat. When he took off his shirt, I could see at once the cause of his problem: His back was broken, with an amazing forty-degree angulation at the fracture site. His peculiar gait was the result of increased reflexes in his legs, an ominous sign that his spinal cord was under pressure and that paralysis was imminent. No wonder, then, that what would ordinarily have been a one-day walk had taken this man four days—hardly the recommended treatment for an acutely fractured spine!

I told him he would have to be admitted to the hospital, but he threw up his hands and said he couldn't possibly stay: He had no *saathi* (friend) to stay with him and cook his food (as was the custom), he had only enough money left to buy food for the way home, and besides, all he had come for anyway was an injection and some *mollish* (menthol-scented Vaseline) to rub on his back. It was not hard to convince him to stay, however, once I pointed out to him that he would be totally paralyzed before he reached home. He could believe it too, because he had been getting progressively weaker each day. So he became one of our numerous charity patients, receiving completely free of charge not only his medical treatment but also his food.

Despite my fears, he improved rapidly, and within ten days the pain in his back had gone, and his legs had stopped jumping. As soon as he saw he was going to get better, he insisted on leaving. Lectures, pleadings, threats, promises of food—nothing could persuade him to stay. So we wrapped him in a plaster-of-paris jacket to provide some semblance of protection for his incompletely healed back and sent him off with the uneasy feeling that he would take the plaster off himself as soon as he got home and that the next time we saw him he would be completely paralyzed. But he never came back, which can mean either that he recovered or that he did not. Either way, he wouldn't have been inclined to make that long trip again.

Orthopedic practice in Nepal is not limited to broken backs, of course. We have seen everything from smashed toes to smashed skulls—like the recent case of a sixteen-year-old boy who fell headlong out of a tree onto a pointed rock, sustaining a severe compound depressed skull fracture. He was finally brought to us ten days after the injury, unconscious, extruded brain caked on his face. He recovered completely.

Trees aren't the only cause of fractures in Nepal. Nepal's innumerable cliffs provide us with plenty of business—as long as the victims don't die at the bottom. One day during a lunch hour, I actually watched two young women fall from a thirty-foot cliff on Liglig Mountain when the ledge they were sitting on gave way. We could hear them screaming. Some of our hospital staff went out with stretchers to fetch them. One had only a broken leg and was treated and discharged. The other had a badly lacerated face, together with a shattered jaw that we had to wire together. So much for cliffs.

One source of broken bones unique to Nepal is the Nepali version of the Ferris wheel, the Nepali *ping,* a homemade contrivance whose four wooden seats rotate on an axle suspended between two upright piles. During the main festival month in autumn, nearly every village assembles a *ping*. Its free-swinging seats revolve at a reckless speed, banging heads, knocking out teeth, breaking bones, and even hurtling unsuspecting riders for surprising distances through the air. One young boy was flung from a *ping* onto his outstretched hands and ended up with two compound wrist fractures. But the most astounding *ping* injury of all happened to a young girl who somehow got her long hair tangled up in the works, which ripped off the entire thickness of the scalp from her skull. We have no need of the automobile here to liven up our casualty department!

Some of the more agonizing cases we encounter are the result of obstetrical complications, so common in medically underdeveloped areas. Each year we see dozens of women in labor who, after spending days at home in agony, finally arrive at the hospital in critical condition. I remember the eighteen-year-old young woman who had been in obstructed labor for several days and who was brought by her family only after the protruding head of the infant had turned black and gangrenous. We removed the baby, but the young mother's entire pelvis was severely infected, with large communications present between the bladder, vagina, and rectum, causing incontinence of stool and urine.

She remained desperately ill for weeks and nearly died on several occasions. It was her first child, and her young husband, also eighteen, manifested unusual tenderness and love for her to a degree rarely shown by husbands to their wives in this society. It wasn't on his account that the young woman had come so late; he would have brought her sooner. But in Nepal, a young wife is completely under the jurisdiction of her mother-in-law, and the young husband has almost no say in what happens to her. The mother-in-law, who more often than not was herself treated harshly as a new bride, makes no effort to make it any easier for her daughter-in-law. After all, it's her turn to enjoy life now; let the younger one labor. Thus, this particular mother-in-law had balked at taking the young wife to the doctor: It was too expensive and just plain inconvenient. So the poor woman had remained all that time at home, and her husband had been powerless to do anything about it.

Even when the mother-in-law finally relented, they were further delayed because they couldn't find porters to carry the woman. Giving birth makes a woman "unclean," and those coming in contact with her have to undergo costly rites of purification. Even if porters can be found, they charge double the price. It's no wonder we see labor cases so late.

During the young woman's first few days in the hospital, her relatives were attentive and caring. But once it became apparent that her childbearing potential had been lost, the family—with the exception of her husband—lost interest and no longer came to the hospital to see her. The young husband was obviously touched, even encouraged, by the love and concern of the hospital staff for his wife, who would ordinarily have been cast off as useless. He stayed with her alone, week after week, until his savings were exhausted and he had sold his possessions to pay for the treatment. After that we began giving the medical care free, and members of the church helped with their meals. We constantly wondered how vigorous (and costly) our treatment should be, considering the young woman's bleak outlook and her need for several further operations and months of hospitalization.

As time passed, however, the husband grew discouraged: He could see no end to her ordeal. When at last he took her home after six weeks in the hospital, she was still debilitated and in great pain. Nevertheless, she had been showing faint signs of improvement, and we even had begun to hope she might make it. It was not to be: After suffering at home for several more months, she finally died. It was a sad ending to an all-too-common sequence of events.

Nepalis regard surgery as a very special and awesome form of treatment. Nepalis are happy to take pills; they have been doing it for years. They are delighted to receive injections, believing them to possess a special potency deriving from their painful method of administration. Some come from a day away just to receive a vitamin injection, and many other patients can be expected to ask for one if we have neglected to prescribe it. Even the lancing of boils is readily submitted to, because in their everyday experience Nepalis have learned that when the evil material is released, the pain and fever subside and the wound heals.

But an operation is another matter. Surgery has had to earn its acceptance. We have had to contend with several popular prejudices, among them the belief that witches can enter the body through an operative wound and thereby "possess" the patient. Also prevalent is the notion that following surgery a person won't be able to carry loads, have children, eat meat, and do a lot of other things that are considered important and enjoyable. Gradually these superstitions have been overcome as more and more people have had surgery without experiencing these undesirable consequences. In fact, the chief remaining barrier to the acceptance of surgery is the expense. Most Nepalis find the cost of surgery prohibitive, even at the low price of twelve dollars for a major operation. This is particularly true when the less productive members of society, such as the elderly, require surgery. The average family can't afford to spend that much on someone who can't work, even when the condition is easily curable.

A common problem is the many elderly Nepalis who are blind with cataracts and end up sitting out their last years in a dark corner of the house. One sixty-year-old man had been for many years not only blind from cataracts but also deaf. Most of the world had been shut off from him, except for the love and devotion of his two sons. Having heard that we operated on cataracts, they brought their father a two days' journey to the hospital, the old man protesting all the while that he would have nothing to do with any operation. The patient presented a serious problem for us since we could not communicate with him except through his sons, who had to shout directly into his ear at the top of their voices just to gain his attention. The old man was stubborn and irascible, and what's more, to make up for the loss of his sight and hearing and to keep in touch with his environment—and perhaps, at times, just to entertain himself—

he kept up a loud and steady barrage of pontifications on every imaginable subject, including, of course, the sufferings he was undergoing at the hands of "these hospital people."

He finally gave his vague agreement to surgery; but when he got to the operating room, he promptly retracted it, claiming he had been "tricked." The sons managed to calm him down and with great difficulty persuaded him once more to go through with the surgery. The operation turned out to be a more hair-raising one than either he or his surgeon had bargained for. Cataract extraction is a delicate procedure, and in Amp Pipal it is done under local anesthesia, which eliminates the risk of general anesthesia in an elderly patient. It was therefore necessary to station one of the sons next to the old man's ear to scream instructions at him and to keep him from sitting up, moving around, shaking his head, and generally impeding the progress of surgery. This worked more or less satisfactorily until, at a critical juncture in the operation, we heard a dull thud on the floor. The son had passed out. We called for the other son to help, but when he saw his brother being carried out, he refused even to enter the operating room.

Left alone with his "tormentors," the old man grew more and more contentious. First he was thirsty and demanded water. Next he announced he was suffocating, so an extra assistant was assigned to hold the drapes off his nose. Then he said he was leaving at once and going home and demanded to be released from the ropes that tied him to the operating table. When we made no move to release him, he began to assail us with a lifetime accumulation of abusive expressions, interspersed with threats, ultimatums, and repeated denunciations of his worthless sons for deserting him so shamelessly—all of this accompanied, of course, by furious yankings on his restraints. Somehow, in spite of the incessant jerking of his head, I managed to remove one of his cataracts (I certainly wasn't going to try for the second), and to everyone's relief and amazement, the result in the end was excellent. Most gratifying was the extraordinary change that occurred in the personality of that old man as he saw his sons and his surroundings for the first time in eight years of blindness.

The hospital staff also treat many congenital anomalies, ranging from club feet—some of which, in adults, are so deformed that some patients actually walk on their ankle bones instead of their heel—all the way to an exotic case of bladder exstrophy in a thirty-two-year-old woman. Since birth this woman's bladder had opened out on her abdominal wall, a glistening giant raspberry attached just above the pubis. For many years, out of shame, she had assumed the dress and mannerisms of a man, and when we first saw her, she was miserable, lonely, and pathetic, her clothes reeking of urine. It's hard to say whether we were more surprised by the success of the rather formidable operation that was required or by her ensuing social rehabilitation as a woman.

The most satisfying congenital defect to treat, however, is the cleft lip, or harelip. A cleft lip is an ugly enough anomaly at birth, but when it remains uncorrected, the nose and mouth become progressively distorted, and by the time a child reaches maturity, the upper lip and nostril have widened into a fixed and repulsive deformity. Since there had never before been a surgeon in this part of Nepal to repair these defects at birth, most of the early patients we saw were adults and older children, who by then had become grotesquely deformed.

My first cleft-lip patient at Amp Pipal was a fifteen-year-old girl whose parents were unsuccessful in marrying her off because of her disfigurement. They had gone for advice to a missionary couple, Gary and Barbara Shepherd, who suggested taking her to the Amp Pipal Hospital. The parents were reluctant to go that far away to an unfamiliar place (no one from their area had ever been to the hospital), and the girl herself was terrified at the prospect. In the end they agreed to go only on the condition that the Shepherds would accompany them.

The girl's deformity had left internal as well as external scars. She was unhappy, withdrawn, and emotionally unstable. She was frightened by everything she saw at the hospital and broke into fits of screaming at the least provocation. The mother shared many of her daughter's anxieties and was therefore no help when it came to quieting the girl down. Although they must have known before coming that the only treatment was surgery, it seemed the farthest thing from their minds. Only with the greatest difficulty could they be persuaded to have the operation, and then only after the Shepherds promised to stay with them until they were out of the hospital.

I had some qualms of my own about the case, though I hadn't let on. I had never repaired a cleft lip before. I had never even seen one repaired. I had a book, though, that showed me what to do. It wasn't the first time I had met with a case I had never seen before, and it wouldn't be the last. In fact almost half of the operations I did in those early years at Amp Pipal were operations I had never seen. It's called learning by experience— great for the surgeon, but not always so great for the patient.

The major problem was not my inexperience—you can teach a monkey to sew up a lip—but the anesthesia. My book said to use general anesthesia, which for us meant ether. However, the only staff person who could administer a general anesthetic was our Indian lab technician, and for him it was merely a sideline, if that. Sideline or no, this was the last case for which he ever gave ether. Giving anesthesia has been described as hours of boredom interspersed with moments of terror. But it's the terror you remember, and in this case the memory turned out to be too much for our lab technician.

Things started off well enough. After a brief struggle with the four assistants who were holding the girl down, she fell asleep. But a few minutes later her larynx suddenly went into spasm, as if someone had stuffed a large wad of bubble gum into her windpipe. She strained to breathe, but no air passed. She turned blue, her heart slowed. The lab technician panicked and called me out of the adjacent room where I had been reading the section on cleft lip in my plastic surgery book. I quickly passed an endotracheal tube through the obstruction, and the crisis was over.

The repair of the lip itself went well, and as I was putting in the finishing stitches, I was quite pleased with the result. I had only to remove the endotracheal tube, and the procedure would be finished. The ether had been turned off for some time, and the girl had begun to wake up. I wanted the tube out before she began to cough and gag on it and possibly split apart the wound I had just spent two hours suturing. But to our dismay, the instant the tube was withdrawn, her larynx again went into spasm. Some people are peculiarly sensitive to ether, and of all people, this girl had to be one of them. In her case, we had pulled the tube too soon. Coughing and gagging would have been nothing compared with what she began to do now. And to reinsert the tube—if I *could* reinsert it—would require putting strong pressure right where the lip had been sewn, surely splitting it apart. And even if I dared give her more ether, trying to fix that lip the second time would be a disaster.

I had no time to ponder. The girl was blue and getting bluer. Aware of the saying, "The operation was a success, but the patient died," I ripped off my gloves, pried open her mouth, and again pushed down the tube, even as the lab technician was saying he could no longer feel the pulse. A few good puffs from the breathing bag, however, soon brought her heart back, and as soon as the patient and I had taken a breath, I looked at the lip. It was intact! Not a stitch out of place.

The patient was wide awake when we finally took out the tube the second time, and no problems occurred. As I walked up to our house, where the Shepherds had been waiting with Cynthia, I couldn't wait to tell them how great the lip looked.

I thought as I went how lucky I had been to get that tube through the constricted larynx that second time, and without even hurting the freshly sutured lip. When I got home, Cynthia and the Shepherds had just finished praying. They had been praying through the whole operation. That was unusual; although we often prayed earnestly and repeatedly for our patients, none of us had ever prayed through an entire operation before. Had they sensed my qualms in the beginning? Or was it because the young missionary couple had so much at stake in the success of this girl's treatment? Whatever the reason, I knew in my heart where my "luck" had come from.

The patient was happy too. As in the case of the old man with cataracts, the resulting transformation in the girl's personality was almost more gratifying than the success of her surgery. I won't forget the joy on her face when she looked at herself in a mirror on the day she went home. Much more than her lip had been healed.

The Balloon Man and Other Stories

F OR EVERY PERSON who shows up at the hospital for treatment, at least three or four other people needing treatment do not show up. As a result, whenever we travel to outlying villages, we see many people with curable conditions who later decide to come to the hospital because of our visit. Just seeing the doctor in the flesh overcomes much of their hesitation: He is not a strange monster from another planet; he even speaks their language and knows about their illnesses. Fears are dispelled, and patients come.

In one village a day's walk away, I encountered a seven-year-old boy who six weeks earlier had suffered a thirty-percent burn covering his entire chest and abdomen and one arm. The boy was a skeleton, wracked with fever and pain. In accordance with local custom, his family had withheld food from him because of the fever, and they had applied a foul mixture of dried leaves and cow manure to the wound on the advice of a village "practitioner." It was a wonder the boy had survived, considering the extent of his burns and the nature of the treatment he had been given. Yet he had now clearly come to the end of his road.

I debated how strongly I should urge the father to take his son to the hospital. We had seen so many patients treated at home like this until they were almost dead, and then when they were finally brought to the hospital, we would watch them die the same day or the next, partly as a result of the journey. The hospital was in danger of becoming known as the place where people went to die instead of where they recovered. At any rate, I certainly couldn't do anything for the boy in his village. I told the father that his son would die soon if he was left at home, but he might have a chance to live if he was brought to Amp Pipal Hospital.

This set off a heated discussion among the many villagers who had gathered around in the meantime, each of whom offered strong and long-winded opinions about whether or not to follow the "Americani" doctor's advice. Since in rural Nepal most important decisions are made by the group and not by the individual, it was perfectly natural for the father to listen patiently while his neighbors all had their say. It was hard to follow the general drift of their arguments, however, because not only did the opinions of different people conflict with each other, but also the opinions of any one person were likely to change from moment to moment. Thus a man could be heard denouncing a position he himself had vigorously advocated only minutes earlier. The local *pradhan panch* (mayor), who had also joined the crowd, changed sides with himself so often that I couldn't tell where he stood in the end, and most probably neither could he. No one was at all bothered by his own or anyone else's inconsistencies. The upshot of all this debate, to my surprise, was that the father should take his son to Amp Pipal the very next day. I groaned inwardly; once again the hospital would be on trial.

The boy arrived at the hospital the following evening, having withstood the trip without difficulty, and we promptly cleaned up his wounds and started him on a program of intensive feedings. Although we thought he might die several times during the first few days, he began to rally, and by the end of the first week he was on his way to recovery. The father, however, had not counted on the long time required for burn wounds to heal, and several times during the ensuing weeks he almost lost patience and took his son home—which would have quickly erased all gains he had made. In the end, though, they stayed, and after six weeks of treatment, which included extensive skin grafting, the child was restored completely to health. His recovery was to change the attitude of that village toward our medical work from then on; no longer would their debates about going to the hospital last two hours. And so it has been: Each successfully treated case has served as an advertisement for modern medicine, and gradually, village by village, the prejudices against the foreign hospital have melted away.

Another disease we find difficult to treat is tuberculosis, which is different from most other infectious diseases in that its treatment must extend over many months, a concept quite foreign to Nepalis, who are accustomed to taking the village remedies for only a few days at a time. They often stop taking their medicine as soon as they feel better. In many cases they get away with it, but not when it comes to TB: The disease almost always returns with greater vehemence than before. Our biggest hurdle, then, in treating TB is convincing patients to stay on their treatment for the full course of eighteen months, and to do this we offer several incentives, such as free drugs and various concessions on the patients' medical bills. American churches and friends also contribute to a special fund that helps to underwrite the cost of treatment for poor patients. Nonetheless, it's a great deal to ask village Nepalis to keep making the long trip to the hospital month after month to renew their prescription even when they're feeling fine, and thus many simply stop coming. And when months later they finally return, they are far worse off than they were to begin with.

When Shanta Kumar showed up at the hospital extremely ill with tuberculosis, our first question was whether or not he had ever been treated for TB before. And, as is often the case in Nepal, his answer was yes. He had started treatment a year earlier but had not taken the medication for the prescribed eighteen-month period. He had begun to feel better, so he had stopped after four months.

Now, eight months later, Shanta was a hollow-eyed, dried-out wreck, gasping for breath and barely able to stand; he was worse than he had been before he started the medication. He had been carried to the hospital by some village friends; his only living relative was his wife, a bewildered young woman, who was nursing two babies, one of whom, we soon discovered, also had tuberculosis. She was not only frightened and inexperienced, she was devoid of intelligence. The prospects for treating this family successfully were gloomy indeed.

Shanta's left pleural cavity turned out to be filled with pus, and the lung on that side was a fist-sized mass of collapsed, necrotic tissue. We put in a chest tube and drained off two quarts of pus, but after that was done, large quantities of air continued leaking out the tube from the damaged lung. Usually this kind of air leak seals over in a few days, but in Shanta's case it did not. We were forced to leave the tube in day after day, then week after week, and still the air kept coming. All during this time Shanta received intensive anti-tuberculous therapy, supplemented by a nutritious diet and other supportive measures, all designed to help him combat his life-threatening infection.

At the beginning of the third week, the air leaking from Shanta's lung into his chest cavity and out the tube now also began to penetrate beneath the skin of his chest, neck, and face, gradually giving him the bloated and puffed-up features of a toad. Shanta was distressed not only by his inflated appearance but also by the fact that he felt as if there were cracked eggshells under his skin. He had developed a condition known as subcutaneous emphysema, an infrequent complication of tuberculosis.

This condition always bothers the patient more than the doctor, for it is usually self-limiting and goes away on its own. However, with this young man the puffiness did not subside but increased more and more, until finally his face became so distended he could no longer see through his eyelids. At this point the young wife could stand it no longer; early one morning she ran off with the children and never came back. My doctor friends won't believe it, but the air continued to accumulate under Shanta's skin until it had spread to every part of his body—right to the base of his toenails! He was so blown up, he looked as if he would float off the bed, like one of the balloons in Macy's Thanksgiving parade. Even his conjunctiva protruded an inch from between his puffed-shut eyelids—filled with air bubbles! His appearance was monstrous. And then, as if someone had released a hidden valve, the air went away and left him looking again like the desiccated cadaver he was when he had arrived, except that now his skin was even more crinkly.

After the air was reabsorbed, Shanta's general condition began to improve, though air and pus continued draining out through his chest tube. But suddenly one day, he also decided to leave; perhaps he was prompted by loneliness, or perhaps he was disoriented from one of the drugs he was taking. Whatever the reason, he got out of bed early one morning and walked down the long corridor leading to the front entrance. Since he was still hooked up by his tube to a drainage bottle, he simply dragged the bottle along with him, shattering it as he went up the front steps. Fortunately, someone apprehended him before he could get out of the hospital and despite his loud protests, returned him to bed. But now he required constant watching, an added burden for our chronically overpressed nursing staff. It seemed only a matter of time before he would escape from the hospital for good.

Shanta, however, surprised us by once more becoming rational and even cooperative. It turned out to be one of the medicines that had caused his strange behavior after all, and once this was stopped, he became normal again. At this point, since the tube was obviously not adequate, I decided to open his chest and take out a rib, thereby providing wide-open drainage for his continuing infection. This I did under local anesthesia.

The entire pleural space, where the left lung should have been, was just a gaping cavity, at the bottom of which Shanta's heart could be seen beating steadily. And there also, near the root of his shrunken fibrotic lung, was a tiny hole through which a small catheter could have passed into his windpipe and out through his mouth. This was the cause of his air leak and persistent infection. I stuffed the cavity with sterile strips of cloth torn from old sheets, and when I had finished, I had put enough stuffing into his chest to fill two Christmas turkeys.

Shanta really picked up after that—until he began to lose his appetite because of the smell from his wound. This could be controlled by changing his packing each week, but after two months the cavity hadn't even begun to fill in. Shanta, however, was by this time well enough to walk home, so we discharged him with strict instructions to return once a month to have his packing replaced.

For several months Shanta appeared faithfully, though it was not easy for him to make the day's walk up the mountain. We tried to get him to bring his child back for TB treatment, but his wife refused to have anything to do with a hospital where patients filled up with air. Then he stopped coming. We sent him letters, but we received no response; and gradually, as the months passed, I forgot about him. Then one day a year later, he turned up, healthy and husky and as delighted to see me as I was to see him. He had been packing his own chest, he said, using the same material over and over, merely washing it periodically in the village spring. He had come for new cloth this time because the old had begun to wear out. He also said that he was getting his medicine from another village near his home. As far as I could tell, his tuberculosis was cured; only the hole in his chest remained, now down to one-turkey size. It caused him no trouble; it didn't even smell anymore. For all intents and purposes, he had fully recovered.

A complicated or exceptional case? No more so than many other TB cases we see. Tuberculosis is never simple, and it's always deadly. It is only one disease, but it has a thousand faces.

Bear mauls are simpler: no long drawn-out illness, no long months of fever and cough and pain. Just one stroke and it's done. Those that survive come to the hospital because even the most backward villager knows there is no other treatment besides getting sewn up, and that service is offered only at Amp Pipal Hospital.

We see bear-maul cases three or four times a year, and most of them have one thing in common: The bear has gone for the face. I've always marveled at those powerful claws that can rip through the hide of an elk or a moose. Compared with that, the human face is like tissue paper.

The worst bear maul any of us had ever seen arrived at the hospital at eight o'clock one Sunday morning, the busiest day of the week during our busiest season of the year. Two emergencies had come in the evening before so the staff were already taxed before the day began. I had just started rounds when the head nurse called me to see a patient whom they had brought in just five minutes earlier. There on the table lay a twenty-year-old man with the most ghastly face I ever want to see. In fact, it wasn't the face so much, it was its absence that was striking—or rather, I should say, its *location,* for what was left of the face had been stripped away from the facial bones and was laid back, flesh upward, across the patient's neck and upper chest, attached only at the edge of his lower jaw like a long beard that had been dipped in spaghetti sauce. His right eye was gone; only its empty socket stared blankly ahead. The fleshy part of the nose was gone, too, leaving two gaping nostrils covered by their mucous membranes. The left eyeball was intact and uninjured, but the lower eyelid on that side had been ripped away and was lying together in one piece with cheeks, lips, and chin on the patient's chest. Dirt and bits of grass stuck to the raw surfaces. The two rows of teeth, with their pale gums were completely exposed. The young man remained motionless except for his one eye, which followed me without expression. Then his teeth moved and said, "Give me some water." It was like a voice from the dead.

Fewer than twenty-four hours earlier he had been out chopping firewood with his two brothers. He had become slightly separated from the others when he was suddenly attacked by a large Himalayan black bear. The brothers, hearing his screams, ran to him. They found him lying face down; the bear was gone. They had then run the three-hour distance to their home, alerted their father, gathered together friends and neighbors, and returned to the site of the accident. Finding the injured man still alive, they decided to carry him directly to the Amp Pipal Hospital. A few men went to a nearby village for lanterns and flashlights that they would need for the all-night journey. And the rest of that day and all that night, they had run, covering in just fourteen hours a distance that would ordinarily have taken two full days—and that, carrying a patient in a hammock in the dark.

three

Once the staff saw the patient's condition, we forgot the rest of our day's work. The operating team sprang into action, and for the next five hours we attempted to put back together what remained of the young man's face. Considering what we had to work with, the result was better than any of us had hoped for: at least he looked human once more, even without his eye and nose. The wounds healed without infection, which was remarkable since they were a day old when we operated and had been caked with dirt and grass.

As the face healed, the upper eyelid on the left was slowly drawn down over the remaining eye. We could find no way to correct this except through major, multi-staged reconstructive surgery, which the patient had already turned down when I had suggested rebuilding his nose. So I made in the eyelid a small hole through which he could see; and three weeks from the day he arrived, he walked home, terribly mutilated, but alive, healthy, and able to work and provide for his family.

Strong as my impression remains of that young man's injury, stronger still remains my impression of that father's love. Night and day he attended his son, his rough, hardened hands trembling and gentle as he learned to feed him and clean his lips and nostrils and even his eye. Bent with labor and age though he was, he did not spare himself or give thought to his own comfort. What a horror to have to look on such a face, and of one he loved so dearly. May we never think that these unsophisticated villagers feel less acutely or love less deeply than we do. And should they at times appear to be indifferent, it is only because they have learned to accept with resignation the sorrows that come their way.

I remember the day a father brought his ten-year-old son, who a few weeks earlier had been bitten by one of the countless stray dogs that infest Nepali villages. The boy seemed normal enough, except that whenever he tried to swallow, his face became contorted in an unnatural grimace, as if something were choking him from inside. We gave him a glass of water to drink, but before he had even raised it to his lips, he began to gag and to salivate profusely. His head and neck writhed uncontrollably.

34

Unable to speak, the son expressed with his eyes the pain and terror he was experiencing. The terrible truth was all too apparent: He had contracted rabies, for which there is no known cure. Rabies can be prevented by administering antiserum immediately after exposure, but once signs and symptoms have developed, nothing can be done. Virtually all rabies victims die, usually within a few days.

I called the father, together with the villagers who had accompanied them, into another room and told them the boy had rabies. The news didn't surprise them: It was exactly what they had feared. Only a few days earlier a boy with the same symptoms had died after having been bitten by the same dog. Indeed, rabies was well known to them, better known to them than to most Western doctors, who rarely get to see a case. Not that any doctor should want to: It is a terrifying disease, one in which the victim is gripped by a relentlessly progressive series of spasms or seizures, without losing any awareness of what is happening. And doctor and family can only stand by helplessly—and not too close, lest the patient in frantic thrashing should transmit to them the fatal illness.

The faces of the father and the men with him showed little emotion when I told them to take the boy home at once, that we could do nothing for him. They talked among themselves for a while, much like men sitting over tea in a teashop, discussing the price of a bag of fertilizer. In fact they were discussing other people who had died of rabies. Joining in their conversation, I took the opportunity to teach them a little about the prevention of rabies. I reminded them that their own government had passed a law instructing every *panchayat* (local governing council) throughout Nepal to eradicate their stray dogs—and this in a Hindu country, where, according to popular belief, a dog might be somebody's deceased aunt or uncle. Then the father asked what he could do for his son, how he should care for him until he died, what should or shouldn't he give the boy to eat and drink. He asked this in a matter-of-fact manner, as if it were someone else's son he was inquiring about. With my thoughts still occupied in tracking down stray dogs and

three

preventing new cases of rabies, I told him it would be best if people didn't go near his son—he might try to scratch or bite them as he became more wild—and I suggested he be locked in a room by himself. (Like a mad dog, I might as well have added; the effect was the same.) I caught myself, but too late.

The father was staring at me horrified, as if he couldn't believe I meant what I said. Then his composure vanished, as the awful truth suddenly broke in on him that not only was he going to lose his son, but he wouldn't even be able to comfort him in those final hours. Tears filled his eyes. He stepped forward and impulsively threw his arms around me, his body shaking with repressed sobs. The other men shifted uneasily, eyes to the floor, embarrassed by this outbreak of emotion. The father looked up and asked only once: "Isn't there anything you can do?"

"Nothing." I tried to say it gently and compassionately but with finality.

To the father I was the last hope. From his point of view, what good was it knowing that, in fact, God alone was his last hope, and the doctor's, too? What difference was it going to make? And I thought, as I stood there holding on to that father, the two of us equally helpless and perplexed, that Jesus would have cured that boy, with just a word.

Not all of the cases we see are dramatic. Most of our time is spent in treating the large numbers of patients who are not so seriously ill and who do not readily engage our sympathy. It is when we deal with these patients—frequently neurotic, querulous, impatient, insistent, and unappreciative—that we realize how truly deficient we are in the love of Christ, without which our ministry of medicine is but an empty shell.

The Thin Man

*O*NE DAY the thinnest man I ever saw was brought to the hospital. It wasn't just that he lacked flesh: something about his skin lent a peculiarly macabre cast to his appearance. It wasn't dried and crinkled as one might have expected the skin of a starved and wasted person to be. Rather, it was stretched taut, smooth and waxy, hugging the contours of his bones. So extreme was his thinness that his skin came together, front and back, between the bones of his forearm; and his lower abdomen was hollowed so deeply that the promontory of his sacrum (backbone) could be plainly seen jutting forward between his visibly pulsating iliac arteries. I even could feel the grain of his bones beneath his skin.

This man's relatives and friends had carried him three days from a remote village in a neighboring district. Although he was forty-five years old, he looked seventy or older. He was barely alive. It was an effort for him just to open his eyes and move them about. He lay motionless on my examining table, motionless except for his slow, creaky breathing. His legs hung more than a foot over the end of the table; he was all of six feet—exceptionally tall for a Nepali. His height made him look even thinner.

The relatives accompanying the man included his two sons from his first wife—she had died in childbirth some years earlier—along with his second wife, a frightened young woman whom he had married the year before. In addition to the relatives, a large number of friends and acquaintances had come four

with the man, mainly to get medicine for themselves, but also to demonstrate their concern for the dying man and his family.

When I asked the sons what was wrong with their father, they told me that for over a year he had been vomiting everything he ate. He would eat a meal, or even two or three meals, and then a day or so later he would vomit it all back up. They could even identify things he had eaten three and four days earlier. His bowels moved twice a month—little rock-like lumps—and now it had been a full month since they had last moved.

One gray-haired man who had come with the sick man pushed forward and informed me that the patient's problems could all be attributed to a lack of "cold" foods in his diet. The others nodded their assent. Now that he couldn't eat anything, "hot" or "cold," nothing could make up for this deficiency. They had brought the patient for an injection: A shot of "cold" medicine was all he needed, they said; that would get him well in no time.

When I said that I didn't really think that was the problem, I overheard one of the group murmur to the others, "See, I told you he wouldn't understand our diseases. He comes from a different country."

Rural Nepalis think most diseases are related to an imbalance of "hot" and "cold" elements in the body. Thus, if the "cold" elements predominate, one might catch a common cold, for which aspirin ("hot") would be appropriate therapy. Arthritis, on the other hand, is a "hot" disease, and aspirin, on this theory, shouldn't be given. Thus some of our patients throw their aspirin away when we give it to them for their aching joints.

All foods fall into either the "hot" or "cold" category. Often common sense seems to determine what a particular food will be: Spices are "hot," while yogurt is "cold." Unripe fruit is "hot," while ripe fruit is "cold." But in other instances the choice is harder to explain. Garlic is "hot"; onions are "cold." Chicken is "hot," duck is "cold." Cow's milk is "hot," but buffalo milk is "cold." This is said to be because cows drink less water than buffalos do, and too little fluid in the system makes a cow, along with its milk, "hot." The fact that the thin man also had little fluid in his system—he was as dry as a pretzel—was considered further evidence that his disease was a "hot" one. Its treatment: replenish the "cold elements," which he had been vomiting up for so many months.

The "consultants" gathered around the examining table were, for that matter, not so far off as might be supposed. As I soon found out, the patient was suffering from a stomach ulcer, a condition that is certainly exacerbated by hot spices and "hot" aspirin. I thought it would be wise in this instance to go along with their disease theory, a shift in approach that helped restore my damaged credibility.

When I examined the thin man, I found two other abnormalities. Around his umbilicus I found a cluster of puckered scars, some of them still oozing. The patient had been branded with a hot iron rod, a common therapy village practitioners used to cure abdominal pain. The second abnormality was more noteworthy: The patient's entire upper abdomen was filled with an enormously bloated stomach, whose peristaltic waves could be seen churning across his body from left to right. The cause of his problem was obvious: a densely scarred ulcer had constricted the outlet of the stomach, permitting only a trickle of liquid to pass into the intestines. The patient was in a terminal phase of starvation.

The only treatment for such a condition was surgery. I would have to create a new passageway between the stomach and the proximal small intestine, thus bypassing the obstruction altogether. The operation could even be done under local anesthesia. It would take a week to get the patient ready for surgery, if he lived that long. He needed large amounts of intravenous fluids; and if he could tolerate a milk diet, that would be even better. But even with adequate preparation, an operation in such a debilitated person would be an extremely risky undertaking. I wasn't looking forward to it.

When I had finished examining the thin man, I turned to the assembled friends and relatives and carefully explained the problem and what I proposed to do about it. After a brief interval the gray-haired man, who appeared to be the group's spokesman, said, "If an operation will cure him, then operate. If it won't, then we'll take him home."

This was the usual response. "It's not as easy as that," I said. "The operation is extremely dangerous for someone so sick. It may not be successful. He has only a one-in-three chance to survive if we operate. He has no chance if we don't." Ordinarily this kind of statement would be enough to settle the issue in favor of taking the patient home. A long discussion ensued, in which the participants weighed every conceivable factor except the opinion of the patient himself.

The young wife had no part in the decision. From the moment I mentioned the word "operation," she had started an uninterrupted high-pitched wailing, signifying not so much love for her husband as fear of becoming a widow, a circumstance that for a Nepali woman was the worst of all possible fates. It would mean the loss of her home, her land, even her friends. A widow, especially a childless widow, had no status, no self-respect. She was considered to be in some way personally accountable for her husband's death; she was a disgrace both to his family and to her own. She was not permitted to remarry. In short, she faced a lifetime of unrelieved sorrow and privation. It was no wonder that this young woman, scarcely twenty years old, should dread the prospect of her husband's death.

Finally the patient himself, in a faint, croaking voice, ended the discussion by announcing that he would rather die than go home the way he was. "Go ahead and operate," he said. "If I die, I die. If I live, I live."

This seemed to satisfy everyone but his wife, who broke into a fresh outpouring of tears. After soundly rebuking her for raising so much commotion, the friends and relatives trooped off in a body, leaving the sick man and the weeping wife alone in their new surroundings.

By the time a dozen bottles of intravenous fluid had run in, the patient's condition had improved markedly; he was alert and responsive and had begun to take an interest in things around him. But he couldn't take the milk we tried to feed him. Everything he drank came up with explosive force, much to the distress of those occupying adjacent beds. After the first day he made no further progress, and by the third day it seemed pointless to delay surgery any longer. So I passed a large tube through his nose into his stomach and attached it to a suction apparatus, at the same time instructing the young wife to give him nothing more to eat or drink; his stomach had to be empty for surgery. I then scheduled the operation for the next day.

The surgery went smoothly, except that the stomach was filled with a large quantity of biscuits that the patient had consumed two hours beforehand. "He was hungry," the wife told me later. "Besides, when you told me not to feed him, I thought you meant only rice." In spite of the biscuits, I quickly constructed a new passageway between the stomach and intestine, and within an hour the operation was finished.

To my surprise, the thin man tolerated the surgery without any difficulty whatever. That evening he was bright and cheerful, probably for the first time in months. The next day he took his first food and held it down. By the fourth day his appetite seemed limitless, and he began to eat as if making up for lost time. His wife kept busy just cooking for him, and whenever we saw her, she waved and smiled at us gaily. Her former tears of sorrow had been replaced by tears of joy. On the seventh day, the patient's stitches were removed. A relative came to inquire how he was getting along and was sent back to the village with word that four porters should be sent the following week to carry the patient home.

"You are our *bhagwan* (god)," the relative said to me, expressing a common sentiment after any successful treatment, a sentiment we took pains to deny.

In the middle of the night of the eighth postoperative day, the patient got out of bed, stood up, passed out, and fell full-length onto the concrete floor of his room. The assistant nurse and the night sweeper lifted him up and put him back in bed. They left him sleeping quietly. The wife, asleep on a bench next to his bed, had never wakened. Within two hours the patient was dead from a cerebral hemorrhage.

I remember standing there by the bed that night, staring

four

down at the patient's face, thinking how much healthier he looked—even in death—than he had when he first came to the hospital. He had filled out, his eyes were no longer sunken. I almost expected him to open his lids and look up at me. It all seemed unreal. I even thought for a moment I might be having a nightmare. But I wasn't.

We left the body in bed, fearing to move it lest we rouse the wife, whom we preferred to leave sleeping until morning. If she were to awaken and find him dead, she would wake up the whole hospital with her wailing. Besides, after daylight, more people would be around to comfort her.

The young wife woke up at dawn, and seeing her husband lying peacefully in bed, she got up quietly and went out to prepare his morning meal. When I arrived on the ward, she was just returning with a steaming plateful of rice and vegetables. As soon as she saw me, she sensed something was wrong. She put down the plate and ran to the bed and tore back the sheet. For a long while she just stood there, the tears welling in her eyes. Then she sank down on her knees, and putting her face in her husband's upturned palm, she began to sob.

For the next two days she sat guard outside the dead-house, where the corpses are placed. She had waited on her husband through their married life, through his illness, and here she was, waiting on him still. On the third day, as we had previously arranged, the dead man's two sons came to take their father home. With them were a few other relatives and four porters whom they had hired to carry their father. By chance I met them as they were arriving outside the hospital entrance. We recognized each other from our first meeting at the time of their father's admission. They had heard the good news of his successful operation, and they came up to me now with smiles of gratitude on their faces to thank me for bringing their father back to life. They were robust and honest-looking young men with the sweat and dust of three days' walking caked on their features. I can't say what I would have given to have been able to tell them that their father was alive and well.

They took the news without outward emotion. Their glad

42

anticipation slowly turned into a numbed disappointment. They quietly paid their bill, went to the dead-house, and with deliberation and respect laid the body in the hammock they had brought with them. Then, together with the other relatives and the dead man's widow, they filed slowly away and passed out of sight down the steep winding trail that led from the hospital to the valley below.

five

A Sore Toe

*T*HE WEDNESDAY-NIGHT prayer meeting was over before ten o'clock, and the eight of us who had met together set out in different directions to our respective homes. The trail down to the hospital led for a few hundred yards along the top of the ridge, and in the moonlight the valleys that fell off to either side seemed strangely far removed. In the distance the snowy mountains, rising to 26,000 feet, glistened silvery-white against the darkened sky. No need for a flashlight on a night like this.

As I descended, I approached the old farm, its buildings set precariously against the steep hillside. Once a busy agricultural center, the farm had been closed by the government the previous year, and now the buildings were rarely used. As I passed the lower storage sheds, I thought I heard a long, low moan. It was too distinct to be the wind. It came again, still louder, until gradually it became a cry, like the cry of a wild animal. I knew that leopards and jackals used to raid the farm chicken coops in the past, but the farm no longer had chickens, and the predators had little reason to visit the mostly abandoned buildings. Once more I heard it, and as I stopped to listen, I could hear a voice repeating over and over: "Hari Ram, Hari Ram, Hari Ram."

I went to the shed from which the voice came and peered in through the partly open door. There lying on a table and rocking from side to side was the figure of a man, one knee clasped in both hands, his leg drawn up against his buttocks. On a stool beside him burned two incense sticks. The room had a sweet sickly mustiness about it, and as I stood in the doorway, I

44

thought I smelled dead flesh. I accidentally knocked loose a clump of dirt from the wall, and at once the man on the table sat up and struck a match to light his small kerosene lamp.

"What do you want?" he asked.

"I'm a doctor," I said. "At the hospital."

"Oh, I know you." The "you" was emphasized, unpleasantly. "Well," he said, "I don't need you. What did you come here for?"

Smoke hung heavily in the room. On the stool next to the burning incense stood an offering plate on which was placed red powder, uncooked rice, and various other grains. And on the dirt floor, fresh blood and feathers were all that remained of a recently slaughtered chicken.

I only slightly knew the man on the table. He was Gopal Adhikari, a former *panchayat* council member who had fallen on bad times. He had sold most of his land to pay off debts, it was said, and now he was having difficulty feeding his wife and five children. The government agricultural officer responsible for the farm had arranged for him to watch over the buildings at night, for which Gopal received a meager stipend. But as to the calamity that had reduced him to lying there in the dark, moaning with pain, I had not a clue.

"What's the matter?" I asked, ignoring Gopal's obvious displeasure at my arrival.

He said nothing, but slowly straightened out the leg he had been holding. I noticed a dirty piece of rag wrapped around his big toe. "What's under that?" I asked.

"It's nothing," he said. "It's getting better."

The odor of dead flesh once more arose, mingling with the smell of incense. Gopal took out a cigarette, lit it, and began to smoke rapidly, as if to dispel the nauseating atmosphere of the room. "Let me see what's under there," I persisted.

Gopal finished his cigarette in silence, and when he was done, he slowly unwrapped the rag. Even in the dim light the toe was a remarkable study in red and black, black at the tip and red at the base: gangrene with secondary infection.

"How long has it been like this?"

"A month. Maybe two."

"You need to come to the hospital," I said. "It's only twenty minutes down the hill."

"It would take me longer," said Gopal. "Besides, the *jhankri* is treating me." The *jhankri* was the local shaman, or witch doctor. "The priest has also been here," Gopal went on. "He said not to go to the hospital. He and the *jhankri* know what to do. They said it was just a matter of time."

I felt for the pulse in Gopal's foot but found nothing. Except for the red swollen area, the foot was cold. Clearly the arterial blood flow to the foot was blocked, almost certainly the result of a malignant form of arteriosclerosis, a condition made worse by smoking.

Gopal took out another cigarette and lit it.

"That's bad for your foot," I said, pointing to the cigarette. "Furthermore, that black part is dead and needs to come off. If not, your whole foot will become infected. People have lost their entire legs because of this disease."

"Are you saying you'd cut my toe off?"

"Just the dead part," I said.

"It's not dead; it's just discolored. Besides, I don't have enough money to go to the hospital."

"What are you paying the *jhankri* and the priest?" I asked. "And for these chickens you've been sacrificing?"

"That's different; it's our custom," Gopal said sullenly.

Seeing no point in talking further, I turned to leave, but as I stooped to go out the door, I thought of something else. "We have medicine to lessen your pain if you want it. You can send someone to the hospital to fetch it for you." I waited a moment, and getting no response, I walked out, leaving him puffing on his cigarette.

I learned a few days later from one of our community-health nurses who lived near the farm that Gopal had been moaning in pain night after night for the past two months. She said that twice a week the *jhankri* would come, go into a trance, kill a chicken that Gopal had provided, and then rub the dead chicken on the affected foot. Not only that, she said, but the priest had told Gopal's family that one of the gods was displeased and required daily offerings of rice and ghee if the disease was to be reversed. The services of the priest and *jhankri* were not offered free, even for a poor man like Gopal, and over a period of time the payments had mounted up.

The next day my interest and concern were aroused when a man came to the hospital to get pain medication for Gopal. Several evenings later I went back up to the farm to see him. If anything he was worse, but at least he seemed willing to talk. He explained to me that a spirit had caused the disease in his toe and that the *jhankri* had so far been unable to identify it and drive it out. I thought I detected in Gopal's manner a little less confidence in the treatment he was getting, and I once again urged him to come to the hospital. I said that his problem was in reality caused by arterial thickening that in turn reduced the blood flow to his foot. I told him his toe was dying because of lack of blood.

Gopal nodded. "The *jhankri* comes tomorrow night," he said. "I'll tell him that."

I was about to say it was no use telling the *jhankri* because he wouldn't understand anyway, when I hesitated. Did I know what caused arteriosclerosis? Yes, cholesterol plaques accumulated in the arteries, but where did the plaques come from? I thought of the times I had scoffed at the *jhankris* and their ideas that spirits were behind every illness. Yet didn't we Christians teach about spirits, especially evil spirits? I left without further comment.

I didn't go up to see Gopal again, but I knew from others that he was continuing to groan and smoke his way through the nights as before. Then I heard that another more renowned *jhankri* had been called in and that just the previous night the *jhankri* had performed a major healing ritual, with Gopal's family and other friends in attendance. The ceremony had lasted from dusk to dawn. The famous *jhankri* had gone into a trance in order to communicate with the spirit world and enlist the aid of one or more deities in identifying the evil spirit causing Gopal's illness. Once identified, the evil spirit could then be called forth and compelled to leave the victim.

five

In Gopal's case, the spirit troubling him was identified as a *bir,* the spirit of someone who had died without proper funeral rites, one of the more malevolent varieties of spirit. To exorcise the *bir,* the *jhankri* prescribed the sacrifice of four chickens, blew magic formulas onto the infected foot, and went into repeated trances.

When these measures failed to alleviate Gopal's pain, the *jhankri* had tried to drive out the spirit by striking Gopal's foot with a small straw broom in the belief that only the spirit felt the broom, not the victim. All these proceedings had been accompanied by the beating of a tin plate, the chanting of prayers, and the frequent offering by Gopal's family of quantities of uncooked rice, which the *jhankri* periodically threw at Gopal's leg. By the next morning, however, Gopal was not better. Two days later he showed up at the hospital.

The Amp Pipal Hospital hadn't been open very long at this point, and for the average villager it took a leap of faith to trust these strange foreign doctors and their equally strange methods of diagnosis and treatment. It was widely known, for example, that the foreigners felt the pulse in only one wrist, instead of both, as was the practice of any competent village shaman, or *jhankri.* Villagers also complained that the hospital people listened to their hearts instead of their stomachs, the latter being considered more important. Furthermore, it often took days for the foreigners' medicine to work, whereas the average villager expected to be cured within hours. And beyond that, it was rumored that the hospital staff sometimes cut off parts of a person's body; what was done with the parts was unknown. Most people, of course, sensibly refused to submit to such treatment.

It would be a few more years before the shamans and priests learned to discern which illnesses were best treated at the hospital. They would soon discover that for cuts, fractures, and gangrene a quick trip to the hospital would save a lot of chickens, not to mention the arms, legs, and lives of their patients.

When I saw Gopal in my office, his toe looked the same, but I could see telltale red streaks of infection running up his leg. I told him we would have to admit him for a few days, and then when the infection had subsided, we would put him to sleep and remove the dead part of his toe.

"I can't stay," he said. "I have my animals to look after during the day, and if I'm not on duty at the farm at night, I don't get paid. I've come for an injection."

His request was typical; Nepalis believed injections would heal anything. But I knew an injection wouldn't do anything for him. When the injection failed, he would only be convinced that going to the hospital had been a waste of time after all. It was better to give him no treatment at all than to give him ineffective treatment. Yet he was finally acknowledging the failure of the shaman to cure him, and it seemed a shame to let him slip through our fingers.

I thought perhaps he just needed persuasion. Using the blunderbuss approach, I fired off five minutes of fragmented Nepali at him, mixing together bits on septicemia, gas gangrene, arteriosclerosis, the use of antibiotics, the dangers of smoking, and the folly of killing chickens when what he needed was to have his toe cut off.

"I've come for an injection," he repeated. He stood in my office a little bent over, leaning on a crude cane. He looked older than his forty years, and he was obviously in pain. I imagined him lying in the shed again that night, having gone to the hospital and received no treatment. But it was his own fault; he had refused the only treatment that was going to help him. And if I gave him treatment that wasn't going to help, he would probably never come back to the hospital again. I could give him a painkiller, but it would offer only temporary relief, and of course it would do nothing for the disease.

He waited patiently. Finally I prescribed a penicillin injection and a week's course of penicillin tablets and sent him off to the cashier's office. The cashier came to me a moment later to say that Gopal would pay only for the injection, not the pills. I told the cashier that I would pay for the pills, but that under no circumstances was Gopal to go without them.

I didn't see Gopal again for almost a month. I heard that his foot had improved slightly for about a week but then had begun to hurt again, worse than before. The *jhankri* had been invited back. The priest had prescribed new and greater sacrifices and offerings by which to appease the offended deities. Then I heard that Gopal had become dangerously ill, with high fever and toxemia. I decided to go up to his house and see him.

He was lying on a straw mat on his veranda when I arrived. "Gopal," I said, "do you think the priest and the *jhankri* can save you now?"

"Who knows?" He shrugged. "What happens happens."

"I believe the true living God can save you," I said. "He's the one responsible for building the hospital. Some people who have gone there would have died if they had not come. You could get well if you would come to the hospital."

"I don't have any money."

"I'll see that your treatment is paid for," I said. "Whatever it takes."

Gopal looked up at the thatch covering of the veranda. His wife had come out of the house, followed by two runny-nosed children. The three of them stood and stared at me. "All right," he said, "I'll go. But I can't walk."

I knew that the headman in Gopal's village owned a *doli*, a simple hammock suspended from a long pole, by which a sick person could be carried. I promised to see the headman at once and arrange for Gopal's transport down to the hospital.

Later that day Gopal was carried down and admitted to the ward. After two days of treatment his toxemia had subsided and his temperature was back to normal. On the third day, under general anesthesia, I removed the dead portion of his big toe. When I visited him on the ward later that evening, I found him sitting up in bed, smoking. A newly opened box of Himal cigarettes lay on his bedside table.

For the sixth time I gave Gopal my lecture on smoking. The fact was that smoking caused a reflex constriction of the blood vessels, further impairing blood flow to the extremities. If Gopal didn't give up cigarettes, ultimately his recovery was doomed. I warned him that if he continued to smoke, I would stop treating him.

Next morning when I came on rounds, Gopal was gone.

Gopal's house was on the path going up to church, so the next Saturday morning on our way to the worship service I stopped by his house to see how he was doing. He was outside in his bare feet, hoeing his field. The bandage I had wrapped on his still-open wound was half unraveled and saturated with mud. He seemed in good spirits.

"It doesn't hurt so much anymore," he said cheerfully. "It'll be okay now."

"Did you know you had an open wound on that foot?" I asked. "You need to have it cleaned and dressed twice a week at the hospital." He said that he would come to the hospital the very next day.

He did not keep his word. The next time I saw him was two weeks later, again on my way to church. He was lying on the veranda; this time he was not so cheerful. Instead of the bandage, the wound was covered with a layer of pulverized leaves mixed with raw egg. The foot was grossly swollen, and it was obvious that the bones at the base of the big toe had become infected. He hadn't been able to work for a week, even as a night watchman. The *jhankri* had been by but said he could do nothing more for him. The *jhankri* had suggested that Gopal return to the hospital, but he had been embarrassed to do so. Perhaps he didn't want another lecture on smoking.

When Gopal finally agreed for the second time to be carried to the hospital, the entire inner side of his foot was infected and draining. Chronic sepsis had left him weak and emaciated. He had lost his job as night watchman, and the few fields he still owned had been left untended, even unplanted. When I met Gopal's wife at the hospital, she assured me that from now on he would do what I told him.

Indeed, along with the change in Gopal's physical state, his attitude had changed as well. He felt genuinely sorry that he had disregarded my instructions. He promised that he would not repeat his mistakes, if only I would save his foot. To live in the hills of Nepal with only one foot was indeed a prospect to be dreaded.

Gopal stayed in the hospital two months. I amputated the remainder of his great toe and cut away the infected bone along the inner part of his foot. Because of the markedly diminished blood flow to the area, the wound was slow to heal; but even so, Gopal never once agitated to leave the hospital. Morning and evening his wife brought him a heaping plate of rice and lentils. He was encouraged and befriended by Dil Kumar, the Christian cashier of the hospital. Along with Gopal's general health, his spirits also improved. While he was in the hospital, he was re-elected to the Amp Pipal *panchayat*. A steady stream of visitors came to see him, some on business, others just to chat. Word circulated that illnesses even the shamans and priests were powerless to deal with could be cured at the mission hospital.

Also during Gopal's stay, the old farm that had been closed down by the government was unaccountably returned to the mission for use by the community-health team as a nutrition center. On my assurance that Gopal would be able to function adequately as a watchman, the community-health director agreed to give him back his former job, this time as a regular employee of the mission on a full salary. When the day of his discharge from the hospital finally came, Gopal had good reason to be beaming: Not only had his foot been saved and his health restored, but he had regained both his job and his former position of leadership in the community. And it hadn't cost him a thing. His entire medical bill for two months, amounting to less than fifty dollars, was covered by a gift from some Christian friends in America.

Given the villagers' perception about Gopal's condition, it was no small matter to them that a man afflicted with an evil spirit should enter the mission hospital and come out free of his affliction. Gopal's case was one of many that over the years gained for the Amp Pipal Hospital the reputation of being a place where evil spirits did not flourish.

Two Medical Nightmares

*I*T WAS A memorable week and still remains my candidate for the "worst week ever." We were treating two young women with illnesses that were atypical and alarmingly progressive. In neither case was the diagnosis evident. Looking back, I can think of no two cases that perplexed and drained us more than these.

The worst of it was that we knew both young women so well; they were our sisters in the church, special friends for whom we had a deep attachment and concern. One was a Christian Nepali, the other a missionary nurse. And there they were, getting sicker and sicker before our eyes, while we remained stymied, unable to figure out what was wrong with them. It would have been bad enough caring for one of them, but to have them both in the hospital at once was far more than double the strain.

To add to our troubles, a major flu epidemic had incapacitated over half the hospital staff, with most of the remainder either coming down with the flu or getting over it. The nursing staff was functioning at one-third strength; the hospital was in a state of demobilization.

We were unusually busy in the regular clinic that week, not only with the victims of the flu epidemic but also with a multitude of other complicated medical and surgical problems. We had fifty inpatients in the hospital, some of them lying on straw mats in the corridors. But the center of the drama remained these two special patients.

Both young women had become ill early in the week. Initially, the missionary nurse seemed to have the flu, but her condition worsened. She had a high fever and severe aching throughout her body, followed by a gradual loss of consciousness. When we had done all the available diagnostic procedures and still didn't know what was causing her illness, we decided to send her to Kathmandu on the Saturday plane, at that point three days away. We didn't know if we could keep her alive that long or if she would survive the four-hour trip down to the airstrip in a hammock. And, of course, we had no way to communicate with the doctors and mission executives in Kathmandu or with the nurse's family. At that time our area had no roads and no telegraph.

The second woman, a twenty-year-old Nepali named Maya, came from a prominent Hindu family. She was unusual in two ways: She had graduated from high school, a rare accomplishment for a girl in the hills; and even more rare, she was a Christian, one of a few dozen believers out of more than a million people in our area of central Nepal. Back then there couldn't have been more than three or four Christian female high-school graduates in the entire country. Christians and Hindus alike loved and respected Maya. Hers seemed a model life, one toward which any Nepali girl might well aspire.

Maya was admitted to the hospital with what also appeared to be a severe case of the flu. But her condition also steadily grew worse.

By Friday our anxiety for both these women had reached a maximum. There was much to be done to get the nurse ready for her journey to Kathmandu. We had to write medical letters as well as hire porters to carry her, her medicine, the intravenous solutions, as well as her personal belongings. The nursing superintendent would accompany the nurse to the airstrip and then to Kathmandu. We prayed that the weather would be clear next day so that the plane could land. An overnight stay at the airstrip was an experience to be avoided even in the best of health, let alone the worst.

On that Friday, Maya's condition suddenly deteriorated. I had two operations that morning, and my colleague, Dr. Helen Huston, was swamped with an unusually large load of outpatients. At about noon Helen called me abruptly out of the operating room to see Maya, who had just stopped breathing. She was thrashing about like a drowning person, unable to take a breath. We instantly recalled that she had had one of these thrashing spells the previous night, but we had dismissed it as an anxiety attack and the spell had quickly passed away. Now it was the patient who was passing away, from what appeared to be an obscure form of respiratory paralysis. Since she was about to die, we had no time to cogitate and philosophize. Within a few minutes Maya's struggles weakened, and she lost consciousness.

The immediate question was: to do something—or nothing. I was for doing nothing, because in Amp Pipal, if a person can't breathe on his own, he has pretty much come to the end of the road. I presented the cool, objective viewpoint of a surgeon. Helen thought otherwise and wanted to prolong Maya's life in the hope that she would recover spontaneously and begin again to breathe by herself. Since Maya was primarily Helen's patient, I was content to follow her lead by inserting an endotracheal tube into the young woman's windpipe and artificially ventilating her by means of a respirator bag. Our hospital staff had become quite adept at handling emergencies like this, and we were soon able to bring Maya back to life and consciousness.

Now that we had committed ourselves to breathing for Maya for an indefinite period, we needed to instruct her family, and whoever else was willing, how to care for her. Because of the flu epidemic, we didn't have enough regular staff available to tend to her. Our young Nepali maintenance man volunteered to help, so we put him in charge of the respirator bag.

And so the scene took shape: twenty or more relatives and friends standing around wide-eyed, while the maintenance man pumped on the respirator bag, and Maya's younger brother repeatedly removed saliva, secretions, and regurgitated gastric contents from her nose and mouth by means of a suction tube connected to a foot-operated suction pump. All the while Maya remained completely alert.

All Friday afternoon Maya was kept alive by the uninterrupted pumping and sucking of her relatives and the maintenance man.

The question in everyone's mind was how long we should keep this up. After finishing up the forty patients still waiting to be seen in the regular clinic, I went down to see Maya again with the hope of weaning her from the respirator. But whenever I disconnected the bag and let her try to breathe on her own, she would take a few spasmodic gasps and then frantically signal to me to start breathing for her again. I was basically the respiratory mechanic, called on to keep this young woman alive until some medical or spiritual illumination might descend on us and show us what to do next.

Meanwhile all of Maya's Christian friends and most of the missionary community had arrived to pray, sing, and give advice and encouragement. It was hard to know what was going on inside Maya's mind, but I believe she apprehended all that was taking place around her, as well as what would happen when we pulled out the endotracheal tube.

Helen had scheduled a special prayer meeting at four o'clock, and at five it vaguely got under way. Many people were too sick, tired, or upset to pray, but for those who attended, it was a time of renewal and refreshment, if not enlightenment. Nearly all of us felt that God wanted to restore this young woman, but somehow no one really believed He would. We all believed He *could,* but that was quite another matter. We prayed for wisdom and guidance, and I believe we obtained a portion of it— enough, anyway, for us to keep Maya alive from hour to hour.

Helen and several other Christians decided to spend the night at the hospital. In the morning we would confront once more the question of whether or not to pull the tube. Throughout the intervening spare moments, Helen and I continued our effort to figure out what disease could possibly account for Maya's bizarre symptoms. We considered any number of syndromes, including bulbar polio, myasthenia gravis, and multiple sclerosis. We thought of poisoning, but we didn't know of any poison available in Nepal that would selectively knock out the respiratory mechanism; furthermore, both Maya and her family consistently denied she had taken any poison.

Saturday morning it was pouring rain, not what we needed

for the sick missionary nurse and her trip to the airport by hammock. The porters were two hours late, guaranteeing that they would miss the plane—though no plane could have flown in that weather anyway—all of which assured the nurse a disagreeable night at the airstrip. However, because of the remote possibility that it wasn't raining at the airstrip or that the weather might clear by the middle of the day and the plane would come after all, we had no choice but to send her down the mountain and hope she wouldn't be dropped too many times along the slippery way.

At the hospital, events were rapidly progressing to their conclusion. Word of the unusual patient who was being kept alive with a rubber bag had spread all over the area, and many curious onlookers had swelled the ranks of those attending Maya. Considering that she was such an exceptional patient and so cherished by all who knew her, it was a highly charged time for all concerned. In addition, everyone was exhausted, and still either coming down with or just getting over the flu.

We decided to let the family's wishes guide us. As they couldn't see much future in what we were doing, we agreed to pull the tube and let God either raise her up or take her. We all gathered in her room; the young maintenance man was still pumping the respirator bag. After much singing and praying, one of Maya's closest friends told her what we were going to do. She talked to her for twenty minutes about heaven, about the Lord, about His forgiveness and His reward; it was a moving scene. Almost everyone in the room was weeping, even hardened and wrinkled old men who were hardly related to her.

When the time finally came to remove the tube, the family requested that we first get her properly dressed. All the men, including the maintenance man, left the room, and Helen herself pumped the bag while Maya's family dressed her. The dressing took a long time; perhaps those involved were unconsciously putting off the terrible moment, or perhaps they were just functioning inefficiently, unable to concentrate or even to see clearly for the tears in their eyes. To add to the distress, Maya's lungs suddenly ruptured from the prolonged squeezing of the bag. Before anyone realized what had happened, she had blown up like a balloon. In the end it didn't matter.

The tube came out at last, and the final minutes of anguish passed quickly. Helen was sitting next to the bed with the respirator bag between her knees. Maya began to try to push on the bag, though of course it was disconnected from her. Then she clutched at Helen, and a moment later began to strike at her. After several minutes she became unconscious but continued twitching and convulsing for many minutes more. When all movement had ceased, the relatives, without a word, took her outside and laid her in the rain. It was not suitable, according to their custom, to leave the body inside. The family seemed to have regarded Maya as a Christian while she was alive and hadn't interfered with the singing and praying of her Christian friends. Even when some relatives arrived early Saturday morning to perform certain Hindu rites and had been prevented from doing so inside the hospital, they had accepted it without protest. But now that Maya was dead, her family assumed responsibility. Having settled their bill, they wrapped the body in a white sheet and strapped it onto two bamboo poles. Then, forming a single file, they carried it slowly off into the rain.

It was now about noon. I felt I should walk down to the airstrip to see how our missionary nurse was doing, as it was all but certain that the plane wouldn't be coming on such a stormy day. I packed some extra bottles of intravenous solution, along with spare medicine and syringes—in case the plane didn't come the next day either—and got ready to set off, planning to spend the night at the airstrip and return early Sunday morning in time for the regular outpatient clinic.

After a brief nap and some lunch, I started down the mountain, arriving three hours later at dusk, covered with mud and leeches. My progress had been slowed because of the rain, which had transformed the trails into channels of slick mud. I had no desire to slip—which would have landed me neatly on my packful of IV bottles. To my surprise and pleasure, the nurse's condition was somewhat improved. The main airfield "waiting room" had been converted into a temporary hospital, and the Royal Nepal Airlines' chief clerk had kindly provided the mobile airplane steps to serve as shelves for medicine, IV bottles, and other paraphernalia.

After satisfying myself that my assistance was no longer required, I retired to a nearby hotel—a thatched hut with walls of dried leaves and twigs, a mud floor, uneven slat beds, and a wonderfully pungent aroma of smoke, spices, animals, and unwashed humans like myself. The beds were jammed together, three in all, and mine was the middle one.

On the bed to my right two grizzly men were asleep; the one nearest me managed to cough all night long into my face, raising every few minutes great mouthfuls of sputum, which he attempted with indifferent success to deposit down through the crack between our beds. (A month later he arrived at the hospital with advanced tuberculosis.) Not to be outdone, the man in the bed to my left passed the night generating the most remarkable profusion of snores I have ever heard. A flea-bitten dog shared my bed for part of the night, and a large number of chickens occupied the space beneath us, periodically flapping their wings with great vehemence, perhaps in response to the noise reverberating over their heads or possibly in appreciation for the large quantity of sputum contributed by our consumptive sleeping companion, which they quickly gobbled up with evident relish.

Meanwhile, the hotel owner himself was engaged for much of the night in a verbal skirmish with his wife and some other women in another corner of the establishment. As a result, I got less than an hour of fitful sleep. Of greatest inconvenience, however, were the bedbugs, which left their marks on me in twenty places. I arrived back at the hospital the next morning at nine o'clock, just in time to diagnose a perforated typhoid ulcer and operate on it.

To everyone's relief the plane came that Sunday, and I was spared a second trip to the airstrip to check on my patient. Three weeks later we received word that the nurse had made a satisfactory recovery and was ready to return to work.

Maya's death had deeply moved all those present. The Christians shared in the common sorrow but also experienced a joy born of the assurance that Maya's suffering had somehow not been in vain. All through Saturday afternoon and evening they had spent many hours together praising God for the life and testimony of this brave Nepali girl who had faced death so courageously and had made such a powerful impact on the community. The people had been confronted with the eternal; indeed, in some way they may have been more profoundly affected by Maya's death than they had been by her life.

Then on Sunday afternoon two things happened, both of which together had the effect of a bomb going off in the pit of my stomach. First, a neighboring shopkeeper casually announced that a week earlier Maya had bought two cans of *dalf,* a locally available bedbug poison, whose mechanism of action was the same as that of the nerve gas developed by the Nazis in World War II. Second, we received our first copy of the *Nepal Medical Association Journal,* a small quarterly publication to which we had just subscribed. The lead article was about thirty-one cases of *dalf* poisoning treated at the government hospital in Kathmandu over the preceding year. Needless to say, the symptoms described in the article were identical to Maya's symptoms. My heart sank as I read the treatment: atropine, of which our hospital pharmacy had a full supply. It was all too sickening to think about. Her inspiring death had degenerated into a pointless and depressing suicide. And we had watched her die with the treatment close at hand.

It wasn't long before we understood the reason for Maya's action. Shortly after becoming a Christian, she had been married off by her parents to a Hindu man whose family was adamantly opposed to her Christian faith. At first she didn't live with him, but finally she could no longer put off moving to the home of her husband and his family. On that day she had bought and taken the poison. Not fully realizing the implications of what she was doing, she had chosen to escape from a life of anticipated sorrow into a life of anticipated joy. In a way, who could blame her?

But disturbing questions linger on. We are all too eager to write radiant accounts of our accomplishments and stirring portrayals of Christians enduring all manner of trials for the sake of Christ. But we would do better to temper our enthusiasm and to beware the delusions into which we so easily drift in our attempt to justify and advertise our missionary enterprise. If our work is to be judged solely on results that can be seen with the eye, it will never stand. Often when I hear of dramatic conversions and thrilling answers to prayer, I think of Maya and wonder what I've not been told. It's so easy to talk only in terms of the new life, the abundant life, the power, the peace, the joy that is to be found in Christ. But we also need to reckon with the misery, the despair, the isolation that can result from becoming a Christian in a country like Nepal.

Don't misunderstand me. I have no regrets about Maya, for I believe that she is with God. And that, after all, is the ultimate point in becoming a Christian. However, her death reminds us that the Gospel is a two-edged sword and that we need to bend every effort to see that the wounds from becoming a Christian are not needlessly incapacitating. This means that in a country like Nepal we will, in so far as possible, adapt our presentation of the Gospel to the national culture; that we will anticipate the areas of conflict in which new believers are likely to be vulnerable; that we will make greater efforts to witness to entire families and to preserve the community ties that keep young Christians from being cut adrift from their cultural moorings; and that, above all, we will seek to nurture in believers a deeper spiritual life, which will enable them to count all sufferings but joy for the sake of Christ.

Building Stones of
the Church

Church on Trial

I WAS LATE. I never did allow enough time on Saturday mornings for my medical rounds. I had worked up a good sweat on my way up from the hospital to the top of the ridge, and now, just outside the small stone building, I paused to catch my breath. The assorted sandals and flip-flops were piled in the doorway as usual. Inside, the worn straw mats were laid out on the damp mud floor. I saw some room in the middle to sit down, but the best "seats"— those against the walls—were all taken. There you had something to lean against even if the whitewash did come off on your shirt.

Adding my sneakers to the pile of footwear in the entrance, I spied a vacant section of straw mat not too far inside. Stepping over a dog lying quietly near the door, I made my way between the seated Nepalis, taking care not to touch anyone with my feet—something to be avoided in Nepal, where feet are considered contaminated, and quite rightly. That was always a trick, because all the other latecomers sat bunched together right near the door, presenting an impenetrable barricade to still later stragglers like me. Usually it was the women who blocked the entryway—the men were more bold to move farther in—and there they would sit with their shawls pulled over their heads, as immovable and unresponsive as wax figures in a nativity scene, their colorful saris flowing out onto every spare inch of floor space around them.

The room contained about fifty people, among them a dozen or so missionaries. Some of the young Nepali men sitting along the wall had come from villages two and three hours away. Ten or more children rounded out the group, one fussing here, another crawling there, still another contentedly sucking its mother's milk. The missionary children busied themselves with their books, which they read fitfully, passing them back and forth and rustling the pages noisily. A few villagers looked in through the windows from the path outside. At the front, beside a plain wooden pulpit, the only piece of furniture in the room, stood Pastor Abraham, a Nepali Bible balanced in the crook of his withered arm, slowly intoning a passage from the Psalms in a rich, mellifluous voice. The weekly Saturday-morning church service was under way.

Pastor Abraham began to pray. He was interrupted by a loud rip as little Rajendra tore a page from the hymnbook. He had gotten away from his mother and fetched up one of the Nepali hymnbooks lying on the floor. After a brief struggle, more ripping, and some loud screams, the mother grabbed the child up and made for the door. It took a while, of course, getting through the barricade, during which time little Rajendra let it be known just how dissatisfied he was with the state of things. The eight women blocking the doorway slowly moved aside and then, as soon as mother and child had passed, shifted back again to their original places. Three minutes later the process was repeated as mother and child came back in and sat down—a little ritual performed several times each service by different players.

We sang some hymns, and then the collection was taken. After that two Nepali assistant nurses stood up and sang a song, the words and music of which they had composed themselves. It was beautifully done. After another hymn it was time for the sermon, which could be expected to go on for forty-five minutes, if Pastor Abraham was up to form. People settled into different positions, and Abraham started in.

Abraham never failed to amaze me. It wasn't his preaching— it was the man himself. He had originally been a traveling singer, a *gaine,* one of the lowest caste groups. Converted to Christianity in an Indian mission hospital where he had been treated for polio, he had returned to Nepal and had begun preaching up and down the hills of his native land. He had been to every corner of Nepal, and now in his late fifties he was still spending part of each year on the trail. That he could get around at all with his paralyzed arm and leg was remarkable enough, but that he was able as well to travel far and wide year after year on preaching journeys I could only attribute to the power of God resting on the man. Many younger men with two good legs couldn't keep up his pace.

Only a few months earlier he had been out in a remote part of western Nepal when he had been struck with cholera. He was a long way from the nearest settlement and felt convinced he was going to die on the trail. But, as he put it, God restored both his faith and his body, and now here he was back preaching as usual, with no sign of slowing down.

Our services were always full of diversions to keep people alert. Fifteen minutes into the sermon, the dog came to life with a long and penetrating howl. It was being poked with the steel tip of an umbrella. A moment later an equally penetrating odor spread across the room. The dog had gas, and the woman sitting next to it, not wanting to be implicated, was trying unsuccessfully to drive the dog out the door. Last week a loose chicken had managed to hold the interest of the congregation for the better part of the sermon. Dr. Helen's cook, Tata, had brought the chicken to the service—it was to be Helen's dinner. The chicken evidently had other ideas.

The sermon rolled on. Soon eleven-month-old Mika of Finland was creating a new focus of attention near the front of the room. His mother had shut her eyes for a moment, and Mika had taken the opportunity to start crawling toward an inviting tambourine that was used during hymns to liven up the singing. Mika drew out the suspense by stopping to turn around and look at his mother every few moments. He had a lot of second thoughts, and it took him several points of the sermon to get within range of his objective. The entire front of the room held its breath as Mika reached for the prize—then, whump! His mother had him by the foot, and the game was up. We were back to Pastor Abraham just in time for the final prayer.

The people filed out the door, collecting their shoes on the way, and after a quarter-hour of visiting, they began to scatter in different directions. Those who came from a distance would be invited to somebody's house and then stay for the afternoon service and evening Bible study.

To an observer passing by, this crude stone church and the trifling band of mud-splashed, barefoot believers would have offered little worth noting. Yet at that time, this small group was the only Nepali Christian congregation in a surrounding population of more than a million people, a tiny church set alone on one among a thousand hills. That was enough to make it unique. And throughout the entire land there were only a dozen other congregations, mostly in the cities. Twenty years earlier, there had been none.

Until 1950, Nepal had been without a church, essentially without even a Christian presence. For most of its history Nepal had remained closed to foreigners, particularly foreign Christians. The earliest recorded missionary work in the country began in 1707, when a small group of Capuchin fathers arrived overland from Rome. Their efforts continued until 1769, when the first king of Nepal banned all further missionary activity. From that time until the opening of the kingdom in 1951, there was no settled missionary work within its boundaries.

Yet during this period God was not without His witness to the people of Nepal. As Nepalis migrated to India to work in the tea plantations and served as mercenaries in British armies all over the world, they inevitably became exposed to the Christian Gospel. In addition, missionaries with a special concern for Nepal began to settle along major trade routes near its border, gaining access to the growing number of Nepalis journeying to and from their country. Much of this ministry was carried out by expatriated Nepalis who had been converted in India and elsewhere.

During this same period, many unsuccessful attempts were made to penetrate the country. One of the best known of these occurred in 1914, when the famous Indian evangelist Sadhu Sundar Singh entered eastern Nepal, only to be arrested, placed in wooden stocks, covered with leeches, and left until he was "bled" nearly to death.

From 1920 on, foreign mission boards increasingly began to focus their attention on Nepal, then one of the few remaining "closed" countries in the world. By 1950, more than ten missions were operating on the periphery of the country, waiting for the time when they would be permitted to enter. Little did anyone suspect that the first breakthrough would come as a result of a bird-collecting expedition conducted by ornithologist Robert Fleming and his physician-wife, Bethel. It was largely out of their concern over the enormity of the suffering and deprivation they witnessed among the Nepali people that permission was finally granted for foreign Christians to undertake medical work in Nepal and subsequently to establish schools and other development services. This modest beginning has since expanded to include not only the United Mission to Nepal, with its four hundred workers in a dozen different projects, but also a number of other Christian groups engaged in leprosy work and other services.

Also during this period many Nepali Christians previously living in India entered Nepal and formed several congregations in different parts of the country. It was under the leadership of these men that a truly indigenous Nepali church came into existence. This church, essentially a loose-knit fellowship of independent congregations and scattered individuals, has developed free of foreign control. Missionaries have never planted churches, baptized new believers, or taken official positions of leadership in the Nepali church. The church is self-supporting and self-propagating. Across the land in ever increasing numbers, believers are meeting in scores of tiny isolated groups to worship a Lord that a mere forty years ago had been virtually unknown.

While foreign mission organizations have no formal administrative connection with the Nepali church, missionaries naturally are available to serve as ordinary members of local congregations in the areas where they work. Nepal places no restrictions on religious practice and expression—as long as no one changes his religion, or causes others to change theirs!

Until recently, it was against the law for any Nepali citizen to become a Christian, and any Nepali doing so was liable to a year's jail sentence. Those accused of converting others to Christianity could go to jail for up to six years. The purpose of the law, of course, was to prevent outsiders representing rich, powerful nations and institutions from coercing or enticing the Nepali people to depart from their religious traditions and also at the same time to discourage Nepalis from succumbing to such coercion and enticement. The law doesn't take into account, however, the essential fact that it is not by human agency that men and women are converted to Christ but by the Holy Spirit, who is hard to silence and harder still to throw in jail.

A traditional missionary would find little welcome in Nepal. The country doesn't give visas to pastors and evangelists. All missionaries working in Nepal today have full-time jobs in "secular" professions. We are not restricted, however, in what we do with our free time in our own homes, and many of us find ample opportunity to share our faith privately with our friends. Indeed, any limitation on personal witnessing has come less from the law of the land than from our own diffidence, as well as from fatigue and lack of time.

One of our greatest joys in Amp Pipal has been to teach in the local church. For most of the time the church has had no regular pastor, and members of the congregation have taken turns giving the Saturday-morning message and conducting the Saturday-evening Bible studies. The church has been run by a committee of elders made up of Nepalis and sometimes a Westerner to represent the missionaries. Our little church has been blessed with a number of fine young leaders over the years, though many of them have since gone on to bigger and better things. In fact, a disproportionally large number of Christian leaders throughout the country have originally come from our district, back in the early days of the Amp Pipal project.

In the hospital, opportunities to speak about spiritual matters are more limited, largely because of lack of time. This is especially true in the outpatient department. However, at ten o'clock each morning we hold a prayer meeting, open to anyone, in the hospital prayer room, and usually a dozen or more outpatients wander in to see what's going on. Literature is available, though for books a fee is charged so that we don't give the appearance of promoting our religion through gifts. On the ward the opportunity to talk with patients is greater, of course, than in the outpatient department, but here we must be even more circumspect lest we be accused of "preaching to a captive audience." The government would take a dim view of our using the hospital to take advantage of its citizens.

Yet the hospital is known far and wide as a Christian hospital. Indeed, that is one of the reasons patients come in such large numbers. Healing is more than just curing the body, and though it's the latter that most people come for, those wanting more than that sense they can find it at Amp Pipal Hospital. As more than one patient has said: "The demons have no power here." Before the hospital even opened, Dr. Helen, its founder, was given a prophecy that this was to be a hospital of the "living Word," and so it has been.

That is not to say all Nepalis are happy that the Amp Pipal Hospital is a Christian hospital. A few years ago students from the local high school broke into the prayer room and took out all the hymnbooks and other literature and burned them in a great bonfire in front of the hospital entrance. Yet most people viewed this as an act of vandalism and disrespect for others, and it gained for the perpetrators the contempt of the community. In the end far more good than harm came of it, which is usually God's way.

That wasn't the first instance of bookburning at Amp Pipal, and it probably won't be the last. Part of the community's outrage over that episode can no doubt be ascribed to the fact that we are foreign guests, entitled thereby to consideration and respect. Nepalis are not so solicitous, however, for their own people who adopt the "foreigners' religion." When Nepali believers are victimized by Christian-baiters, the onlookers will generally applaud.

A few years ago, during an otherwise ordinary Saturday-morning service, the church was unexpectedly attacked by an angry mob of two hundred students wielding heavy sticks. The Nepali worshipers were driven outside and told that if they ever met in the church again, they would be beaten and reported to the police. The Nepalis took the threat seriously—the students were obviously capable of backing it up—and the church building was closed. Services were moved to the house of Prakash, our anesthetist. Only two of the Nepali Christians, along with Dr. Helen, stood to confront the students that day: Prakash, and a courageous young woman named Moti Maya. Nonetheless, from that day on it was abundantly clear that the Christians were without protection or legal redress; they could be harried and hounded with impunity, and then sent off to jail as well.

Under circumstances such as these, then, a Nepali might well think twice about becoming a Christian. For one contemplating such a step, fear of imprisonment has probably been the major deterrent. Although only a small percentage of Christians have actually wound up in jail, the possibility has been real and has hung over the head of each new believer. Up until recently, at any one time you could have counted on a dozen or more Nepalis being in jail—simply because they had become Christians.

Whereas only a few Christians have ended up in jail, they have all experienced ostracism. In a society so centered on family and community life, it is a devastating blow to be forced out of one's village, disowned and disinherited by one's parents, and abandoned by one's friends. Yet this has happened to young Nepali Christians over and over again, and it's still happening.

The persecution takes many forms. One high-school boy, three months from graduation, was expelled from school when he acknowledged that he had been baptized. Some Christians have had their personal possessions confiscated or destroyed. Still others have been publicly mocked and even beaten in their villages. Many have had to leave the place of their birth and look for employment elsewhere. And if jobs are hard to find for the ordinary person, imagine what it's like for a Christian to find one. New Christians, in short, find themselves alone, often with inadequate spiritual and material support. Becoming a Christian under these circumstances is very much like walking the plank. This is why the ceremony of baptism is such a significant event for Christians in Nepal: It is the single public act that brings down on their head the condemnation of society and family. It's little wonder that some new Christians have gone across the border into India to be baptized, while others simply remain secret believers, afraid to openly profess their faith.

It's easy to see that any Nepali who becomes a Christian means business. The Christians of this land have counted the cost—and are paying it. And as has happened so many times through history, adversity has only made the church grow faster.

Once people take the step to become Christians, they face another more subtle pressure, a pressure from within the Christian community itself: to conform to the standards of behavior set by the church. Let new believers slip or falter once, and they find themselves almost as severely censured by their fellow believers as they had been by society when they first became Christians.

The reason for this is understandable. A rudimentary Christian community in a country where the Gospel is largely unknown is extremely vulnerable when one of its members misbehaves. It is such a giant step for these few, frightened, and isolated Christian Nepalis just to embrace their new faith that many of them are unable at first to grasp the more awesome fact that through their visible behavior they are now the principal means of making Christ known to other people. Thus when a church member—either Nepali or foreign—falls into disrepute, it is a staggering blow to the reputation of the tiny local church and effectively negates the witness of the rest of the congregation. Looking back on the short history of the church at Amp Pipal, it must be confessed that one after another of us has so stumbled and fumbled that if God hadn't had other means of maintaining His honor beyond our uneven performance, He would have found Himself in a bad way in Amp Pipal.

The greatest challenge to any Christian community is that its members live like Christians. The greatest deterrent to the spread of the Gospel is that many who profess to be Christians don't live like Christians. The one great witness we can offer to our non-Christian neighbors is that Christ makes a difference in our lives. And we can be sure our neighbors are watching us closely to see if it's so—especially in a place like Nepal.

One of the major areas of difficulty for new Christians in Nepal is the matter of giving up their former Hindu practices. Hinduism is a syncretistic religion, and many Hindus happily "accept" Christ by adding Him to the list of deities they worship. They see no conflict in this; the idea of exclusivity is foreign to them. The Nepali church, however, is emphatic in its acknowledgment of only one Lord and demands of its new members a total break with Hinduism.

The problem is that Hinduism is intimately woven into the fabric of Nepali life. Nearly every activity or relationship is in some way defined by Hindu belief and practice. Simple respect for parents demands attention to numerous Hindu rites— especially at their death. Marriage ceremonies, feasts, illnesses, even the love between brother and sister, are all clothed in explicitly Hindu ritual. The job is to strip away the ritual and still have left something with which new Christians can culturally identify.

In Nepal today, believers face the same situation faced by the first believers in New Testament times. Enduring ridicule and persecution from the society around them and struggling to find and maintain their identity as a Christian minority in a Hindu land, Nepali Christians are providing an example of courage and faithfulness that we Westerners would do well to emulate.

They are also providing an example of unity. The painful fragmentation that has affected the Christian church in nearly every other country on the globe has yet to leave a permanent mark on the Nepali church, which remains fundamentally united on all important issues. These new, unsophisticated Christians, whose only guiding coordinates have been the Bible and the testimony of the Holy Spirit, gaze with incredulity out on a splintered Christendom; and when we lamely try to explain away the rifts that have separated professing Christians and caused them to discredit one another's faith, they remind us simply that Jesus accepted anyone who acknowledged Him as Lord and did the will of the Father. They have studied the Bible and have found that for every biblical passage instructing them to "be separate" and to "come out from among them," dozens of other passages command them to "judge not" and to be united. With minds unmolested by the posturing and competing claims of this and that Christian camp, they are learning, as a minority church in a hostile society, that they won't be heard unless they speak in unison. They, more acutely than most, understand the danger of letting the demand for doctrinal "purity" in peripheral matters diffract the single beam of the church's oneness.

Christians on Trial

S OME TIME AGO we invited to supper a missionary couple and two single missionary women, members of our team at Amp Pipal. Cynthia had prepared a special meal for the occasion, with plenty to eat. On this particular evening, as our amply dressed and nourished guests entered the house, a fifth figure appeared out of the darkness behind them. In contrast to the missionaries, he was lean and bony, and as he stood shivering in the cool November air, he wrapped his arms around his chest to keep out the cold. His only clothes were a thin, short-sleeved shirt and a pair of short pants.

It was Mohan, nineteen years old, who had just walked an hour from his village to attend the Friday-night Nepal Christian Fellowship meeting, which was held in a hospital staff member's room. As Mohan tried to follow through the door after the guests, I stopped him. I knew he was hoping for a meal before he went to his meeting, and I knew he wouldn't get one anywhere else. Yet I turned him away—in spite of knowing we would have food left over.

Mohan didn't eat that night or the next morning. He stayed for the Saturday-morning church service, which lasted three hours. Then he went home, hungry but cheerful, intending to return Tuesday for the evening Bible study. Which he did.

Mohan was obviously a believer. He was eager for every opportunity to hear God's Word and had asked to be baptized. He was also desperately poor. He had six younger brothers and sisters and got little to eat at home. We had, in fact, fed him on similar previous occasions but had begun to notice that he was spending more time with the foreign missionaries than with the local Nepali Christians.

We had said to Mohan, "You can count on getting God's Word when you come here, but not food. You must either eat before you come or bring your own rice."

"I'm not coming for food," he replied. "I need work too, but I'm not coming for that either. My family and neighbors ask me why I come here, what benefit I'm getting. I tell them it's to find God, to receive His Spirit, to be His disciple. If I get food or clothes or work here, how will they know the real reason I come?"

How will they, indeed? How will even Mohan himself know? The lure of material gain is stronger than we imagine; it pervades the consciousness of the poor. How do we protect this new spiritual plant from being choked by thorns—and at the same time fulfill our basic obligation to provide for those in need?

It's a dilemma that rich missionaries in a poor country need to sidestep by referring the matter to national Christians, who are better able to assess the motives of seekers and inquirers than we. Furthermore, the Nepali government frowns on people becoming Christians for *any* reason, let alone for material gain. We run the risk not only of producing "rice-Christians" but also of being expelled from the country.

We steadfastly refused to give Mohan any material assistance. Each time he came, we would refer him to one of the Nepali Christians, usually to Tika Ram, the assistant cashier, who lived in a small rented room near the hospital. Tika Ram, though but a new Christian himself, was already a leader in the local church and had shown on many occasions considerable discernment in dealing with cases such as Mohan's.

Tika Ram was not poor by Nepali standards, but he had learned the cost of discipleship in other ways. He was from a strict, high-caste family, who hadn't objected to his believing in Christ until they realized it meant he was no longer a Hindu. The year before, when Tika Ram failed to show up at home for the main Hindu festival of *Dasai,* opposition from his family and village had begun in earnest. They had abused and reviled him, and tried to prevent him from coming to work. Then some time later men sent by his father had gone to his room near the hospital and removed all his belongings, including his bed. The family had hoped thereby to force him to live at home, where they would be able more readily to dissuade him from following this foreign religion. When other Christians provided for Tika Ram's needs, thus thwarting his father's intentions, the father threatened to deprive Tika Ram of his inheritance. Now, a year later, the conflict continued unabated.

What better person than Tika Ram, then, to teach Mohan what it meant to be a Christian, how "anyone who loves his father or mother more than me is not worthy of me"? Who better than Tika Ram to tell Mohan to "seek first God's kingdom and His righteousness" and then "all these things will be given to you as well"?

Soon Mohan stopped coming to our house. We felt some qualms about this but reflected that he was better off associating with the Nepali Christians, who had less in the way of material goods to offer him. But it wasn't long before he had stopped coming to meetings altogether. One day I asked Tika Ram what had happened.

"Oh, he's not a believer," was the reply. "He's a fake." Tika Ram explained that Mohan had finally admitted that his parents had put him up to coming to Amp Pipal and posing as a Christian just to get a job with the mission. It was an all-too-common occurrence. Mohan's story had one difference, though: He was the only one who ever owned up to his duplicity.

Of course, who ever came to God from entirely pure motives? Most inquirers no doubt believe they are sincere; if some temporal advantage should also accrue from their association with Christians, so much the better! And if they believe they're sincere, who are we to doubt them? Woe to us if by our hardness we drive away those whom God has called.

Life would be simpler for missionaries if they had nothing material to offer anyone. Missionary theorists talk about going to the people with "empty hands." Well, that might be fine for many places, but we wouldn't get far in Nepal with empty hands—we wouldn't even get visas to enter the country. We are welcome in the country only because we have something to offer *other* than our religion, be it medicine, education, jobs, scholarships, or *gobar* (manure) gas plants. So, in Nepal anyway, there is no escaping the problem of people like Mohan.

Our only recourse is to be scrupulously impartial in dispensing our favors. In actuality we end up discriminating *against* those who show an interest in Christianity. Suppose, for example, that two young men, equally qualified, apply for a job at the hospital. One begins coming to Bible studies. The other gets the job! Otherwise, we open ourselves to the charge of playing favorites and enticing people to become Christians with job offers—charges that would be hard to refute. Even toward those who are already Christians, we must take care to show no partiality in the exercise of our administrative duties, something they find hard to understand. It's not just a question of who gets the job. Nepali Christians rightly ask: Is this a Christian hospital you're running or not? Do you want Christians in positions of leadership or not? A Christian mission needs to say yes to these questions, and somehow remain impartial at the same time.

Aside from the need to avoid partiality, we need to exercise care in granting benefits to Christians for an even more important reason: They easily become vulnerable to the corrupting power of this world's goods. More than once have we seen a vibrant young Christian turned aside by the liberality of a well-meaning foreigner. More than once the foreigner has been myself.

Regardless of our honest efforts to be impartial in giving jobs, a disproportionate number, perhaps 10 percent, of the hospital staff are Christians. There are good reasons for this. Some of them became Christians after working with us for years. Others, already Christians, were hired because they were the best qualified for the job. A few were transferred from other projects.

The problem appears, however, when we look at the membership of our local church: Almost all the members are either employed by the mission or related to those who are. So people will charge that we have not only rice-Christians but also a rice-church! The charge is easily rebutted; we are, after all, in Nepal, where there are relatively few rice-Christians. The hardship endured by Christians in this country is too high a price to pay in exchange for any kind of rice. But in the eyes of the Hindu community around us, the church is merely the ward of the mission, with no independent life of its own. The Nepali Christians are regarded as opportunists, or worse, like Mohan, frauds—until, that is, they have had occasion to suffer for their beliefs. Then, and only then, is the Hindu community convinced that their faith is genuine. In fact, the Christian who has suffered and stood firm is held in esteem by the community; and Christianity suddenly becomes attractive, authentic.

In the early years of a mission project there is no way to avoid having a church full of mission employees. Amp Pipal had no church at all before the mission came, and it was inevitable that the people first attracted to Christianity should have some connection with the mission. On the other hand, it's also true that a church that remains indefinitely in the shadow of a large mission project will have difficulty developing its own strong and independent leadership. At Amp Pipal we have witnessed the gradual emergence of a viable church with its own leaders, a process that has been hastened by the determination of the missionaries to remain in the background and keep their hands off.

Our experience in Amp Pipal has highlighted some of the problems inherent in setting up mission institutions in a country like Nepal, in particular the tendency of such institutions to retard the development of an independent national church. Some missionary strategists would prefer to do away with mission institutions altogether and go into countries not as managers but as servants, working alongside the nationals in *their* institutions. And that approach has merit.

However, Nepal had very few national institutions at all when the United Mission was first invited into the country. Moreover, the mission's purpose was to "minister to the needs of the people," and to do that, the mission needed to establish institutions. And it was natural that these institutions be "Christian" institutions, managed and directed by Christians. An institution, after all, is only as "Christian" as the people who work in it.

However, the situation in Nepal today is changing rapidly. Government programs in health, education, and economic development have come into their own. The need for foreign-run projects is decreasing. Thus missionaries, together with national Christians, have begun to work with the government on its projects. Furthermore, all foreign missions in Nepal work with the understanding that the government will gradually take over their institutions, a process euphemistically called "Nepalization." The United Mission, in fact, is actively committed to this process, and for years it has been recruiting and preparing suitable Nepalis to take leadership in its projects. But as "Nepalization" takes place, the role of "Christian" institutions will inevitably diminish. Christians in Nepal, then, both foreign and national, need to prepare themselves for the day when they *all* will be working for government or other non-mission organizations. That will be a time of further testing: Leaving our Christian "compounds" is never easy.

The church in Amp Pipal owes its existence to the establishment of a mission project. Some of the first Nepalis to become Christians in Amp Pipal, in fact, were healed of serious illnesses at the first dispensary, long before the hospital was ever built. Such was the case with Dil Kumar, whose first introduction to the mission came the day he was brought to the dispensary, nearly dead from tuberculosis. The disease was far advanced in both lungs, making him pant for breath even while lying down. He was started on treatment, and for months he lingered between life and death. Several times his lungs collapsed, nearly killing him on the spot; at other times he coughed up so much blood that he almost died from blood loss. He continued to fail in spite of treatment. Medically his case was hopeless.

Those of us who deal with the seriously ill develop a feeling about patients, a sense of whether or not they're going to make it. We're not always right, of course, but very few patients for whom we've lost all hope survive in the end. In rare cases, however, we've seen patients so far gone that death has seemed but seconds away, yet for no apparent reason they have suddenly picked up and gone on to recover.

Dil Kumar was such a patient. Those caring for him, including Dr. Helen, attributed his healing to divine intervention. Dil himself came to the same conclusion; and as a result of his illness and his close brush with death, he found faith in God and became a Christian.

This created a considerable stir in the village, because Dil was an influential and highly respected member of the community. At first the villagers didn't trouble themselves about it—Christianity, after all, wasn't something to be taken too seriously—and furthermore, they were awed by his amazing recovery. They were prepared to believe with him that he had been healed by God's power. And if Dil wanted to call God "Christ," that was all right too.

Not long after that, however, Dil's father died, and Dil was called home to perform the Hindu funeral rites. He refused. The community was outraged: No one refused such a fundamental duty, especially to one's own father. But Dil stood fast, and suddenly his former friends and neighbors realized that Dil's new religion wasn't something to joke about: Indeed, it was vitally opposed to their most firmly held beliefs.

The angry villagers retaliated, and Dil soon found himself an object of scorn, assailed at every hand. He lost his land, his inheritance, his friends, and his standing in the community. He had become a public enemy, a disgrace, even a criminal. Only his wife stood with him. Indeed, she had become a Christian before he had, and while nursing him back to health had shared her new faith with him.

Having lost everything and having no means of support—he was too weak to do manual labor—Dil accepted a job at the mission dispensary. He couldn't read the English names of the different medicines, but he could count pills and wrap them in old magazine pages to give to patients. Gradually as his strength returned, he was given more and more responsibility, and before long he was collecting the money. His English improved too, and a few years later, when the hospital opened, he became its first cashier.

As the months passed and the villagers saw that Dil was not dissuaded by their abuse but endured it patiently, their attitude slowly changed. They began to see Dil as a man who had been somehow touched by God, as a man who had the courage of his convictions. Little by little their anger against him was replaced by a grudging respect, and in the end his enemies treated him once more with friendliness and even deference.

For many years Dil remained the sole male Nepali Christian in Amp Pipal. It was a lonely position. But he endured, and slowly, one by one, a small group of Nepali believers gathered around him to form a congregation. During this time the missionaries also came to rely on him for much more than just the handling of cash. His judgment and his knowledge of local affairs proved invaluable in helping the missionaries through many crises. By the time Cynthia and I arrived in Amp Pipal, Dil was not only the acknowledged leader of the church but also the confidant and chief advisor of the missionary team. And on the day early in my career when I almost killed a cow, Dil was there. It was he, more than anyone else, who was responsible for calming that angry crowd and explaining to the villagers that missionaries were not only human, they were often dumb. Had it not been for Dil, I believe my career at Amp Pipal would have come to an abrupt and ignoble end.

Others, like a young Brahmin named Rudra, had a more tenuous connection to the mission. Rudra was an independent thinker who provoked controversy in his village by trying out new things: new crops, new fertilizers, new methods of irrigation. Some villagers considered him an innovator; others called him a crackpot. When his agricultural ventures proved successful, his neighbors became jealous and sabotaged his efforts by stealing his produce and diverting his irrigation water into their own fields. They let their animals eat his cabbages and fruit-tree seedlings, and when someone's goat died from eating one of Rudra's recently sprayed trees, the village held Rudra responsible and made him pay for the goat!

Rudra didn't limit his independent thinking to agriculture. During high school he had heard about Christianity from a teacher in one of the early mission schools, and what he learned had remained in his mind. He was disillusioned with Hinduism as practiced in his village and felt that it served merely as a barrier to progress. Eager to learn more about Christianity, he set out for Amp Pipal to see if he could find a book about this religion and perhaps meet one of the missionaries.

He arrived on a weekday and eventually found his way into Val Collett's community-health office. Though she was busy, she took a few minutes to chat with him and loaned him a Bible to take home and read. She suggested he come back Saturday for the church service, after which people would have more time to talk with him.

Rudra came Saturday and attended the service, but somehow no one had much time for talking. Everyone, I think, had assumed I would spend the afternoon with Rudra since I was the only man in the project at the time and Dil and Pastor Abraham weren't around. But Cynthia and I had guests that day, so I wasn't free either. After talking with Rudra for a few minutes, I excused myself, mumbling something about guests, and said I would be happy to meet with him next week, same time. (It was only a two-hour walk from his village, after all.) We could hardly be accused of "pushing" our religion!

The next week Rudra didn't come to church. But just before supper that evening, he and a friend showed up at our house. That was awkward, as we had invited some people to eat with us; the best I could do would be to sit and talk with them until supper was ready. I told them I had been expecting them earlier, that now I could talk with them only briefly. They assured me they would be grateful for whatever time I could give them. Although they didn't show it, they must have been put off by our way of having to fit everything into a schedule. Certainly no one who had walked two hours to *their* village would get treated that way.

We had an amiable conversation, and I was favorably impressed by the young men. What's more, they seemed genuinely interested in Christianity. Rudra said he had been reading the Bible Val had given him, and to prove it, he had a number of questions to ask me on some difficult passages. I didn't know about his friend, but Rudra certainly didn't seem to be angling for a job: He was well-off and had plenty to do keeping his various agricultural projects going. He wasn't about to go off for more schooling, so he didn't need a mission scholarship. And here he was walking two hours to talk with me for thirty minutes about Christianity. They planned to walk back home that evening—they could just make it before dark. If anyone was inquiring about our religion without ulterior motive, surely it was Rudra, and probably his friend too. Rudra said to me, "We would like you to teach us the Bible. Can you give us classes?"

I invited them to our Tuesday-night Bible study and told them we could even help them with sleeping accommodations if they wanted. I was reluctant to include food in the offer—that would be an "enticement." They left saying they would be back Tuesday. Sure enough, two days later they showed up at our house for the Bible study, having eaten just before in a nearby teashop. We had eleven young men in the class that evening, and we talked late into the night. It was a lively and stimulating time. I was happy that finally these two new fellows had gotten a kick out of our church and heard something to challenge them. They had gotten off to a slow enough start with us; this helped make up for it.

It was midnight before the meeting broke up, and I still had to arrange a place for Rudra and his friend to sleep. The guest room on the ground floor of Dr. Helen's house was vacant, so I put them in there; Helen lived on the second floor, with a separate entrance into her quarters. As I said good-bye to the young men, I hung the padlock back on its latch, clicked it shut, and pocketed the key. "I'll lock the place up tomorrow," I said. "Just close the door when you go out." I knew they wanted to leave as soon as it was light in the morning, and this way they wouldn't have to worry about where to leave the key at that hour.

Rudra and his friend didn't go straight to bed, however. Instead they went down to the hospital to see one of Rudra's relatives who happened to be a patient at the time. Since the relative was asleep, they sat for a while in the nursing station and visited with the night nurse, a Nepali they knew slightly. As luck would have it, Dr. Helen arrived at that moment, having just remembered something about one of her patients. At the sight of Rudra and his companion she drew up, sniffing a scandal in the making. Not knowing who they were but suspecting the worst, she told them sharply to get out, that they had no business sitting there having tête-à-têtes with young women in the middle of the night, and so forth. Rudra and his friend sheepishly retreated to the bedside of Rudra's sleeping relative.

Meanwhile Helen went back to bed. She was no sooner asleep than the door to the downstairs guest room began banging in the wind. Again waking up and thinking that robbers were trying to break in, Helen went outside and down the path to the guest room below. Finding the door open and the padlock hanging locked on the latch, she went out, fetched another padlock from her room, closed the door, locked it, and then went back to bed.

It was raining when Rudra and his friend finally returned to the guest room to sleep. They were surprised to find the door locked, and after debating for a moment what to do about it, they came up to our house to get the key from me. I greeted them with a trace of grumpiness. Between their embarrassed stammering and the rain beating on the tin roof, I sleepily understood something about the wind locking them out and, finding no reason to question it, I gave them the key and went back to bed. Of course, it was the wrong key: In the dark they hadn't noticed that a new lock had been put on the door. Seeing no point in arousing me again, they went back down to the hospital and slept the rest of the night on the cement floor outside the prayer room.

Such were the sleeping arrangements we had worked out for

eighteight

our visitors. The next day after we all realized what had happened, I wondered if they would ever return for an evening Bible study—or any other meeting for that matter. They had hardly been received as honored guests.

I needn't have worried. They returned for the next Saturday service, and for the next Bible study as well. They kept coming back until they were satisfied that this new religion was indeed for them, at which point they went ahead and became full members of the church. In the succeeding years we have lost track of Rudra's friend, but we have watched Rudra develop into a mature and consistent Christian, a new kind of innovation for his village. And though he has not suffered the persecution that Dil Kumar experienced, he has nonetheless had to endure the daily sniping of his jealous neighbors. Worse, they still steal his crops. They have evidently found it easier to harvest the fruit of another man's labors than to grow it themselves.

One by one the church increases. Our fellowship has few "ordinary" people. There's the man whose leprous feet prevent him from doing heavy labor or walking long distances. He works as a night watchman for the grounds outside the hospital, and on any given night we can hear him reading the Bible out loud to himself or singing hymns from the Nepali hymnal. There's the former alcoholic, one of the church's most eloquent spokesmen, who mortified everyone two days after his baptism by going on a binge and regaling the crowds at the hospital with wondrous accounts of his religious experiences. It was a shaky beginning.

And there are many more friends like these, all of them with their own stories to tell. Through these distinctive people God is building His church in the hills of Nepal.

nine

Ram Bahadur

*T*HE SUPPER invitation was for six o'clock at the house of Ram Bahadur's parents in Rip Gaun, a fifteen-minute walk up the mountain from the hospital. Ram himself lived elsewhere, but whenever he had guests, he invited them to his parents' house. When I asked if cooking for guests was too great a burden to be laying on his aging parents, he replied, "Oh, no trouble at all." Nonetheless, I was secretly relieved on his parents' behalf when the other two families Ram had invited to supper were unable to go.

Rip Gaun, the village nearest the hospital, was one of the villages least receptive to modern medicine, modern education, and progress in general—not to mention Christianity. This resistance to change was undoubtedly due in part to the influence of Rip Gaun's chief shaman or witch doctor—Ram Bahadur's father, to whose house I had been invited for supper. Ram was the shaman's eldest son and would ordinarily have been expected to inherit his father's position. A younger brother, Gopal, having finished tenth grade at the mission-founded school in Amp Pipal, had become the leader of a militant Communist youth organization devoted to destabilizing Nepal's social, economic, and political institutions as a prelude to full-scale revolution; included as one of its prime targets was the Amp Pipal Hospital. We received no end of headaches from this young agitator until one day he was hauled off to jail for two weeks for attempting to disrupt the balloting during a nation-wide constitutional referendum. After that, his revolutionary zeal dampened.

nine

When I arrived at the house, Ram Bahadur was not there. But I was welcomed warmly by his mother, who laid a *gundri,* or straw mat, out on the front porch for me to sit on. Ram's father, the shaman, appeared from a nearby vegetable patch, and giving me a slight nod, sat down next to me on the *gundri.* Our relationship over the years had been strained because of his younger son's antics and also because his own medical practice had frequently run counter to ours—much to the detriment of some of his patients. Tonight, however, if not exactly amiable, he was at least gruffly civil, and we were soon engaged in a wide-ranging conversation that gradually passed from matters pertaining to this life to those that pertained to the next.

An hour and a half passed, and Ram still hadn't shown up. Had he forgotten? Then one of his sisters came bouncing along the path with news that Ram was at a youth meeting and would be down soon. Since the food was ready by this time, Ram's parents invited me inside the house and promptly served me a large tin platter heaped with steaming rice, accompanied by four small bowls containing spiced vegetables and, especially for the occasion, indiscriminately chopped up pieces of goat—muscles, tendons, skin, bones—all dished up together in a tasty sauce. In Nepali homes the guest eats first, with all the family members in attendance, watching to see that his plate and various bowls are continually replenished. It's worse than attending a duchess's luncheon: There you only *feel* that all eyes are on you; here, they actually are.

By the time I had finished eating, darkness had fallen outside. The interior of the house was illuminated only by a tiny alcohol lamp and by the embers of the fire glowing in a small depression in the center of the floor. The light barely suffused into the fifteen-by-fifteen-foot room that constituted the ground floor. Above was a crude loft where the family's grain and seed were stored. The "ceiling," consisting of irregularly split slats laid across rough beams, was blackened with the soot and smoke of many fires—and thereby protected from termites.

Even at noon the room would have been dark. Aside from the narrow doorway, the only other source of outside light was a

tiny window opening onto the low-roofed porch and covered
with a thickly latticed wooden shutter. We sat on the floor. The
house had no furniture—no table, no chair, no stool, no
cupboard, no shelves, no bed, no pictures on the mud walls. A
few straw mats for sleeping were rolled upright in one corner;
two beat-up baskets for carrying manure and a newer basket for
carrying the water jug to the spring ten minutes away stood in
another corner. A few coils of homemade rope for tying up the
family's goats and buffalos lay nearby. Piles of straw and
unthreshed millet were strewn here and there. Along one wall lay
a wooden plow. Except for a large copper cauldron, all the pots,
plates, and glasses the family owned were in use. One ladle and
one spatula were the only implements I saw; we ate with our
fingers.

On the floor near the door were a few tattered school books
belonging to the two daughters. They had begun to eat, their
guest having finished, and were deftly propelling handfuls of rice
into their mouths without dropping so much as a kernel. I had
fared less well on that score: If the kernels I dropped had been
gathered, there would have been enough for another small
helping.

Two and a half hours had elapsed since I had arrived, and we
had all been fed, except the mother, who like all Nepali
housewives always ate last. Ram still had not appeared. The
conversation faltered. I found myself reflecting on the spareness
of this "upper-middle-class" household and wondered why the
chief shaman of Rip Gaun indulged in no more amenities than
did his poorest neighbors. Had his medical practice suffered with
the arrival of the hospital? Probably not. Most villagers in Nepal
invest whatever income they manage to accumulate in land and
livestock, not in luxuries. Certainly the shaman illustrated this
truth.

As I began uneasily to contrast this unembellished home with
the mission house in which we lived, a voice became increasingly
audible in the darkness outside. It was someone approaching
with a transistor radio. No, it wasn't a radio; it was a cassette
recorder. The speaker's voice became louder and louder—the

whole village could have heard it. Then I realized the man's voice was reciting a portion of Scripture—in fact, Paul's first letter to Timothy—one of a series of tapes of the New Testament in the Nepali language. The voice came booming at full volume right up to the door, and in walked Ram Bahadur cranking a small hand-operated playback machine we had loaned him some weeks before. He seemed glad to see me, and sitting down to his meal, he began to eat and talk all at once as casually as if he had been three minutes late instead of three hours. The youth meeting had been fabulous, he said, twenty or thirty present, great singing, terrific fellowship, a real blessing. His parents looked as if they had heard it before. The sisters took up the playback machine and cranked us through Second Timothy and on into Titus, making further sustained conversation impossible. By the time we reached Philemon, I decided it was time to leave, having already stayed two hours longer than I had intended. Ram joined me, since his lodgings were also near the hospital; and as we walked, the remainder of Philemon rose voluminously into the starry night.

As the two of us walked, I thought back to the first time Cynthia and I had met Ram Bahadur twelve years earlier, shortly after we had arrived in Amp Pipal. We had been in the process of starting our garden, and knowing nothing about gardening, we had hired Ram to be our gardener. We were soon to regret our choice. It would be hard to imagine anyone less suited to gardening—or any other kind of physical work for that matter.

The first sign of trouble had appeared when Cynthia had asked him to dig a hole three feet wide and three feet deep in which to plant a fig tree; the hole that resulted after two hours of labor would have nicely accommodated a partially inflated volleyball. Other examples had followed, and we were finally forced to conclude that this was the most indolent, slow-moving fellow we had ever encountered. This deficiency was compounded by the fact that he knew nothing about gardening—at least, our kind of gardening. After several weeks of making excuses for Ram—our meager ability to speak his language, rocky inhospitable soil, poor equipment—we had finally let him go. Although he had remained unfailingly cheerful and courteous, we had not seen a particle of improvement in his work.

Fortunately, there had been no repercussions from Ram's dismissal, in spite of the fact, as we later discovered, that he was the son of the most influential shaman in the area. People in rural Nepal don't take kindly to losing their jobs, especially when jobs are scare. Such "loss of face" often results in retaliation, like cutting the mission water pipes and electrical lines or filling the hospital water tanks with mud and stones.

The next time Cynthia and I ran into Ram Bahadur had been three years later, when he was a patient in the hospital. For several months we had been hearing reports of Ram's strange behavior—his refusing to speak or eat with anyone, and walking naked about the village, often disappearing for days on end. Instead of showing the kindness and sympathy customarily afforded the mentally ill, the villagers had treated Ram with contempt and abuse. They regarded his sickness as a form of depravity and perverseness. School children threw stones at him. He withdrew further into his troubled world, spending days at a time hiding in the jungle without eating. His father, pressured by the community to disown his son and throw him out of the village, began to lose both hope and patience.

Before dawn one morning, gaunt and wild-eyed, Ram had appeared at Dr. Helen's house to seek help. Since Helen was away at the time, Dr. Eleanor Knox, who knew nothing of Ram or his problem, sent him down to the hospital to be admitted by the doctor on call. The Nepali nurse on duty had told Ram to wait outside until eight o'clock, when the doctor would be coming down to make his rounds. Perhaps the nurse thought Ram had been drinking; perhaps she thought he was dangerous; perhaps she simply didn't want to bother the doctor. At any rate, Ram left and did not return.

When Cynthia heard of Eleanor's early morning visitor, she knew at once who it was. For several days Ram disappeared from sight, and when he finally turned up at his father's house one night, he could barely walk. He was allowed to lie out on one end of the narrow side porch where the goats were tied up, and there he remained, neither eating nor speaking, growing progressively feebler with each passing day.

A week elapsed before we learned that Ram was at his father's house. Cynthia, together with Dr. Eleanor, who was experienced in psychiatric disorders, decided to go up to Rip Gaun and see him. They found him lying in a dark corner, incoherent, disheveled, and wasted. With his father's permission, they proceeded to talk to him, and to everyone's amazement he began to speak for the first time since he had visited Eleanor that early morning the week before.

"I came to find help from the Christian doctors," Ram said faintly. "I believed that your God would heal me. But I became afraid. No doctor came. I thought people from my village would come and find me and beat me. So I ran away."

"Do you still believe God can heal you?" asked Dr. Eleanor.

"Yes, I believe it," he answered, almost inaudibly. "I want Him to heal me."

The gravity of his condition was plain to see. Since the family seemed disinclined to take any action, a Nepali Christian living nearby volunteered to carry Ram down to the hospital, where he could receive proper medication and be fed, if necessary, by means of a stomach tube. The Christian neighbor, arriving at the house shortly thereafter and finding that Ram had changed his mind and was no longer willing to go to the hospital, simply picked him up in his arms, slung him over his shoulder like a half-empty sack of rice, and marched off with him down the hill.

I had been a bit apprehensive on hearing that yet another psychiatric case had been admitted to the hospital; we generally discouraged the admission of such patients since they were extremely difficult to manage under the best of circumstances, let alone in a busy, minimally staffed general hospital in the hills of Nepal. Some of our mentally disturbed patients have broken down doors, ripped out light fixtures, shredded expensive foam-rubber mattresses into tiny pieces, and generally created so much commotion that the staff have been unable to attend to their regular duties. One fearful young woman periodically eluded her "tormentors" by climbing onto the multi-leveled tin roof of the hospital, where the attempt to recapture her was like a rerun of one of those old movies of police chasing thieves across the rooftops of Paris.

However, Cynthia's compassion and spiritual intuition prevailed over my administrative misgivings, and Ram was admitted to one of our two private rooms. Members of the Christian community took turns attending him in the absence of his family, and more importantly, they prayed for him. For days his condition remained unchanged. The whole church, both missionary and Nepali, individually and in groups, persevered in prayer that Ram might not only recover from his illness but also come to know and love the God in whom he had so recently placed his faltering hope.

Whether one ascribes the cure of such patients to time, prayer, medicine, or a combination of the three, it doesn't alter or detract from the fact that within four weeks Ram Bahadur was completely healed. He had become a new person, talking freely, eating ravenously, and deeply grateful to the Christians who had shared God's love with him. On the day he left the hospital, Cynthia sat with him in his room and talked to him about Jesus, leaving with him a small copy of Mark's gospel. In the end, she prayed that he would follow the light that had shone on him even in the depths of his sickness and that he would keep following it until he had reached its source.

After that we didn't see Ram for several years. He tried first to enlist in the army, but failing that, he had gone off to India to find work. He had been away from home almost three years when one day his mother came to a special meeting at our church. She said that her son hadn't written for six months, and she asked us to pray for him and for her—that he would write and relieve her anxiety. A devout Nepali woman named Battini, illiterate but full of faith, happened to be attending the meeting that day, and she, together with Cynthia, took the mother aside and prayed that Ram might be kept from harm and that he would write home soon and reassure his worried family. They also had prayed that Ram would come to know the Lord who had healed him. After they had prayed, Battini said, "Go home now in peace. You will hear from your son."

Months went by, and no word came. Cynthia became uneasy whenever she encountered the family, fearing to hear yet again the same negative reply to her inquiries. Then one day, four months after Battini and Cynthia had prayed that Ram would write, a letter arrived from Ram stating that he was well and had a good job in northern India. The letter, however, had been written and posted four months earlier—within the very week, in fact, that Battini and Cynthia had prayed with the mother.

When Cynthia visited the family some days later to follow up this answer to prayer, she found the mother had gone off on a pilgrimage of thanksgiving to a famous Hindu shrine a day's journey away. After the mother had returned, Cynthia went again to their home and chided the shaman and his wife for having received a benefit from one god and then given thanks to another. "Do you suppose," Cynthia said to them, "that the living God who has healed your son will be pleased that you have done this?"

A year later Ram Bahadur, having tired of the heat and bustle of the densely populated plains of northern India, returned to his home in the quiet and familiar Himalayan foothills. His disposition was again bright and cheerful, as it had been before his illness. After trying in vain to get a job at the hospital, he went to work as a dutiful son in his father's fields.

A year had passed this way when Campus Crusade, an organization new to Nepal, announced a month-long evangelism seminar to be held in Pokhara and invited the churches of western Nepal to send suitable candidates for training. The only Amp Pipal church member who was free to go was an assistant in the hospital pharmacy. Somehow Ram also heard about the seminar and asked if he could go along too. As the pharmacy assistant wanted a companion, the church committee somewhat hesitantly agreed—providing that Ram would pay his own way, since he wasn't a church member.

The seminar turned out to be the occasion for which the church had been praying, for it was there that Ram met the Lord and committed his life to Him. He also caught something of

Campus Crusade's vision—and their exuberance. No sooner had he arrived back in Amp Pipal than he invited to the very next Wednesday-night prayer meeting a dozen of the neighborhood children, infusing the session with unaccustomed evangelistic fervor. Others who had known about our meetings for years and never attended suddenly began to show up—having been urged by Ram to come. Even his revolutionary younger brother, Gopal, started attending sporadically.

Some months later Ram was formally accepted into our church fellowship and has since gone on to become a valued member of the congregation. Because he has had no regular job to tie him down, he has been free to do a variety of activities that in the past no one else had time to do. He has remained willing and available to run errands, carry messages, and perform cheerfully even the most menial services that might be asked of him. He has made more use of the church tapes than anyone else; in his hands the playback machine has rarely been at rest.

Recently Ram has been instrumental in forming a lively Christian youth group, a development that has had a resuscitating effect on the entire church. Their meetings have been well attended, and some of them have run hours beyond "schedule"—more accurately without schedule. One of those meetings happened to have coincided with my dinner engagement that night at the home of Ram's parents—and had been the cause of Ram's showing up three hours late.

This is only the beginning of Ram Bahadur's story. The real story is yet to come. For the future, Ram has talked about going to Bible school in order to be better able to share the Good News with his family and neighbors. His enthusiasm is infectious; his vision is ever-expanding, undimmed by his parents' coolness and the threats of beatings from his brother's former friends.

But Ram Bahadur is not alone. There is in Nepal an increasing number of young men and women like Ram Bahadur. They are the fruit of the labor of many groups of believers working in this land. They are the building stones of a new church.

Tanka Prasad

O F ALL THE Nepali members of our church, Tanka Prasad is the one with whom I have had more dealings than with any other. When we first came to Amp Pipal, he was the assistant building supervisor at the hospital, which was still under construction at the time. Slight of stature, like most Nepalis, with black hair and dark complexion, he possessed little in the way of physical characteristics that would have set him apart from his fellows. He had the typical features of a Brahmin—a narrow face, sharp nose, pointed chin—and when he fixed you with his eyes, you had the feeling that he looked inside you instead of at you. But it was never for long: His eyes were restless, like the rest of him. He was intense, high-strung, always in motion—ideal, I suppose, for a hospital building supervisor.

Tanka Prasad wasn't a Christian back then, when we first knew him. He was brusque and overbearing, self-confident, self-important, and cocky to the point of rudeness. I couldn't understand what he was saying most of the time; I always felt whenever he spoke as if someone was blowing peas in my ear through a peashooter. Even though I seldom crossed paths with him in those early days when I worked only half-time at the hospital and had no administrative responsibilities, I rarely missed knowing when he was nearby, for he was continually peppering his workmen with a sharp, staccato volley of comments and criticism that ricocheted along the hospital corridors from one end to the other. The workmen put up with him good-naturedly even though he was much younger than they were: He could read and write, while they could not. Furthermore, as a Brahmin he could demand and expect to receive the respect of the lower castes.

Behind Tanka Prasad's quick tongue was an equally quick mind. He took his work seriously and drove himself as hard as he drove anyone else. He held a responsible position, helping to supervise forty or fifty men, all of whom were more experienced in their particular jobs than he was. He had learned the different aspects of the work rapidly, however, and by the time the hospital building was completed, he had acquired many of the skills himself.

My first direct contact with Tanka Prasad came after we had been in Amp Pipal several months. Although we had a hospital generator that provided electricity for both the hospital and the various staff houses, we found that we had no electric outlet in our own house for plugging in appliances. Therefore, I asked Tanka Prasad if he could run a cord to some convenient but inconspicuous place in the house and connect an outlet for us. Ever courteous to the missionaries, who paid his salary, he said he would be happy to do it, he would get to it the very next day, not to worry.

The next day I was off to Lapsibot, a six-hour walk to the north, for one of our regular monthly village clinics. When I returned the following evening, the first thing that met my eye as I walked in the house, tired and hungry, was an ugly, fat, off-white electric cord running right down the middle of our living-room wall, ending in an outlet fixture a yard off the floor. The cord must have been hooked up to a hot current because the second I saw it, it blew fuses in both my cerebral hemispheres. I can't say why that cord troubled me so; my aesthetic sensibilities couldn't have been offended that much, seeing that the wall itself was made of mud and buffalo manure. Nonetheless, it caught me at a low moment, and all during supper I found myself staring at that wretched cord and thinking up suitable ways of settling the score with that cocky building supervisor.

In the midst of creating this problem for myself, I was suddenly struck by the thought that Christ is sort of like that cord, cutting right across people's lives—and there at the end is that outlet, inviting them to plug in. I had gotten unplugged all right. But the crisis soon passed, and never did I say a word to Tanka Prasad.

After the hospital construction was completed, Tanka Prasad stayed on as our maintenance man, a job that he was by that time well-equipped to handle. But he helped out in other ways too. For example, he was there in the operating room, holding down one of my first intestinal obstruction cases—until the patient suddenly died on the table. And it was Tanka Prasad who had pumped the respirator bag during the final hours of Maya's life—a life brought to an untimely end by the ingestion of two cans of bedbug poison.

Several weeks after Maya's death, Tanka Prasad called me over our local battery-operated phone circuit and asked me to come to see him at once. He was calling from the house of another missionary, and over the phone he sounded frightened about something. He begged me to come quickly.

I was shocked to find Tanka on the verge of hysteria. His normally quick and nervous movements were grossly accentuated. He was perspiring, twitching, and looking distractedly this way and that with wide, frightened eyes. And no wonder. Only half an hour before, he had swallowed half a can of bedbug poison—the same poison Maya had used—and now he was having second thoughts!

How anyone could have watched Maya's slow and terrible death for so many hours at such close range and then have gone and taken the same poison himself was utterly beyond me. I knew that Tanka Prasad had been turned down for a mission scholarship and was discouraged about his prospects for furthering his education, but that hardly seemed sufficient reason for resorting to this.

We hastily got Tanka Prasad down to the hospital, pumped out his stomach, and gave him some injections of atropine to counteract the effects of the poison—we knew the treatment this time—and he was spared the consequences of his rash act. In fact, he experienced only a few minimal symptoms of poisoning, and these lasted only a matter of hours.

Tanka Prasad remained unsettled, however, and his work deteriorated. Finally he quit and went off to another city to try his hand at something new. Shortly following his departure we discovered that he had been misappropriating certain hospital supplies, and not long thereafter we heard that he had gotten into some kind of trouble and had fled across the border into India to avoid arrest.

We lost touch with him after that, and several years went by before we caught up with him again. He was in Kathmandu this time, working with our mission headquarters in the supply office. Somewhere along the line, through all his troubles, Tanka had become a Christian. The most profound influence in his life had come during his stay in India, where he had met up with a team of Christians working with Operation Mobilization, an evangelistic organization consisting mainly of young people. The leader of the team happened to be a Nepali, a Brahmin like himself, who invited him to join the group. So for several months Tanka Prasad traveled through India with his new companions, learning about Christianity and also finding out what it was like to live as a disciple of Christ. By the time Tanka left them, a process had been set in motion that would change his life for good.

Tanka Prasad did well in Kathmandu and eventually became second in charge of the mission's central service department. There he proved himself able, industrious, and honest. He became a member in good standing of one of the Kathmandu congregations. He also studied on the side in an attempt to earn his high-school diploma. Indeed, it looked as if he had tapped into that popular formula that says if you do good, you'll be successful. For him it had apparently come true.

One thing changed the equation for Tanka Prasad, however: He returned to Amp Pipal. He had begun to have a hankering to go back to his village near the hospital. He felt a burden for his own people, for his parents in particular, and believed God was calling him to share with them his newfound life in Christ. At the same time that this conviction was forming in his mind, we were having a major staffing crisis at the hospital, with a number of our senior people, including missionaries, all leaving within a short time. We urgently needed a replacement for our purchasing officer and our maintenance supervisor, both of whom were departing, and the only person I knew of capable of holding down either post was Tanka Prasad. In fact, I thought he could take care of both jobs at once; but even if he couldn't, he would be far better than nothing, since we had no other prospects in sight.

Our biggest hurdle was persuading the mission to release Tanka Prasad from his job at headquarters; they were naturally reluctant to lose such a reliable worker—though they had a much better chance of finding a similar person in Kathmandu than we had in Amp Pipal. Conveniently for us, the king had recently launched with great fanfare a nationwide "Back to the Village" campaign to encourage talented young people to leave the cities and return home to aid in the development of their own communities. Jumping on the royal bandwagon, we urged headquarters to get in step with the king's campaign and send Tanka Prasad back to his village. In the end they agreed to let us have him.

Others on the hospital staff, however, were not so eager to have Tanka back on the staff. They remembered how he used to be, and they were quick to note that his personality and some of his mannerisms were little changed—as if they had expected a green apple to ripen into a peach. Thus Tanka Prasad met with a less-than-gracious reception on his return to the hospital, and this discouraged him.

Even less gracious was his reception by the village, especially by his own family. It was known that he had become a Christian, and the fact that he was a Brahmin only heightened the offense. The father was torn between his love for his son and the village Brahmins' demand that he disown him and throw him out. The Brahmins won, and Tanka Prasad, having finally returned home after an absence of more than five years, was turned out of the house by his tearful parents and forced to take a small room near the hospital.

Tanka Prasad had been prepared for such treatment. He knew through his reading of Scripture and the testimony of other Nepali Christians that his conversion would result in personal hardship and possible persecution. At first he seemed almost spurred on by his troubles, believing that God was favoring him by giving him this opportunity to suffer for his faith. He spent much of his spare time trying to persuade his former friends that Christ was the answer for all Nepalis and that Christianity was not a foreign religion but had actually originated in Asia and was just as much for Asians as it was for Westerners. His efforts, however, won him only more enemies, in part, perhaps, because of his brash manner. Eventually becoming disheartened, he withdrew from active confrontation with the community and devoted himself to his responsibilities in the hospital and the church fellowship.

For a while opposition to Tanka Prasad died down, and it looked as if his troubles might be coming to an end. But within a few months trouble struck again. And this time I found myself caught in the middle of it.

One day, without any forewarning, I emerged from the operating room to find the entire outpatient area packed with an excited crowd of shouting, pushing people. The clinic had been totally disrupted, and everyone was crowding toward my office to see what was going on. I heard some people asking "Where's the doctor, where's the doctor?" and others near me saying "Here he is, here he is," as they shoved each other aside to make way for me.

As I got closer to the office, I sensed the crowd's staring at me with what seemed like morbid curiosity, and when I got still closer, it began to look more like anger. What had I done to cause this? I couldn't make a thing out of the hubbub since everyone was talking at once. But I wasn't to remain in the dark for long. Pushing my way into the office, I saw Tanka Prasad and a policeman. Angry Nepalis had crammed into every available space. I noticed the X-ray technician, one of Tanka Prasad's chief detractors, standing in a corner smiling contemptuously. And then I saw the cause of the commotion: On my examining table lay a young woman, face up, fully clothed but without a sign of life.

Oh, God, I thought. *She's dead.*

Then I asked out loud, looking at Tanka Prasad, "What's going on here?"

"We're being arrested," Tanka said.

"Who's being arrested?" I said.

"You and me."

"For what?"

"For conspiring together to murder my wife."

His wife? Yes, I recalled he had a wife in the village, but she had gone back to her own family as soon as they had gotten word of his religious conversion, and she hadn't had a thing to do with him since. And certainly I hadn't had anything to do with her. I didn't even know her.

A murder case! I glanced at the woman again. She looked dead enough; I could detect no motion, not even a quiver. She lay straight and rigid, her face wax-like, drained of blood. But as I kept looking at her, as if hoping to see one little twitch or flicker, I realized that she was breathing. I felt the blood returning to my own face. At least it wasn't murder—not yet, anyway.

A short swarthy man wearing a frayed vest and the usual coarse white loincloth stepped forward and pointed a finger at me. "That's him, sir," he said, addressing the policeman. "He poisoned her. She's been like this ever since she left here." He added an exclamation point to his sentence by spitting at my feet.

"That's her father," Tanka Prasad whispered to me. "My wife was here two days ago, and you gave her medicine. They say it was poison and that I had asked you to poison her for me. What on earth did you give her?"

"How do I know without looking at the card," I said. "Are you sure I saw her?"

"That's what they say."

I had the sick feeling that maybe I had given ten times the dose of some medicine or other, misplaced a decimal perhaps. Usually the pharmacy workers picked up that sort of mistake and checked with us. Or maybe she was having a drug reaction.

The father scowled at me malevolently. He was a singularly unpleasant man, unshaven, with straggly hair sticking out from beneath a dirty, shapeless topi. The others with him scowled also, as if trying to outdo each other in looking disagreeable. Most were relatives of the young woman on the table, but other enemies of Tanka Prasad had come along as well.

The policeman turned to me, "Doctor, did you treat this patient two days ago?"

I had no recollection. She could have been any one of fifty or more patients I saw that day. "I have to see the card," I said. "I can't say anything until I've seen her card." I looked around for Sita, the office assistant. "Sita, Sita," I called. Where had she gone just when we needed her most?

"I'm here, I'm here," came a high-pitched voice from the middle of the crowd pressing at the door. "I'm bringing the card." Sita was always six steps ahead of me.

Sure enough, Tanka Prasad's wife had been to the hospital two days earlier, and I had been the one who had examined her. But then I saw with relief that I had written only for worm medicine, the safest and most common treatment we gave at the hospital. And the dose was right, too. The card said she had complained of mild stomach pain and that the physical examination had been normal. The stool report showed roundworms.

Tanka Prasad read the card over my shoulder.

"There's something strange going on here," I said.

"That's what I think," he agreed. "Someone is framing us."

It was fine for him to say that. But he wasn't responsible for the half-dead young woman lying on my table. Even if it hadn't been my fault, it could still have been a pharmacy mistake. Besides, these people could say anything they wanted. They could say I wrote worm medicine to cover up what I had really given her. I was satisfied I had done nothing wrong, but it was the others who needed convincing—like the policeman, and who knows who else after that.

Everyone seemed to be waiting for me to do something, now that I had seen the card. Tanka Prasad suggested I had better at least examine the patient. Maybe she needed treatment.

It was a quite reasonable suggestion. I had forgotten that I was also the doctor on the case. I told the policeman that I couldn't examine the patient until the crowd was out of the office. I insisted that everyone leave except Sita, Tanka Prasad, the father, and, of course, the policeman.

I told Sita to undress the young woman. The father and Tanka Prasad had to help, since the young woman just lay there without moving, and even with the three of them working, it took them a long time to get her clothes off. I then slowly and deliberately went over her from head to foot. I found virtually nothing except that she was in a coma. I found only two other unusual signs, her slow breathing and a low blood pressure, but they were both within the lower limits of normal.

But all this time my suspicions had been increasing. The whole business didn't fit together. I had never seen anybody this deep in coma before without other physical findings to go along with it. I suddenly thought to myself: *This patient is hysterical*. To test my idea, I shook her a little. When that produced no response, I began to prod her, punch her, pinch her, and finally to yell at her. I told her to get up, that I knew she was acting, that nothing was wrong with her. But she just lay there. The father meanwhile got angry and said I was lying and that I had better stop mauling his daughter or he would press charges for that, too.

Of course, hysterical patients don't usually respond to poking and pinching—I knew that, actually—but all the same I was a little disappointed that it hadn't worked. Maybe she wasn't hysterical; maybe I'd missed something. And how was I going to convince anyone else if I wasn't even convinced myself?

Tanka Prasad was looking more and more worried. Right at that moment I formed a resolution: I would try to call their bluff even if it meant bluffing some myself. It was a gamble, but if it worked and I turned out to be right, we could save ourselves a lot of trouble. I didn't want to spend a night or a week at some police station, and I knew that Tanka Prasad wanted to avoid the prospect more than I did; he could expect far worse treatment than I would be given.

Putting on my most professional air, I said to the policeman in as positive a tone as I could produce: "She's bluffing. She's faking. This is all an act." Then I turned to the father, and working up steam as I went along, I said, "You've made up this whole business. You've come here, stirring up all this commotion, disrupting the entire hospital just to cause trouble for Christians and for foreigners who are trying to serve your country. These are all lies you've been speaking. You've put your daughter up to this. This is the rottenest thing I've ever seen in my life. You're the one who ought to be put in jail!"

My performance wouldn't have won an Oscar, but it was evidently good enough for the policeman. He looked from me to the young woman, then to the father, and back to me again. Then he said apologetically, "We've caused you much inconvenience today, Doctor. Thank you for helping us with this case. There will be no charges against you, and you needn't come with us to the station. But I'll have to take the husband; we're not finished with him yet."

It was always that way: The Nepali Christians bore the brunt of any trouble. The foreigners got the apology.

The young woman all this time had been lying there like a corpse. I motioned to Sita to begin dressing her. That took twice as long as the undressing, of course, but I thought during the procedure that I detected some voluntary movements by the patient, as if, tired of the game, she was trying to speed things up by being helpful. But I couldn't be sure; what with the three men and Sita pulling her this way and that, she could have had a convulsion and I might have missed it.

We called for the *doli*, and loaded the patient onto it. Out the door trooped the sullen party, with the policeman and Tanka Prasad following behind. As they went out, I squeezed Tanka's arm and said, "The church will be praying for you tonight."

He smiled, but just barely. "What's going to happen to her?"

he said, looking toward the *doli*. "She's the same. They'll still get me for poisoning her. And supposing she dies? Supposing you turn out to be wrong saying it was all an act?"

It was my turn to smile, just barely. "She won't die" was all I had time to say, and he was out the door.

We didn't waste any time getting back to the regular patients, who had been pushed aside during the turmoil. It was the middle of the afternoon. The entire circus had lasted an hour.

At the usual time next day, Tanka Prasad showed up for work. As soon as I heard he had come, I went to find him. He greeted me with a big grin. "My wife woke up as soon as we got to the police station," he said in answer to my questioning look. "The police were disgusted. In the end they fined her father 300 rupees for disturbing the peace. I've never seen him so mad."

"They'll think twice before pulling that kind of trick again," I said.

He nodded. "Yes, maybe they'll realize God is on my side after all."

I wish I could say that things went smoothly for Tanka Prasad after that, but it would be far from the truth. He had many enemies, not only in the village but also among the hospital staff, and they seldom let pass an opportunity to harass him. Saddest of all, though, was the fact that many of his own Christian brothers and sisters, including the missionaries, remained cool toward him.

It was during the many months of Communist-led disturbances, however, that Tanka Prasad suffered his greatest trials. He became the special target of the student mobs that troubled us during that period. Indeed, he was the object of their first major demonstration at the hospital: He was the purchasing officer at the time, falsely accused of cheating some porters, and the students had come down to mete out their own style of justice. There's an old saying that it's easier to die for Christ than to live for Him. That day, Tanka Prasad almost got the chance to test the difference.

As for the difficulty of living for Christ, Tanka Prasad knows more about that than most missionaries do—certainly more than this one.

eleven

Megh Nath and Jyoti

E *VENTUALLY* Tanka Prasad left the hospital to become an evangelist for the Nepal Christian Fellowship. His departure left us without a purchasing officer, and to find someone who could write English and take the required financial responsibility was next to impossible. Such highly qualified Nepalis invariably gravitated to the cities and had no interest in working in rural areas where the pay was low and the conveniences few. We knew of no local person who could begin to take Tanka Prasad's place. What's more, losing him was doubly hard because we had just lost our Nepali business manager also and we could have used Tanka to train the new missionary business manager, who was to arrive soon. It was one of the worst staff crises we had yet faced.

Tanka Prasad had given us the required month's notice of his retirement and even had agreed to stay on a few extra weeks if we were unable to find his replacement in time. The month passed. At the end of his second week of overtime we were no closer to finding a replacement than we had been at the beginning. We didn't even have any leads. Tanka Prasad could give us only one more week, and then he had to leave.

We had begun to make contingency plans in case we didn't find anyone, but these plans were palatable to no one since they involved distributing Tanka Prasad's duties to people already overworked. And, as was usually the case during a crisis, the hospital was furiously busy.

I was out on my lawn writing a final flurry of letters to various people who might on a long chance be able to suggest someone eleven

to replace Tanka Prasad, when a young man about twenty years old walked up the steps to our yard and over to where I was working. I had never seen him before. His manner was brisk and confident. His dress was immaculate.

"I was passing through and heard you are looking for a purchasing officer," he said in passable English. "My name is Megh Nath. I'm interested in the job."

It sounded too good to be true. However, years in Nepal had made me wary. We had heard of instances where young men dropping by like this had turned out to be professional thieves or Communist agitators. Why should a well-dressed Nepali with such facility in English be wandering about in our out-of-the-way corner of the district in the first place? Something was fishy.

"Yes, we need a purchasing officer," I said without letting on how desperate our need was. "What qualifications do you have for the job? Tell me about yourself."

Megh Nath said he had been born in the village of Borang, a day's walk north of Amp Pipal. After finishing middle school, he had gone to live with an uncle in Darjeeling, India, where he completed high school. He had then gone on to Calcutta for college but had to drop out after a year for lack of money. Next, he worked for a short time in Calcutta but soon grew homesick and decided to return to Nepal to look for work. He had just come from visiting his parents in Borang, he said, and as he passed through Amp Pipal, he had heard about our job opening and had stopped to inquire.

Megh Nath's story seemed plausible enough. When he saw that I understood Nepali, he left off speaking English and spoke in his own language. In spite of his outward self-confidence he appeared slightly nervous; he spoke rapidly and generally averted his eyes. I didn't think much about it since this was common among high-caste Nepali men. In fact, I thought he was forthright, and I believed his story.

"We'll need some references," I said. "We can't take people fresh off the trail and give them positions of such responsibility without getting some sort of written confirmation of their past. We need to see your high-school certificate and the transcript from that college in Calcutta. And we need at least one character reference." We usually asked for two, but I didn't want to give him the idea that I doubted his story, lest he take offense. We couldn't risk losing this young man. I had already begun to look on him as an answer to our prayers.

"I will write for the transcripts and for a reference," Megh Nath assured me. They would be weeks coming, I knew, and we would have to make a decision to hire him long before that. But since everyone the mission hired remained on probation for the first six months, the documents would arrive by the time Megh Nath was ready to be confirmed, which was time enough.

"But you shouldn't really need any letter of reference," Megh Nath went on. "I am a Christian. I was baptized in an Assemblies of God church in Darjeeling and later worked with the pastor of a big church in Calcutta. You don't need to have any doubt about my character."

This was amazing; this guy had dropped out of heaven. I could hardly believe it. He was a Christian brother. There weren't ten other Christian men in the district, as far as I knew, and most of them worked for the mission.

"I have no doubt about your character," I told Megh Nath, "but getting character references is routine in any organization. In your case it's just a formality."

I knew, however, that some of our missionary women would be dubious; they had faulted me in the past for making decisions too quickly. They would need to be consulted. I said to Megh Nath, "Please have the pastor who baptized you send us a letter. That would be very helpful to us." I was sure that some of our team members would demand such a letter.

Megh Nath wasn't so sure that he could get such a letter. "How do I know if the pastor is still there?" he said. He couldn't be sure, of course, but I told him to try to get the letter anyway. I then suggested he meet some of our Nepali church members and get to know them. I said we would need a few days to decide, that others on the team would also have to meet him. I then added that I hoped to be able to put him to work in a few days if all went well. He thanked me and left.

eleven

Over the next few days different members of our team interviewed Megh Nath. As usual, those least responsible for the running of the hospital raised the greatest objections to hiring him and wanted to wait for the necessary references. I pointed out that we couldn't wait, that patients and some members of our own missionary team would stand to suffer if we delayed. Furthermore, we would undoubtedly lose him if we didn't give him an answer. A few missionaries said they found Megh Nath shifty; they didn't think they could trust him. They thought his answers were too facile, too glib. I had to agree with them, and some Nepali Christians agreed as well. In the end, however, at my urging and that of the new business manager—who needed a purchasing officer more than anyone else—we hired Megh Nath. Tanka Prasad spent three days teaching Megh Nath his new job and then departed. Our crisis had been resolved. I attributed it entirely to divine intervention.

Megh Nath did not disappoint us. He learned his job quickly and performed it capably. Gradually people's reservations about him lessened, though they did not disappear completely. On the whole, I felt our decision to take him had been vindicated. He was working out as well as anyone could have hoped.

Not long before Megh Nath arrived, the government had assigned three new assistant nurses to our hospital. Since the mission had started one of the government's assistant-nurse training schools, it was only fair that the mission should receive some of the graduates to work in its own projects. At Amp Pipal we had discontinued our local assistant-nurse training program in anticipation of receiving these properly certified government-trained workers. But we never received as many as we needed. So getting three at one time was a record, especially since two others had left us shortly before.

Getting government-trained assistant nurses was a mixed blessing. They were usually short on practical experience and in some cases had been shoddily taught. At the same time they put on airs as if they knew everything and generally resisted instruction. What was worse, they looked down on our locally trained staff, who were doing the same work and usually doing it better.

It came as no surprise, therefore, that after these three new assistant nurses had been put to work, we began to encounter a rash of new and interesting irregularities in our nursing services. Doctors' orders were left undone or imaginatively misconstrued. Alarming errors were made in the dispensing of drugs, particularly in the calculating of dosages. Hardest hit were the decimal points, which were scattered at random and seldom returned to their places. Indeed, the new workers were so weak in math and English (all drug labels and doctors' orders were written in English) that Rigmor, our nursing superintendent, decided they needed remedial help.

To avoid the appearance of singling out the government-trained assistant nurses, the supervisor gave her entire nursing staff a simple test to see where they stood. Our locally trained women all scored over eighty, including one who had been through only third grade. Two of the government-trained assistant nurses scored in the fifties, but one, Jyoti, got only ten out of a hundred!

I was saddened to hear about the test results because, of the three government-trained assistant nurses, I had come to like Jyoti the most. The other two I found a bit prim and snooty for my liking. They were dainty, thin-lipped girls who tiptoed around as if they were walking on worms and who either cried or grew sullen the moment they were corrected. Jyoti, on the other hand, was a plump, full-formed young woman with thick features and a slow waddling gait, who always greeted me with a wide smile and kept on smiling until I had gone. She was the most placid, docile person I have ever met, whether due to natural disposition or to an absence of mental activity I would be hard put to say. But Jyoti was also warm and good-natured. Never once did I see her ruffled or upset. I thought to myself that even if she wasn't such a hot nurse, she would make some guy a pretty nice wife.

But then she went and got only a ten on Rigmor's test, and Rigmor said she would have to let her go. One day shortly after that, I found Jyoti weeping quietly in a corner of the nursing station. She told me that Rigmor had given her a month to shape up or she would lose her job. I sympathized with Rigmor, frankly; Jyoti was a danger to our patients, and that had to be the first consideration. All the same, her tears distressed me, and I tried to comfort her.

"If you really apply yourself, you ought to be able to do better," I said. "You especially need to work on your English and your math; those are your two weakest areas."

"I know that," she said. "But who has time to teach me? I can't learn it by myself."

Suddenly I thought of Megh Nath. He had just come. He knew English better than any Nepali on our staff, and he had also proved capable with figures. Maybe he could tutor Jyoti in math and English. Jyoti agreed to let me ask him.

Megh Nath was skeptical at first, but after I told him it was Jyoti's only chance to keep her job, he agreed to tutor her an hour each afternoon for the next month. They held their sessions in the hospital classroom, where all our training sessions were conducted. It wasn't a private place; people walked by all the time. I occasionally saw them inside together. Megh Nath would be pacing about, waving a piece of chalk and talking fitfully in a high-pitched voice. Jyoti would sit immobile and passive as if expecting without effort to soak up Megh Nath's instruction as a sponge absorbs moisture. It failed, of course, and in the end Jyoti lost her job. But in the process she gained something else: She and Megh Nath fell in love.

Jyoti and Megh Nath made an unlikely pair. She was as sluggish as he was hyperactive. She was dull and he was bright. She was short and pudgy; he was lean and tall. Many might have found Jyoti unattractive and wondered what on earth a handsome Brahmin could have seen in her. Yet, in her own way, Jyoti was voluptuous.

However, Jyoti was not a Christian. Although we never received a letter from Megh Nath's former pastor affirming his baptism, he had been welcomed into the church as a full member and had been participating wholeheartedly in its activities. He knew that the church frowned on any of its members marrying a non-Christian, so he had been trying to teach Jyoti about his faith. But so far she had shown no interest in becoming a Christian.

One day Megh Nath came to me for advice. "I can't wait any longer," he said. "I love her very much. What am I to do?"

I didn't give the answer that Megh Nath was hoping to hear. Instead, I backed up the church's position. I pointed out that the New Testament clearly teaches that believers should not marry non-believers. "The only solution," I said, "is for Jyoti to become a Christian. Perhaps you can find one of the women in the church to talk to her."

We prayed together and then Megh Nath left, visibly crestfallen. A few weeks later, however, he cheerfully told me that Moti Maya, one of the mature church women, had taken an interest in Jyoti and had begun to teach her the Bible. Megh Nath himself frequently went to Moti Maya's house on top of the ridge to be with Jyoti during these informal classes. I was amazed that Moti Maya would prove such a willing matchmaker, knowing how badly she had been used by her own husband. Indeed we felt like conspirators; few others had any inkling of the romance. Our hope was to bring Jyoti to faith and then have a joyful church wedding. Jyoti began to show interest, and Megh Nath agreed to wait.

About two months later, things blew apart. I was sitting outside at my little desk that served as a table, tending to some hospital administrative matters, when one of the members of the church committee came running up the path and said, all out of breath, "A terrible thing is happening right this very minute. You have to go at once and try to stop it. Jyoti and Megh Nath are just moving into the upstairs loft of Ganga Maya's house. They're going to live together there."

In the eyes of the Nepali church such an action was totally wrong. Even in the eyes of the Hindu community around us, living together with one's lover was considered immoral and uncultural. This would be another blot on the reputation of our small and struggling local church. In addition to that, it all seemed so unnecessary. I had been under the impression that Jyoti was on the verge of making a profession of faith.

"What do you want me to do about it?" I asked the church committee member. "I'm not on the church committee myself at the present time. Megh Nath has broken no hospital rule; Jyoti is no longer on the staff. I have no authority to interfere in something that is their private business. Furthermore, it seems as if we are too late to stop it anyway." From where we were, we could look down on Ganga Maya's house; more than the usual number of people had gathered on the path outside, and the buzzing of voices reached even to where we were sitting. It was just like Ganga Maya to be party to something like this. She was also a member of the church, but she had had a similar affair of her own years before, and her Christian testimony was inconsistent at best. Her husband was an alcoholic who only a few months earlier had threatened to murder one of our missionaries. The troubling thing about it was that he had made the threat when he was sober.

The church committee member said, "It's not too late. You can stop Megh Nath if you go right now. You are the only one he'll listen to. Look, there he is now on the path; he's just arriving." Indeed, we could see him. He was carrying a bag over his shoulder, presumably his clothes and bedding.

We ran down the path to Ganga Maya's house. Going up to Megh Nath, I said, "Let's walk up the path a bit. I want to talk to you."

"It won't do any good, Doctor," he said. "I've made up my mind. I'm going to do what I have to do. Jyoti can't live without me. She cries every night for loneliness. She has no job, and she has no friends besides me and Moti Maya. It's my duty to live with her."

I knew that what Megh Nath and Jyoti were doing was a common practice among Nepali young people. It was a lover's expedient for overcoming parental opposition to their marriage. Once such a "love marriage" was consummated, nearly everyone gradually accepted it. However, what Megh Nath and Jyoti did not anticipate was the degree to which they would isolate themselves not only from the church but even from their few remaining close friends. So not just for the church's sake but for their own as well, I attempted as forcefully as I could to dissuade Megh Nath from carrying out his intention.

But Megh Nath remained defiant. Finally he said to me, "Go up and talk to Jyoti yourself. If you can convince her to call it off, maybe I'll listen."

I figured since I had gone this far, I might as well take his suggestion. I climbed up the notched log leading to Ganga Maya's upper loft and ducked in through the narrow entryway. Jyoti was lying on the straw mat that was to serve for their bed. She had pulled a blanket over herself; obviously she hadn't been expecting me.

I hesitated, unsure of what to say. There was a look of triumph in her eyes. She had made her conquest, and she was not about to be talked out of it.

I wished I hadn't come. I said, "Jyoti, what you are doing is not right. You should call this off. You should get married properly."

"I am married properly," she said. "In what other way do you expect me to be married? My parents aren't here to arrange my marriage; my father is dead, and my mother is very old and sick and can't come all the way out here. So we arranged the marriage ourselves." I heard in her voice a hardness I had not heard before.

"The church could have arranged your marriage," I said. "I thought you were about to become a Christian. Why couldn't you wait? Do you realize what you are doing to Megh Nath by marrying him like this? You are cutting him off from the only friends he's got. This marriage is illegal and immoral. Even your own people would tell you that."

"You'll have to ask my *maalik* (master)," she replied, meaning Megh Nath. "He's the one who said we should marry now. I'm only doing what he says."

Seeing that it was useless to proceed further, I backed out the doorway and down the ladder. As soon as I was down, Megh Nath went up without so much as a nod in my direction.

The next day the church committee voted to expel Megh Nath from the congregation and to sever all fellowship with him until he should repent and cease living with Jyoti. Then, if Jyoti herself repented and became a Christian, the church would welcome them both back into fellowship and formalize their marriage.

Months went by. Hardly anyone saw Jyoti. Whenever I bumped into Megh Nath at the hospital, I asked him how things were and his answer was always "fine." But we all knew otherwise. He no longer had any spring to his step. He seldom smiled. He avoided us and buried himself in his work.

One day Megh Nath came to me, asking if I had an extra shirt and pair of pants. When I asked why he wanted them, he said his two brothers, at his father's instructions, had come while he was out and had taken all of his belongings. All he had left were the clothes on his back, and they needed washing. His family in Borang had just found out about his marriage. It was bad enough that he had become a Christian, but his marriage to a non-caste tribal woman was even harder for his high-caste Brahmin family to accept. So they retaliated. His brothers left a note telling Megh Nath that he had been disinherited and that he was not to return to his home in Borang.

Megh Nath looked more dejected than I had ever seen him. I loaned him some clothes. Jyoti also must have been concerned as she watched Megh Nath become progressively cut off from all his former associations and now from his family. Unbeknown to anyone, she began to visit Moti Maya again. She realized at last that only by becoming a Christian could she make Megh Nath happy.

When church members heard about Jyoti's desire to be baptized, most of them doubted her sincerity. She and Megh Nath began attending meetings again, but for weeks people were cool to them. Restoration does not come easily for fallen Christians in Nepal. It was only after Megh Nath publicly confessed his sin before the whole church that the church was open to baptizing Jyoti. The church committee examined Jyoti and felt in the end that her faith was real. The day of her baptism was a joyous occasion. I hadn't seen Megh Nath look so happy in months.

The day after the baptism Megh Nath came to me and said, "Doctor, Jyoti and I want to have a Christian wedding. Will you marry us?"

"How can I marry you?" I asked. "I'm not an ordained pastor."

"There is no one else," Megh Nath said. "We don't want to call some pastor we don't even know to come out here to marry us. We want you to do it. You have been our loyal friend for all this time. You never abandoned us. Please say yes."

It was true that we had no local pastor. The church committee ran the church, and several of us in the congregation took turns doing the preaching. "I've never led a marriage ceremony," I said. "What kind of wedding do you want anyway? Nepali style or Western style?"

"Western style." That was one of Megh Nath's problems. He was always making more effort to relate to the Western missionaries than he was to his fellow Nepali Christians. We Westerners were easier to fool.

"I think it would be better if someone from the church committee married you," I said. "A Nepali elder. How about Prakash?" Prakash, our anesthetist, had been one of Megh Nath's best friends.

Prakash was more uneasy about conducting a wedding service than I was. In the end the church committee decided that I was the best one to perform the wedding ceremony. Ordination was not necessary. The church itself would sanction the marriage.

I could hardly refuse. But I didn't even know the words to say at a wedding. I had almost no recollection of what had been said at my own, and I had been to only one other Western wedding since, my sister's, and that had been twenty years before. Since the wedding was to take place the next Saturday, I had no time to write off for a copy of the service. Cynthia suggested I look in the back of some of our old hymnals, but I found nothing. Then at a colleague's house I found an old tattered Lutheran hymnal, and there in the back was the wedding service all written out. So it would be a Lutheran wedding. Megh Nath was pleased when I told him.

The wedding went off without a hitch. The whole church turned out. I followed the Lutheran script word for word, except in the middle where I added a ten-minute homily on Christian marriage that I had prepared with Cynthia's help. Someone had baked a cake. It was a thoroughly happy time.

Things went well for Megh Nath and Jyoti after that. Megh Nath was given additional responsibility in the hospital business office; he had turned out to be one of our most valuable employees. Six months after the wedding Jyoti gave birth to a six-pound baby girl, whom I delivered by Caesarian section. They were a happy couple, and now proud parents.

Three months later Cynthia and I went home on furlough. We had been home four months when we received a letter from our colleague Dr. Helen Huston, saying that Megh Nath had been fired for major embezzlement carried on over many months. He and Jyoti had left Amp Pipal, and where they had gone, no one knew.

twelve

Kamal and Radha

I FIRST MET Radha in 1973, when she came to Amp Pipal to work as an assistant nurse. I was introduced to her on the path outside Dr. Helen's house in a monsoon downpour, and the smile she flashed at me from under her umbrella was pure sunshine. And the smile wasn't just for me; it was for everyone she met. Within a week she had become known as "Smiling Radha."

Radha was a lovely girl by any standard. Her face radiated warmth and cheer, and I think it cost her some effort just to put on a serious expression. But she was far from frivolous; hidden beneath the sunny disposition was a store of sorrows, the birthright of any female brought up in rural Nepal.

Radha was the youngest of ten children born to a well-to-do Brahmin man who had five wives. Radha's mother, wife number four, had been carried off against her will at a very young age to marry Radha's father, who treated her like a second-class servant. It was largely because of her mother's unhappy marriage that Radha grew up resolving that at all costs she would avoid getting married herself.

After Radha's father died when she was ten years old, she was brought up by her mother and an older brother who loved her tenderly. Radha's mother and brother, however, felt obliged to marry Radha off at the first opportunity to an appropriate suitor. On one occasion they nearly forced Radha to marry the husband of one of her sisters who had failed to produce any offspring. That the wife was always to blame in such cases was an unquestioned assumption, though probably half the time, the fault lay with the husband.

To escape this pressure to marry, Radha eventually left home and traveled forty miles north to the town of Pokhara, where she enrolled in an assistant-nurse class run by the International Nepal Fellowship, another mission agency working in Nepal. Even there, however, she was not safe. She hadn't been in Pokhara many months when her brother came looking for her; the mother and brother had finally arranged a marriage, and they had scheduled her wedding for the following week. The brother gathered together Radha's few belongings and loaded her onto a bus for the two-hour journey back to their village. On the way, as the bus was pulling out of a small roadside hamlet, Radha suddenly got up from her seat, pushed through the passengers crowding in the aisle, and jumped out the back door. By the time the brother could get up to the driver and tell him to stop, the bus was several hundred yards down the road, and Radha was deep into the woods.

She made her way back to Pokhara, walking along back trails. Her brother finally decided it was useless to pursue such an intractable, headstrong girl. Even if he were to succeed in capturing her and forcing her into the hands of this man, she would undoubtedly end up disgracing the family one way or another, either by running off again or by doing something worse. Already they had been embarrassed enough; they didn't care to become more so.

This rebellious act drove a final wedge between Radha and her family. She had never been close to her mother—it was her brother she preferred—but now her mother gave up on her entirely and would have nothing more to do with her. The brother, though more tenderly disposed, also left her alone after that. Radha, meanwhile, finished her assistant-nurse training and began to work in the mission hospital in Pokhara.

Then, once more, the rumor of a new match in the making reached Radha, and she decided that Pokhara was too close to home for comfort. So Radha's nursing supervisor arranged for her to be transferred to our hospital in Amp Pipal, a full day's journey away. Within a few weeks Radha was on her way to the safety and seclusion of our remote mountaintop.

Radha proved to be an exceptionally fine assistant nurse. Maybe part of it was that smile, which, judging from my own reaction, ought to have made any patient get well twice as quickly. But she was also gentle and meticulous in her care of patients. When she was on duty at night, we could all sleep well.

Radha was also a Christian. She had first heard the Gospel from the older brother of her closest childhood girlfriend. She had heard more about Christianity at the mission hospital in Pokhara, and by the time she reached Amp Pipal, she was a confirmed believer. After joining the nurses' Bible class on her arrival, she soon realized from her study of the New Testament that she needed to be baptized. Before that, she hadn't given much thought to making a public profession of faith. Within six months of her arrival in Amp Pipal, she was taking special classes in preparation for baptism and full membership in the church.

The only problem was that when Radha was ready to be baptized, there was no one in our congregation who felt qualified to perform the ceremony. Pastor Abraham had gone. Dil Kumar was hesitant—he was only a layperson, after all. And the missionaries, as foreign guests of the government, scrupulously avoided taking any part in baptisms. That was a matter for the Nepalis alone to arrange.

The local Nepali Christians decided to invite a pastor to come out from Kathmandu to conduct the baptismal ceremony, and at the same time to lead a series of special meetings in our church. They chose Pastor Suman, a well-known and respected leader who had recently spent a year in jail in western Nepal for preaching the Gospel and for distributing literature. He agreed to come, and on Easter afternoon, 1974, he walked with Radha and two other Nepali women from the congregation down to a stream two hours below the hospital and there quietly baptized her.

There was no fanfare: The pastor, after all, didn't care to attract unnecessary attention. The penalty for baptizing someone was six years in prison, and seeing that he had already been a year behind bars for illegal religious activity, he'd likely be given an even stiffer sentence if caught. He was taking a major risk to baptize this young village woman whom he hardly knew. It was even suspected that many congregations were infiltrated by spies looking for opportunities to bring charges against Christians—in particular the charge of baptizing a new convert. But Pastor Suman was more than willing to take the risk; he had been taking it for years.

Radha's family eventually heard of her baptism and were predictably outraged. Then Radha received word that her brother was coming to take her home and marry her to a proper Hindu. For days the church prayed that the brother's mission would come to nothing and that Radha would have the strength to turn him away. But when the brother finally arrived and heard from Radha herself about her new faith, he relented; and although he didn't exactly approve of her conversion, he assured her of his continuing care and love. With this assurance given, he returned to his village, undoubtedly wondering on the way what explanation he would give to his mother for returning empty-handed.

During Radha's second year in Amp Pipal, she developed tuberculosis, and for many weeks she was seriously ill with high fever and recurring accumulations of chest fluid that required frequent pleural taps. Tuberculosis was an occupational hazard for medical workers, and although we tried to minimize the risk to our staff in various ways, it couldn't be eliminated entirely. Radha remained cheerful throughout her illness, however, and her room became a gathering place for many of the female staff, who would drop by at the end of their duties and visit for hours on end. Fortunately, Rhada's type of tuberculosis was not very contagious.

Another visitor to Radha's hospital room during this period was Rudra, the young man whom Dr. Helen had locked out of the guest room one night. Rudra had also been recently baptized and had been coming regularly to Bible classes, and now, with Cynthia's quiet encouragement, he had begun to take an interest in Radha. Cynthia has that congenital predisposition that wants to see every young person happily married, and here, ready-made for her, were two eligible Christian young people right on each other's doorstep—an extremely rare occurrence in the hills of Nepal.

One of the major difficulties the Nepali church faces is finding suitable Christian spouses for its young people. To begin with, so few Christians are available, and what's more, since their families are usually opposed to such matches, the young people have no one to help them get together. In Nepal, social custom prohibits young couples from conducting affairs on their own and demands that older people negotiate for them. This is also the position the Nepali church takes. Thus Cynthia was not meddling but playing a proper and indispensable role; and who better than she, a foreigner, married herself, someone who could be counted on to be neutral and to have the best interest of both parties at heart?

But much to Cynthia's dismay, Radha didn't cooperate. After enduring several of Rudra's visits, Radha finally sent him packing and told him not to call on her again. She was upset with Cynthia, too, and told her that she had no intention of getting married—ever, thank you—and that she was quite capable of managing her own life. It was a setback.

Radha went on to recover from her tuberculosis and once more resumed her duties as an assistant nurse. Some of our single missionary women were openly pleased that Radha had once again escaped the matrimonial trap, for now they were free to set before her visions of their own—namely, further education, with a career to follow. Radha had been in seventh grade when she first left her village and went to Pokhara for her assistant-nurse course. Now she was encouraged to seize the opportunity to return to Pokhara and finish high school. To turn this vision into reality, several of the missionary women set up a scholarship fund to cover her expenses for the remaining years of her high-school education. And so, after having spent two years in Amp Pipal, Radha went back to Pokhara and back to school. She kept in close touch, however, with her friends in Amp Pipal—including Cynthia; indeed, she returned for most of her school vacations to work in our hospital, for which we were always thankful.

A few months before one of Radha's periodic visits, our church invited a young Christian leader named Kamal to come and conduct a series of meetings. He was a short man, even for a Nepali, and somewhat heavyset, with a round, pleasant face and a brisk, efficient manner. Though not imposing in appearance, Kamal was a forceful speaker with an unusual gift for presenting spiritual truth in vivid and understandable terms.

One night Cynthia and I invited him for supper in order to get to know him better. And during the meal and on into the evening we listened spellbound as he told us about his experiences as a Christian in Nepal. He was the son of a Brahmin priest and had received the necessary education to prepare him to follow in his father's footsteps. The medium of his instruction was Sanskrit, the ancient classical language of the Indian subcontinent. For some time he had carried out the duties of a Hindu priest under his father's watchful eye. But even as the major tenets of Hinduism were being inculcated in Kamal's mind, he was becoming increasingly troubled by what he learned. He was particularly disturbed by the fact that "the Hindu gods and their incarnations came mainly to punish and destroy" and that their own lives "were full of sin and treachery." He asked himself, "If all these gods are unholy, who will help me to be holy? If all came to destroy, who will save?"

When Kamal was fifteen, a man sold him a Nepali New Testament, saying: "This is a religious book; it will be good for you to read it." Kamal took his new book home and began to study it. When he came to Matthew 5:43–44, he was surprised to discover Jesus' saying: "Love your enemies and pray for those who persecute you."

"I had been taught to seek out my enemies and destroy them," Kamal told us. "This teaching was just the opposite."

Then he came to Matthew 18:11 and read the words, "The Son of Man came to save what was lost." And in a flash Kamal realized that this was the God who came to save sinners and not destroy them and that this was the God he must follow. "From that day on," Kamal related to us, "I accepted Christ as God and determined to obey Him. I stopped worshiping idols and threw away my holy thread. My father, of course, disowned me and turned me out of the house, telling me that I was never to enter again. So I found work in a government office in the village, but because I kept preaching about the God who saves sinners, the police and the governor of the district came and arrested me. I was released from prison after a few days, but I lost my job. After that I had to leave my village, and even the district, because of the opposition of the police."

Kamal then told us how he had become an itinerant preacher, traveling on foot from village to village, encouraging small isolated groups of believers and sharing the Gospel with anyone who would listen. During this period he was harassed by the police on numerous occasions. Finally, on a trip to western Nepal, he had been arrested and put in jail for thirteen months for preaching and attempting to convert Hindus to Christianity.

"When was that?" we asked.

"I went to jail in the middle of December 1970."

That was precisely when we first had come to Amp Pipal to live; he was going to jail just as we were beginning our work in Nepal. "Were you alone then?" we asked.

"No, I was arrested with Pastor Suman. We were together in jail."

So Kamal had been Pastor Suman's partner in prison! We had known about Pastor Suman and another man going to jail when we first arrived in Amp Pipal; the word had spread quickly through the Nepali church—even to the ears of new missionaries. Then, when Pastor Suman had come to Amp Pipal to baptize Radha, we had heard more of the story directly from him. But we had never learned who the second man was—and here he was sitting at our table.

Pastor Suman and Kamal had gone together on a preaching tour to the far-western part of Nepal and had been passing out literature to anyone who showed an interest. One man who was particularly interested was a local police official. Posing as an ordinary citizen, he approached the pair and asked them for something to read. Suspecting nothing, they gave him one of their pamphlets, whereupon the police official, proof in hand, arrested them for illegal religious activities and clapped them in jail. And there they stayed for thirteen months, out in a little town in far-western Nepal, days away from friends, relatives, and other believers.

Nepali Christians, hundreds of them across the land, prayed faithfully for Pastor Suman and Kamal—though Kamal was known only as "Pastor Suman's companion." As far as anyone knew, the two might be incarcerated for the maximum sentence of six years, since they had been engaged in evangelism. The last pastor imprisoned had served five years. Thus, when news came that the pair were to be released after only thirteen months, many thanks were offered to God for answering the prayers of His people. In addition, we later learned that during their stay in jail the two men had led twenty-six fellow prisoners to faith in Christ.

Once out of prison, Pastor Suman returned to his former leadership position in the Nepali church and continued to preach and instruct the young and growing congregations scattered around the country. Kamal, however, barely twenty years old, unknown, unwelcome in his district and with little chance of finding employment, decided to leave Nepal for a time and travel to India. There he had joined Operation Mobilization and in time became captain of one of their evangelistic teams working in northern India.

"I stayed with Operation Mobilization in India for five years," Kamal told us, "and then God called me back to Nepal. This is my land, and this is where God wants me to serve. And so here I am."

"And you're not married yet?" Cynthia asked.

"No. The Lord has not yet given me that blessing."

Kamal left Amp Pipal several days later, but Cynthia had already figured things out: Kamal would make an ideal match for Radha. He obviously needed a wife, and even if Radha didn't think she needed a husband, she most certainly did! So during Radha's next visit, Cynthia broached the subject.

"Radha, have you thought any more about marriage?" Cynthia started out.

"No."

"Do you mind if I tell you about a possibility that's come to my mind lately?"

"No."

"I know a fine young Christian man who is looking for a wife."

"Are you sure?"

"Quite sure. He's thirty years old, attractive, and gentle and kind. And most important, he's deeply spiritual. He was here recently holding meetings in our church."

"Who is he?"

"Kamal Bhatta."

Radha smiled, then blushed and looked down at the floor.

"Do you already know him?" asked Cynthia, crestfallen.

"Oh yes, I know him very well. We grew up in the same village together. He was my best friend's brother. He's the one who first told me about Christ. And when he went to prison, I wrote him many times. Some of my friends in Pokhara have been telling me I should marry him." She paused and then said, "But I won't marry him. It's out of the question. Besides, I'm not interested in getting married now anyway. Maybe later."

Some months passed, and the church once again invited Kamal to conduct some meetings. Cynthia, not one to give up easily, talked to him about Radha —who also happened to be in Amp Pipal just then for her school break. Neither Kamal nor Radha had known the other was going to be there—and none of us had planned it that way.

Kamal told Cynthia that he had been writing Radha for more than seven years. He said she had been the only one to write consistently to him in jail, and this had touched him deeply. He had decided even then that if God agreed to give her to him, he would someday marry her.

"I wrote to her only several months ago and asked her one last time to marry me. She gave me her final no. Since then, I have determined to remain single. I don't believe God wants me to marry. He has called me to travel to all the churches, and it's hard to do that and make a wife happy, too."

Kamal must have conveyed these sentiments to others as well, because it wasn't long before Radha herself heard that Kamal had decided to remain single. She had been softening a little since turning down his marriage proposal and had even begun to regret her decision. But now she was vexed with Kamal. What business had he going about saying he would never marry? Where did that leave her? Well, if that's how he felt, the thing was really finished now. Such were the feelings, anyway, that Radha expressed when Cynthia tried to get her to reconsider Kamal's offer of marriage.

"He's really heartbroken, you know."

"He is?"

"He has decided to remain single only because you have refused him. He won't marry anyone else."

"No?"

"Maybe you two ought to talk together and get things straightened out, and tell each other how you really feel."

"That wouldn't be proper."

"You can meet in one of our houses, and we'll just step outside and leave you alone. It will be proper enough."

The meeting took place on the day before Kamal was to leave. It didn't last long. At the end of it they had decided that they could both serve God better together than apart.

They had decided on one other thing too, and when Cynthia and I heard it, we were nonplussed. "I have no one I can call my parents," Kamal said to us just before he left. "I'm asking that you be my parents from now on. It would mean a great deal to me to have parents once more."

Then Radha said, "And I really have no parents either. My father is dead. My mother won't speak to me. There's my brother, but he would never approve of my marriage to Kamal. I have no one to give me permission to marry, no one to make it official." Then she said, looking at Cynthia and me, "Will you be my parents too?"

"You mean for the wedding, don't you?" I asked.

"Oh no," said Kamal. "Forever."

Kamal's earnestness disconcerted me. Okay, we'd be happy to be godparents, we'd be honored to be, but why make such a solemn and serious matter out of it? It was a perfectly natural and ordinary request. I was about to mumble something about how pleased and honored we would be when Cynthia, more perceptive as usual, stopped me. "I don't think you understand what they're really saying," she said to me. "They're asking us to be their *parents,* not their godparents."

"That's right," said Kamal. "We are orphans in this world. We are asking you to adopt us, to be our adoptive parents—not just in name, but in fact."

The "pleased and honored" speech dried on my lips. It was plain now why they had treated the matter so seriously. Were we—was I—ready to take on this responsibility? Godparents didn't really have to *do* anything, but this was different. How can you be a proper parent to a mature, spiritual Nepali couple, barely ten years your junior—and the man, even at his young age, one of the top leaders in the Nepali church? In spiritual commitment, in their knowledge of Nepal and God's work in this land, in their proven willingness to endure hardship and persecution for Christ's sake—in these matters they were our elders, not our juniors. I suddenly saw that we were being given an honor far beyond our worth. How could we live up to that?

And what would other people say? We knew some of the missionaries disapproved of developing close relationships to nationals, even Christian nationals. It created dependence; it was paternalistic. And yet weren't we all one in Christ? We would adopt an American couple under similar circumstances; why should we treat this young couple differently?

In any event, it wouldn't do to stand there, as if unwilling or indifferent; surely they would misunderstand our hesitancy, and the fragile bond that had begun to grow between us would be broken. So, taking their request that we be their parents as an invitation from God and having no idea where it would end, we said yes.

If we didn't know where it would end, at least we knew where it would begin: with a wedding. Our first privilege as new parents would be to give away our daughter in marriage to our son.

Both Kamal and Radha returned to Pokhara, where Radha was still finishing high school, and over the next few months wedding plans were worked out long distance between Amp Pipal and Pokhara. Mail took over a week one way. Since most of their friends were in Pokhara, Kamal and Radha wanted the wedding held there. Unfortunately, on the date they chose, the hospital was scheduled to host a major government laparoscopy (family-planning) camp, which involved taking care of a team of fifteen government workers, including two female doctors who were to be guests at our house. We wrote and said we simply couldn't leave Amp Pipal at that time. When Kamal and Radha for various convoluted reasons were unable to change the date, they decided to hold the wedding in Amp Pipal.

This meant that in addition to the laparoscopy team, we would be having twenty or more people coming from Pokhara for the wedding—not to mention the several hundred women, with their families, who would be coming to have their tubes tied! Plus all the regular patients—it was the busiest time of year on top of everything else. It would be like holding the Democratic National Convention in Pierre, South Dakota.

Well, it all happened. Twenty-five people arrived from Pokhara, including our former pastor, Abraham, who conducted the wedding ceremony. Three hundred eleven women came for laparoscopies. The teashops were bulging with people. Local food supplies ran out and had to be supplemented from elsewhere. But everything got done—how, I'll never know. Even our houseguests, the two laparoscopy doctors, came to the wedding reception and enjoyed witnessing the strange anomaly of a Christian couple's getting married in Nepal.

And the wedding? That, like everything else, had its own flavor. The ceremony took place up in the church on top of the ridge. When it was over, Radha, all dressed in white—even to the white slippers donated by Sister Rigmor—was carried down the hill in a special seat to the little playground that had been built for the missionary children years before. During the half-hour journey down the hillside, Radha's entourage—the twenty-five people from Pokhara and our entire local congregation, perhaps eighty or ninety people in all—sang hymns, joked, laughed, and generally disported themselves in a gay and unrestrained manner. Seldom in Amp Pipal had there been such a large and jubilant group of Christians carrying on in public for all the countryside to see. And onlookers commented later that Radha was the first bride they had ever seen who wasn't weeping. Not only that, she was actually smiling. For most girls in rural Nepal, marriage was not a smiling matter.

The chief attraction at the reception was a great feast of stewed goat, tastily spiced, along with the usual fare of rice and curried vegetables—all served up on hand-woven, banana-leaf plates. But for us the most singular part of the celebration was the opening of the wedding gifts. The idea of giving gifts in the first place, I suppose, originated with Westerners, as did many other features of the whole affair. After all, Nepali Christians had few models of their own when it came to putting on a Christian wedding, so naturally, they looked to the missionaries for ideas. In this case we had retained every local custom that didn't have some specific Hindu meaning. Not only that, everything had been done according to the express wishes of the young couple themselves.

The Nepalis added a twist of their own to the gift-giving. All the gifts were opened at the reception, not by the bride and groom, but by a self-appointed master of ceremonies, who on displaying each item for all to see would make jokes about it, at which the Nepalis in the crowd would roar their approval. Some of the cracks were of a most embarrassing nature, and others were positively cruel, and yet the worse they got, the louder the audience howled. Even Kamal and Radha managed to laugh along with the others.

Three gifts, among the finest of all, came to the couple later, when Radha's older brother visited the newlyweds on their return to Pokhara: a watch for Kamal, two saris for Rhada, and a strong suitcase for them both. In a beautiful moment of reconciliation the brother, ever-loving toward his younger sister, gave his full and heartfelt blessing to the marriage and welcomed Kamal into the family.

Happy and fruitful years have passed since then. Kamal still preaches across the land, though he spends up to half his time at home in Pokhara, where he serves the local churches there as teacher and evangelist. On one of his recent visits to Amp Pipal, he told us about a trip he had just taken to the very town in which he had spent thirteen months in jail. He was speaking about Christ to a small group of people when he noticed a face that he thought looked familiar. Afterward the man came forward and said to Kamal, "I believe now what you speak is the truth." Then Kamal recognized him: He was the police official who had arrested him twelve years earlier.

After relating the story, Kamal said, "You know, years ago before I went to jail, I prayed that God would send me into every corner of Nepal to preach the Good News. So He answered that prayer by starting me off in just one corner—that little jail. I wasn't ready to go anywhere else. Now God is sending me to all the other corners, too."

thirteen

A City on a Hill

A HALF-INCH LAYER of fine powder covered the trail, billowing into the air at the traveler's every step. The path wound back and forth up the parched terraces, recently plowed and seeded with spring corn but now waiting for rain. The soil was poor, mostly hard, red clay. Other than cactus, there was little vegetation to break the monotony of the hillside. Far below flowed the Daraundi River, barely visible beneath the midday haze, a silver trickle twisting through the foothills. And upward—the sun, hot sky, and endless dusty terraces.

Cynthia had been walking three hours. She was on her way back to Amp Pipal from Kathmandu, but this time she had come by a different route so that she could visit an isolated community of Nepali Christians who lived in the southern part of our district. Even though their village was only four hours from Amp Pipal, none of us had ever been there before. In fact, after working in Amp Pipal almost ten years, Cynthia and I had only just learned that these Christians existed at all. Their numbers were said to be over a hundred, which would make them the largest congregation in our district, twice the size of the Amp Pipal church. Since we were two lone groups of Christians in the midst of a population of a million people, it was more than reasonable that some continuing contact be established between us. For that purpose, then, Cynthia had chosen to visit this village and let them know that they were not alone.

As Cynthia plodded hour after hour up the hot terraces, no sign of habitation in sight, she could be forgiven the momentary thought that perhaps this village did not exist. Was she on the right trail? For over an hour she had met no one she could ask. Then finally, coming around a shoulder of the hillside, she spied in the distance a large number of houses scattered widely across the terraced fields. This was the place she was seeking, the aptly named village of Duradada, meaning "far hill."

It was a much bigger settlement than Cynthia had expected. She could see over a hundred houses extending for more than a mile along the hillside. The community seemed to have no center, no group of houses clustered around a pipal tree or tiny temple, as was common in other Nepali villages. Cynthia went up to one of the first houses, wondering how she was going to ask where the Christians lived. Perhaps they were "secret" Christians; perhaps they called themselves by another name to avoid detection by the authorities. Out of the house came a short, stocky tribesman with Tibetan features and a round wrinkled face. His expression was warm and open; his eyes twinkled. Cynthia decided to be forthright: "Are you a Christian?"

"Yes, I am," he replied. "Whom are you looking for?"

"I've come to find the Christian village that's supposed to be here," said Cynthia. "Is this it?"

"Well, part of this village is Christian," said the man. "Mainly the houses higher up belong to Christian families; and quite a few Christians live along that far ridge."

Looking in the direction indicated, Cynthia could make out still more houses that she hadn't noticed at first, little bumps barely discernible against the hazy skyline. They were at least an hour's walk away.

"This is a huge village," murmured Cynthia. "How many of these houses belong to Christians?"

"We have about forty houses now," answered the man. "But more and more families are joining our fellowship all the time. It's hard to keep track exactly."

Aside from Kathmandu and maybe Pokhara, Cynthia didn't know of any other Nepali town or village that could boast forty Christian households.

"Where are you from?" the man asked.

"Amp Pipal."

"There's a hospital there, isn't there? One of our people went there last year to get medicine."

"There's a church there, too," said Cynthia. "I've come to bring greetings from the Christians in Amp Pipal."

The man said he hadn't known there were Christians elsewhere in the district, but he was glad to hear of it. He invited Cynthia to come with him to his house, which was another twenty minutes farther along the trail.

"I've just been visiting one of the brothers," he explained. "I'm the leader of the Christians here. I'm very pleased to welcome you to our fellowship."

Cynthia was pleased too. A thousand people lived in this spread-out village, and here the first person she met was not only one of the Christians, he was their leader.

His name was Sukh Bahadur. As he led Cynthia through the village, he talked enthusiastically about his visions for his people: better health for people and animals, a school for the children, clean water, cottage industry, irrigation. But the greatest need of all, he said, was for Bible teaching. Many of the new Christians, he said, were essentially untaught, and he himself felt inadequate to teach them. "If only you could stay with us one or two weeks," he said to Cynthia. "You could teach not only the new believers but the old ones too. People would come every night."

As they went along, Sukh stopped frequently at the different houses, sometimes calling out a jovial greeting in his native tribal tongue, at other times pausing to speak earnestly to somebody inside the house. He seemed to know every member of every household—both children and adults, Christians and non-Christians. When the two finally arrived at Sukh's house, a number of people were waiting outside to see him. He spoke briefly with each one and sent them off. Then he ushered Cynthia inside, laid out a straw mat for her to sit on, and instructed his wife to prepare some tea and a light snack. "There'll be a small meeting tonight," Sukh said. "It will be good for our people to meet you. Maybe you could say a word to them."

"Is this a regular meeting you're having?" Cynthia asked.

"Well, not really," Sukh said. "It's because you're here. But it won't be a big thing. Just some singing and prayer, and then if you have something to share with us, we would be very grateful."

Cynthia was exhausted. Little did she suspect that all those stops along the way to Sukh's house were actually to announce the evening meeting—and the guest speaker who had so providentially arrived to lead it.

Sukh's house was larger than most of the other houses in the village, befitting his role as leader of the community. It had a kitchen area to one side, a small back room where Sukh and his wife slept, and the front room that served as parlor, dining room, and storage space. The greater part of the house, however, consisted of one large room that evidently was used for meetings. Other than some straw mats laid out on the mud floor, this room was devoid of furnishings of any sort. Not that the other rooms of the house could be called "furnished" exactly: There were no tables or chairs in the "parlor," no beds in the bedroom, and the "stove" in the kitchen was merely a bump in the mud floor with holes in it. These people were poor, even by Nepali standards.

What was lacking in material goods, however, was more than made up for in hospitality. In a short while Sukh's wife emerged from the kitchen with a big brass platter filled with freshly prepared popcorn. Sukh was apologetic.

"It's all there is," he said to Cynthia. "I'm very sorry we have nothing else to offer you."

"Oh, this is fine. I love popcorn," Cynthia assured him. Actually she wasn't that hungry: One seldom is just after a hot, strenuous walk. But she did enjoy popcorn, and thinking that this was to be the sole meal of the day, she figured she had better fill up. There appeared to be plenty.

On the second mouthful she broke one of her upper molars on an incompletely popped kernel. She should have known better: Nepali popcorn is rarely fully popped. She was more cautious after that, testing each piece gingerly on the side opposite the fractured tooth.

Some tea was brought, and again Sukh apologized that they had no milk or sugar to go with it. These were luxuries that most poor families did without. But Cynthia was grateful enough for any liquid after four thirsty hours on the trail, and since the tea had been boiled, it was at least safe to drink.

By the time Cynthia reached the bottom of the popcorn platter, she had eaten far more than her fill. It was four P.M. *This will last me until ten tomorrow morning when they'll eat again*, she thought. She was also feeling drowsy. She would have loved to take a short nap, but since several villagers had walked into the room at this point, she felt obliged to take part in their conversation. Thus passed the remainder of the afternoon.

At six o'clock the last of the visitors left, and from the kitchen appeared Sukh's wife bearing a large tin pie platter laden with a mountain of rice surrounded by two dozen small fish—heads, tails, and all—bathed in a pungent sauce: a miniature volcanic island rising out of a sea of sharks. She placed the platter in front of Cynthia. It would have made a good supper for Paul Bunyan, but it was four times the amount Cynthia usually ate even when she was hungry, let alone full of popcorn. Sukh Bahadur and his wife looked on, beaming with pleasure. Cynthia looked at the fish, then at the rice. There was no backing out. If only she had known supper was coming—but she had been embarrassed to ask.

Cynthia picked up a fish and bit off half of it. She had always loved crunchy fried fish, but the only thing crunchy about this fish were the bones. It had a marvelously intense flavor, which the sauce did nothing to obscure. Cynthia swallowed down the rest of the first fish. There were twenty-three to go.

She tried the rice, mushing some into a little ball with her fingers and popping it into her mouth. It took a long time to go down. Sukh looked concerned. Cynthia began on another fish. At this rate she would be doing well to finish by midnight—and already people were beginning to gather for the meeting. Sukh and his wife were crestfallen. Did *Guru-Ama* (teacher-mother) not like the food perhaps? Oh no, that wasn't it. Would *Guru-Ama* like something else to eat? No, not at all. Was *Guru-Ama* not well? Oh, quite well, thank you. And fish by fish, rice ball by rice ball, the agony dragged on. The meeting room filled. The minutes passed. A slight delay was announced: The speaker was still eating. Would they care to sing, please. There were twelve fish to go.

Cynthia gave it up. Sukh graciously refrained from telling her that in fact those fish had been caught that very afternoon and had been served especially in her honor. He was a sensitive host, more concerned to put his guest at ease than to make excuses for the failed supper. Cynthia entered the meeting room.

The rustling and shifting ceased at once as fifty pairs of eyes fastened on the *Guru-Ama* from Amp Pipal. The group was an even mixture of men and women, young and old, but all of them alike were simple villagers. Except for three or four young men who had been away to school, all were illiterate. Some of the women had saucer-shaped gold earrings reaching almost to their shoulders. For many the earrings represented their entire life investment. They considered it safer to hang it from their ears than to put it in a bank.

The most striking thing about the people, however, was their bright and eager faces. Even the older members of the group, wrinkled and worn down by years of hardship and toil, sat expectantly with radiant expressions. Some of the people had walked forty minutes to get there and would have the same walk back in the dark without flashlights. The church in Amp Pipal was happy if twenty came to an evening meeting, even when it was scheduled. Here in Duradada fifty had shown up on the spur of the moment.

After a short opening prayer by Sukh, Cynthia started in. She talked generally about the family of God, the true church, and how all believers across Nepal were united as one body with many members. She spoke for about thirty minutes and then stopped, fearing that if she went on any longer, she would begin losing her audience. That was hardly the danger. An uncomfortable silence followed. Was that all she was going to say? They wanted to hear more. Sukh wasn't sure what to do; he had expected more from his speaker than that. He prayed again. Then others prayed. They sang some choruses. The evening was just beginning.

Then Sukh suggested that if anyone had questions for the *Guru-Ama*, now was the time to ask them. And ask they did—for the next hour and a half—starting with questions about Christian faith and practice and then moving on to matters of health, education, family planning, and economic development. By the time they were through, Cynthia felt like a wrung-out sponge. At the very end Sukh announced that the Doctor-*Guru-Ama* would conduct a general medical clinic next morning for the entire village, after which she would be leaving for Amp Pipal. The assembly was dismissed, and a few minutes later Cynthia was fast asleep on a straw mat in the parlor.

Before Cynthia's visit, no Western missionary had ever been to the village of Duradada. No one, it seemed, even knew of its existence. How then did this community of Christians come into being, springing up, as it were, out of nowhere? The story, as much as Cynthia was able to piece together on that first visit, began fifteen years earlier when a man named Lok Bahadur, a Tamang tribesman from a district west of Kathmandu, journeyed to the town of Pokhara, carrying a load of goods to sell. While he was there, he learned about a mission hospital run by some people called Christians, who were said to be able to cure illnesses simply by praying to their God. They didn't do *puja* (worship of Hindu deities), they didn't kill chickens, they didn't use traditional healers. They only prayed, and people got well.

When Lok Bahadur returned to his village a week later, he found his ten-year-old daughter seriously ill. His wife, on the advice of some relatives, had called in the leading shaman of the village, and for three nights in a row the shaman had carried out healing rituals, but to no avail. The girl had gotten steadily worse. The shaman planned more rituals.

Lok then told his wife and friends what he had learned in Pokhara. He suggested that instead of paying more money for treatment that wasn't working, they try praying to the Christian's God. The relatives and neighbors scoffed at the idea and chided Lok Bahadur for regarding lightly the traditions of the village. But Lok persisted, and when the neighbors became angry and abusive, he drove them out of his house.

That night, alone, Lok Bahadur prayed to an unknown and untried God, asking that his daughter might be spared. He prayed for several hours and then fell asleep. In the morning the girl was completely well.

Lok Bahadur might have thought he had won his point, but the villagers saw it otherwise. They attributed the healing to the efforts of the shaman on the three preceding nights, claiming that the cure had merely been delayed. Lok alone remained convinced that the Christian God had heard his prayer and had healed his daughter.

A week later another child in the village became seriously ill, and as usual, the shaman was called. Within two days, however, the child was near death, and the parents had given up hope. Lok Bahadur offered to pray for the sick child, and as the parents were willing, he came that evening to their house and once again prayed to the Christian God. By morning the child was well.

This second healing created no small stir in the village. Some accused Lok Bahadur of practicing witchcraft, of being in league with demons. Others accused him of following a foreign religion. Many were puzzled. But the parents of the child believed, and they refused to join the rest of the village in deriding Lok Bahadur's new God.

One day Lok Bahadur visited the home of Bir Bahadur, whose wife had been sick for several months with fever and cough. The woman was growing weaker despite the efforts of three shamans and many sacrifices. Lok Bahadur offered to pray for Bir's wife. When Bir agreed, Lok Bahadur once more called on his God to heal the sick woman. The next morning the wife was much improved, and within three days she was completely well. As a result, Bir Bahadur also began to believe in the Christian God.

Several other healings followed, and soon a dozen or more villagers had begun gathering together to worship the Christian

God and to read from a New Testament that Lok Bahadur had brought back from Pokhara. True, they didn't understand everything they read, and their notion of this new God was indistinct to say the least. Yet they knew He was a God who healed, and on that they based their faith. They stopped worshiping their old gods and gradually stopped taking part in the traditional religious observances of the community.

Inevitably their neighbors turned against this fledgling group of Christians. The shamans and other village leaders tried to persecute and punish them. Acts of vandalism took place at their expense, sporadically at first, but then more frequently. Their crops were stolen or destroyed, their fields were ravaged. They were threatened with beatings. One night a fire was set to one of their homes.

It was a time of trial and testing; their faith, their future, their very lives were on the line. They might well have wondered, in the face of all this, how it was that their God should be so ready to heal the sick yet at the same time seem unwilling or unable to protect them from the attacks of their neighbors. They may have wondered, but if they did, they kept it to themselves.

After three years, Lok Bahadur left the village and settled in the southern part of Nepal, where he died a few years later. With Lok's departure, the leadership of the group, now grown to seventeen households, fell to Bir Bahadur. Then one day the male members of the group were summoned to the village center by the shamans and other leaders. When they had gathered, their hands were tied behind their backs and they were beaten with sticks. They were then fined a large sum of money and told that if they continued to follow their new religion, they would be fined again.

Shortly after this Bir Bahadur and several others in his little group decided to leave their village for good. They had heard that in the next district to the west, the government had set apart a large tract of hillside for settlement by Nepalis who were homeless and destitute. So packing together their few belongings, they set out on the trail westward—four families at first, with others to follow—to make a new home for themselves in what for them must have seemed a land of opportunity and promise.

After three days of walking, they reached the long waterless clay slopes of Duradada, uninhabited and uninviting—the promised land their government had set aside. Undaunted, they set about building temporary shelters of sticks and leaves, and then with their crude spades, they began to hack out terraces up and down the unyielding hillside. They chopped down and uprooted scores of trees. And then, when the fields were at last prepared, they sowed their first crop of corn.

During those early days another of the group, Sukh Bahadur, also began to emerge as an encourager and leader of the others. With the corn planted and the rainy season almost upon them, Sukh organized the construction of monsoon-proof dwellings of mud and stone. They had no thatch, so they used leaves for roofing. Then, when the houses were finished, there was millet to be planted, then more terraces to be dug, trees to be uprooted—and bit by bit, under the leadership of Sukh and Bir, the little band of settlers began to make a life for themselves up and down that long hard hillside. The Christian community of Duradada was born.

Once their new community was established, Sukh and Bir Bahadur began making periodic visits back to their old village. During these visits they would be asked to pray for the sick, and as they did so, more healings resulted. Many who were healed at that time decided to join Sukh and Bir and move to Duradada.

As a result of the energy and enthusiasm of those early settlers, the Duradada community not only grew, it also began to prosper. Before long, people were migrating to Duradada for economic reasons alone: the chance to own their own land, to raise animals, to make a new start. People from other villages heard about Duradada and the opportunities it offered for a better life. Soon hundreds of new people joined the original settlers, clearing trees, terracing the slopes, and building houses on the once desolate hillside. And as Duradada grew, more and more new people began to join in the worship of the Christian God. Prayer for the sick became an integral part of the life of the entire settlement, and with each healing, the faith of the people grew.

It was years after Duradada was settled that Sukh and Bir Bahadur made their first regular contacts with other Christians. Two pastors in particular, one a Nepali and the other an Indian, came for short periods to teach the basics of the Christian faith to the Duradada Christians. Later on, some of the community's own young men were sent off for short Bible courses, some to India, some to Kathmandu. When they returned, they taught the rest of the congregation. As the knowledge of the people grew, so did their hunger for still more knowledge; so much so that by the time Cynthia visited Duradada, Sukh Bahadur could truth-fully say that what his people wanted and needed more than anything else was someone to teach them the Bible.

From the beginning, the migration to Duradada was limited to members of one tribal group, the Tamangs, one among the many tribes of Nepal. The Tamangs spoke their own language (in addition to Nepali) and shared the same basic customs and beliefs. Thus when two influential Tamangs like Sukh and Bir Bahadur became Christians, other Tamangs were thereby en-couraged to take the risk and follow in their steps. Duradada was essentially a "people movement," ethnically homogeneous, and this as much as anything else contributed to the rapid growth not only of the community at large but also of the healing fellowship of Christians at its center. True, that same ethnic homogeneity also accounted for the Duradada community's long isolation from other Christians in Nepal as well as their failure to reach out to other ethnic groups. Nevertheless, whatever their limitations, the community at Duradada remained—and still remains—the fastest-growing group of Christians in all of Nepal.

It was a year after Cynthia's visit to Duradada that I first met Sukh and Bir Bahadur. They had come to Amp Pipal to see us and had brought with them three other leaders of their congregation. When Cynthia and I got home from the hospital at the end of the day, they were there waiting for us out in our side lawn. They sat cross-legged in a semicircle on the grass, grim and unsmiling, like five Indian chiefs at a war council. Sukh stood up to greet us; he seemed ill at ease. "We are in serious trouble," he said. "We've come to ask you for advice and help."

Thinking that perhaps they were under persecution for their Christian faith, we assured them we would be happy to help in any way we could and invited them to tell us about their problem.

It was not as we expected. Sukh spoke for the group. He told us that about a year earlier they had started building a new school in Duradada, but partway through they had run out of money. They had then heard from somewhere that a very quick and sure way to raise large sums of money was to sell musk from the musk deer that inhabit the high Himalayan foothills. The musk, used not only as a medicine but also in making perfume, fetched an extravagant price. All they had to do was to trap four or five of the animals, remove the musk from their musk sacs, sell it on the black market, and presto, they would have thousands of rupees—more than enough to finish their school. It was too tempting a prospect for these eager villagers to turn down.

They had problems, however. First, a Christian leader in Kathmandu had strongly advised them against such a venture. Second, the musk deer were protected by law; it was illegal to hunt them. Third, musk deer were not easy to come by. They roamed at altitudes above 10,000 feet, and it was often months before enough deer could be captured to make the effort worthwhile. Large pens had to be built in strategic places into which the unsuspecting animals could be enticed. And obtaining the musk was a delicate procedure that required skill and care. Just to undertake such an expedition would demand an initial investment of several thousand rupees for food and equipment alone. But the vision of many more thousands of rupees falling into their hands in exchange for a few ounces of smelly liquid was incentive enough to go ahead with the plan and silence the counsels of caution and doubt.

To raise money for the expedition, Sukh and Bir Bahadur had collected the gold jewelry and valuable brass and copper cooking vessels of the few comparatively wealthy members of the community and had placed them in bond to a moneylender as collateral for a loan of 5000 rupees ($400). Then Sukh and four companions had bought the necessary equipment and had trekked up into the high mountains in search of musk deer. Three months later they returned, their money and supplies exhausted. They had not sighted a single deer. And now within three weeks they had to pay back their loan of 5000 rupees or their jewelry and cooking vessels would be forfeited.

"It's not just our own loss we're worried about," Sukh said. "Others in the village have also gone in with us, and they'll lose their property, too. But worse than that, the things we've placed with the *sauji* (moneylender) are far more valuable than the amount of the loan—at least twice as valuable. If only we had a year's extra time to raise the money, we could do it. We could knit sweaters and *jholas* (shoulder bags), and we would have goats to sell by then, even part of our crops. But now we have no way to raise that much money within three weeks. And the *sauji* has refused to give us an extension."

Their predicament was acute. For them, 5000 rupees was an enormous sum to raise. Their entire annual income might amount to only a few hundred rupees. We knew how the *saujis* operated: If Sukh and his companions could not pay back their loan on time, the *sauji* was then free to sell their goods—and for twice the value of the loan. Why should he grant them an extension and lose the chance to make a tidy 5000-rupee profit?

"We have made a very great mistake," Sukh said. "We've been foolish. We were advised not to hunt the musk deer. We knew it was against the law. We deserve to lose our property. But the others in the village don't deserve to lose theirs; we talked them into it. Now all of us are about to lose everything."

The five men stared in silence at the grass in front of them. Then Sukh looked at us and said, "We've come to ask you for advice." Which really meant: We've come to ask you for a loan.

Our reaction was immediate and automatic: Give no money. Pathetic though their story was and desperate their plight, to give money to bail them out of their self-inflicted trouble would, we felt, be most unwise. And yet, how sad was their predicament! Their model Christian community, so far "untainted" by outside money and influence, was now in real danger of disintegrating. The leaders had fallen into shame, and because of their folly many others were about to suffer great loss. It was a blow that they could scarcely be expected to survive. Nevertheless, we remained firm in our belief that to give them money would be the worst thing we could possibly do.

We told them so. Not bluntly but gently, spelling out our reasons, expressing our deep sorrow, and offering to help in any way we could—short of giving them money.

After they heard us out, they sat immobile and expressionless, like stone Buddhas. They displayed neither resentment nor disappointment. Two or three minutes passed in complete silence; then I suggested we pray together. When we had finished praying, the five men stood up, said good-bye, and filed down the steps and out the gate. Cynthia and I looked at each other, both of us confident that we had done what was right.

Two weeks later Sukh, Bir, and their three companions were back again. They had been unable to raise any money on their own. The deadline was one week away. They had come, they said, in faith that we would help them. They asked us to reconsider. They said they could understand our reluctance to give such a large sum, and they agreed with our reasons for refusing them. But would we please, this time, help them. Just this once; they wouldn't ask again. It was only a loan they wanted, not a gift. They would pay back every rupee.

Cynthia and I said no, it was out of the question. Again there was silence. Again we prayed. Last of all Sukh prayed, and his prayer this time was strangely moving. He confessed his sins and errors and pleaded for mercy on behalf of himself and his companions. He then implored God to deliver them from the pit into which they had fallen. When he was done, Cynthia and I were shaken.

I said to Sukh, "Let's talk no more now. We'll pray about it overnight, and tomorrow we'll give you our final answer."

Late that evening there came to Cynthia's mind Jesus' words from Matthew 5:42: "Give to the one who asks you, and do not turn away from the one who wants to borrow from you." And as she pondered these words, Cynthia slowly began to feel that God wanted us to loan the 5000 rupees to Sukh and his friends.

Early the next morning I was called to the hospital for an emergency, so I had little time to talk the matter over with Cynthia. At lunchtime I came home for a quick snack in the midst of a hectic clinic. The five men were sitting on the lawn as before. Cynthia took me aside and said that she thought it was right for us to give them the loan. I was hesitant; I could see nothing but trouble and grief coming from it. Time and again we had seen the ill-advised giving of money corrupt first one Christian and then another. And this was such a large sum; we had never given this much before, even within our own church at Amp Pipal. Word would surely get out: I couldn't think of a single missionary or Nepali Christian we knew—apart from Sukh Bahadur and his four companions—who would approve of such a loan.

Cynthia and I talked it over briefly while I ate, and then it was time for me to return to the hospital. "I don't know what to think," I said finally. "I wish we had more time to decide. But if you feel a clear leading to give them the money, I won't oppose you." With that, I left. On my way out I apologized to the five for my haste and told them that Cynthia would be talking with them.

They got their loan, though it took a few days to arrange. They paid back the moneylender with one day to spare, and thus were able to retrieve their possessions—and, at least externally, their honor. As for us, we committed the decision to God and were at peace about it. Whether we had acted wisely or not was another question.

There is less question about what has happened to the Duradada community in subsequent years. Fifteen years later, Duradada now has more than four hundred Tamang Christians, an increase of three hundred percent. Not only that, leaders of the Duradada congregation have made repeated evangelistic trips back to the original district from which the first Christians came, with the result that now in that district there are two dozen new

Tamang congregations totaling over five thousand believers. Altogether the Tamangs make up almost ten percent of the total number of Christians in Nepal.

Sukh Bahadur is still the leader at Duradada. Under his leadership the church and the local economy have prospered. The people of Duradada, while hardly wealthy, are far better off than they were before they moved there. No Christian goes hungry. Every family owns at least a little land, and those whose land is insufficient to feed them engage in various trades and cottage industries to supplement their income. A new church has been built that can seat three hundred people. The school has been completed, with some outside help, and classes go up through the sixth grade. Two young men have been trained in animal husbandry, and another young man has been trained as a village health worker. With some technical help from the United Mission, the community has put in its own water system, piping water from a source several kilometers away into the center of the village. Loans have been negotiated with Nepal's Agricultural Development Bank for the purchase of goats, buffalos, and additional land. Irrigation projects are being planned. And most recently, two young men have been trained in adult literacy and are teaching their first class of sixty adults to read and write.

All this—essentially self-development—has been accomplished with a minimum of Western planning and, except for the school, with almost no Western money. The key to their success has been motivation, and at the heart of their motivation has been Jesus Christ. These people pull together, they care for one another, they sacrifice for one another. They are providing a demonstration of what true community "development" is all about.

Development is much more than increased economic well-being. True development begins with the transformation of people's characters and people's values and then leads on to a transformation of society itself. This is what has happened with the people of Duradada: Their "development" has begun as a spiritual awakening, and it is from that awakening that all else has sprung. God has brought to fruition the tiny seed planted so many years ago by the mission hospital in Pokhara, and it is bearing still.

"A city set on a hill cannot be hidden." Duradada is such a city.

The Grand Survey

Lamjung District

*T*HE ASSIGNMENT was to survey health facilities in two Nepali districts served by the Amp Pipal Hospital. Sounds dull. But this would be no ordinary survey. To begin with, it would be done entirely on foot—over 250 miles of trail. Ninety-nine percent of the trail would take us either up or down, usually steeply so; the longest level stretch would be hardly longer than a football field. The survey would take three weeks—which would turn out to be wishful thinking.

A plan is needed, of course, an itinerary, with places to visit and people to see. Very well. But you quickly discover that the people you need to visit rarely live on the main path. Say you are to go to the village of Neupani, for example, where there are two people to meet. Now Neupani is not like Whippabonscott, Rhode Island, where the streets are divided into blocks and you can walk from one end of town to the other in five minutes. Rather, Neupani is a sprinkling of thatch-roofed houses spread up and down two miles of steep mountainside, and the two people you are to meet will surely live at opposite ends of "town," with the main path running halfway between. So you walk a mile up to the house of the first person, and he has just left to cut wood in the jungle three miles off and will be back that evening. You then walk to the second person's house, two miles and 2000 feet down, and learn that he was there an hour before but has left for another village and will be back in two days. At this point you can't wait two hours much less two days, as you must press on to Bhirsing, where a similar fate awaits you. This is how you do a survey in Nepal.

Cynthia and I got the job. We had just returned to Nepal for our fourth term, and it was decided that before getting back into hospital work we should travel about the wider area surrounding Amp Pipal and collect information that might be useful to the mission in planning for the future. The survey would also give us a chance to meet former patients and to follow up some of those who had heard the Gospel through their contact with the hospital. One drawback to the venture was the time of year, June, usually the hottest month of all. What's more, the rains had come early, adding to the difficulty of travel. And shortly, rice planting would begin, and everyone we would want to meet would be busy in the fields from dawn to dusk. Not an auspicious time to conduct a survey, to be sure, but it was the only time we had.

To do a survey, you need a map. No one plans a trip without knowing where he's going, even in Nepal. The very finest, up-to-date trekking maps are available in Kathmandu for thirty cents, so, of course, we bought one. It was printed in pale blue ink on gray paper and needed strong light. Three quarters of the villages we wanted to visit weren't on the map, and three quarters of those that were on the map were villages that no one had ever heard of or never went to—and that maybe didn't even exist. Or perhaps the cartographer spoke only Sanskrit.

Now any map can be deceptive, especially a map of mountainous terrain, but this map specialized in deception. It was its strong point. Particularly misleading, it would turn out, were the trails that followed along rivers. On the map these rivers and their trails were invariably depicted by gracefully waving lines that could have passed for Interstate 80 running through Nebraska. Rivers in Nepal, of course, don't run in graceful, wavy lines, and most certainly the trails along them do not. Nepal's rivers don't merely twist, they writhe. On one side there will be a narrow strip of land on which to walk; just opposite will be a cliff. A hundred yards farther on, the sides reverse, and now there's a cliff on your side with nowhere to walk except up over the top. This often means a climb of 400 or 500 feet. Sometimes the trail follows along a narrow horizontal ledge halfway up the cliff face. It's exhilarating to walk along one of these ledges with the angry river churning 300 feet below. Even more exhilarating is suddenly to come to the end of the ledge and find it replaced by some long poles laid across the cliff face for the traveler's convenience. Indeed, with all the ups and downs and ins and outs, one can easily figure on tripling map distances over mountains and quadrupling them along rivers. It's wise never to take a Nepal trekking map too seriously.

Armed with our map, two beat-up sleeping bags, a few sets of clothes, a bottle of iodine to purify our drinking water, and a suitcase of books and pamphlets, we arrived at the big bus depot in Kathmandu and boarded a bus for Gorkha District. It was a sleek new bus, not like the old clunkers we were used to, and written in English across its top was "Pashupati Super Deluxe Express." The windows were tinted to prevent glare, so much so that when you raised the lower half for some air the double thickness of glass at the top was completely opaque; and if you wanted to look out and see anything besides the edge of the pavement, you had to hunch way down in your seat. The only trouble with that was that there was no room to hunch. In fact, there was no room to sit. The seats were so close together that it was impossible to sit straight for more than five minutes without getting pressure sores on your knees from the seat in front. We were three on a seat and had to sit sideways to fit. A metal armrest prevented us from spilling into the aisle. To shift our knees from one side to the other, we had to rise in unison—as if the king had just boarded—and then shift all together. After four hours we were finally able to shift to a seat near the door, which wasn't much better because of the press of people crowding onto the bus at every stop. And our "super deluxe express" bus made more stops on this trip to Gorkha than I can ever remember, extending the usual five hours of driving to eight.

One time we stopped on an empty stretch of road for no apparent reason. I hunched down and looked out to see a bus being pulled up out of the river 300 feet below. It was one of two buses that had gone over the edge the previous week with much loss of life and a great to-do in *The Rising Nepal* about safety standards. A little man in a black suitcoat was sitting on the side of the road, pulling up that bus all by himself by means of a cable, a crank, and a "machine" consisting of three rusty gears. It was modern technology at work. At least, at the speed our bus was going, we weren't likely to go over the edge ourselves.

That first night we planned to spend in Duradada, the village of four hundred Christians. It would be my first visit there, and I was eager to see it firsthand. We arrived in the village at six o'clock, after a three-hour, uphill walk from the bus stop, our progress slowed by old acquaintances we met along the way. We were greeted by Bir Bahadur, one of the two leaders of the community, who warmly invited us to his house. After a meal of rice and spiced fish, a bone of which I cleverly managed to drive through my palate, we sat around outside sharing the latest news and watching the stars grow bright in the darkening sky. Not a whisper of breeze relieved the hot mugginess of the evening.

At ten o'clock Cynthia and I were shown to our beds, two straw mats in the loft of a cowshed. All night we drank in the rank odor of cow urine from the stall beneath. All night we struggled to sleep, but no sleep came. For Cynthia it was simply too hot. For me the heat was compounded by itching. Such miserable itching I had never experienced. In vain I looked for gnats, fleas, mosquitoes, and bedbugs, but in the end I concluded that it was only the heat. In the morning as I looked at my excoriated arms and legs, I thought of the times I had scolded my patients for scratching themselves when they itched. "You have to control yourself," I'd say over and over. It was easier said than done.

We had a lot to do in Duradada. We saw old friends and former patients, visited the sick and attended an adult-literacy class run by Bir Bahadur's son. We were shown the new church and the new school that the villagers had built. We were told that all but four of the hundred homes in the village had outhouses, an incredible record in a district where any other village would be doing well to have one. And finally we walked

forty-five minutes to the far end of Duradada to visit Sukh
Bahadur's wife, Sukh Maya, who had been a patient of Cynthia's
and who had stayed at our house in Amp Pipal. We had met
Sukh Bahadur, the other Duradada leader, in Kathmandu a week
earlier and knew that he'd be away on a preaching trip. Though
Sukh Maya was alone, she insisted we spend the night at her
house. Because our bags were still back at Bir Bahadur's place,
we thought we had better return there. But she persisted, and
two young men offered to bring our things, so we gave in and
agreed to stay. Besides, it would be undiplomatic to stay two
nights at the home of one leader and neglect the other.

Sukh Bahadur's house had been built on a narrow ridge that
sloped downward to the Daraundi River 1,500 feet below. Of
the dozen other dwellings strung out along the ridge, Sukh's was
the highest. The crest of the ridge was so narrow it barely
accommodated the width of the houses; and to either side the
ground dropped off sharply, leaving the houses on top exposed.

Sukh Maya was kept so busy tending the animals, fixing our
beds, and cooking the meal that we had almost no chance to visit
with her. While we were there, a young man showed up and
asked Cynthia to come to his house and examine his daughter,
who was sick with dysentery. His house turned out to be
nothing more than a tiny one-room hut made of sticks and
leaves. The man, Sher Bahadur, was a recent arrival in Duradada,
having been driven from home by his father, a shaman, for
refusing to follow his father's profession. Sukh Bahadur had
given him a patch of land just below his own house, and there
Sher Bahadur had settled with his wife and daughter. Seeing
how poor they were, Cynthia asked him if he would like to earn
some money by working as one of our porters for the next few
weeks. Since he had little land and no regular work, Sher was
more than happy to take Cynthia's offer; at a dollar and a half a
day plus food, it was too good to turn down.

Back on the porch of Sukh's house, we watched the late-
afternoon thunderheads forming on the skyline across the valley.
The clouds massed and thickened, black beneath, with white
tops billowing upward into the sunlight, like monstrous fairy

156

castles. New clouds of gold and gray swept in from behind us, adding to the play of shapes and shadows. Sunshine glided in patches across the land, momentarily lighting up this section or that in brilliant green. Below us the contoured terraces of red earth stretched downward to the river, and here and there a little house poked up, surrounded by new corn. To one side, silhouetted against the sky, stood half a dozen tall banana trees, their large splayed leaves arching gracefully above the courtyard.

Then, as we watched, the kaleidoscope of colors faded. A moist breeze sprang up, and a great mass of black clouds moved in from the right. Lightning flashed, and the distant rumble of thunder rolled across the hills. People scurried about, tying up animals, closing shutters, while others made their way in from the fields. Sukh Maya came back from the water tap with a bundle of clothes and hung them on a line at the edge of the porch. Then she caught up two baby goats and placed them in their pen under the banana trees. A young girl washing her feet in a big cooking pot looked up at the sky and scampered home. Mothers called their children. Our recently hired porter hurried past with a full water jug under his arm, intent on getting home before the storm broke. Life was hard in these hills. First the heat, then the rain; all work, up and down, day in, day out. These people had no respite.

"You can't tell the people's burden from looking at their faces," Cynthia observed, as we sat on Sukh Maya's porch. "They always seem so cheerful. Yet I'm sure they'd trade their lot in a second if they had the chance."

"At least they have piped water nearby," I said. "That's more than most people have." Indeed, they had laid a half mile of plastic pipe that carried water from a distant spring to within a few yards of their houses. It lay on the ground, unburied. In any other village an exposed pipe would have long since been cut to pieces.

Soon the wind came. It started as a far-off moan, sighing from somewhere across the side valley to our right. As it grew in intensity, we could see in the distance trees being flattened and limbs flying through the air. Then the hurricane struck with full fury. Sand and dirt filled the air, stinging the eyes, as the wind roared across the top of the ridge. An empty basket bounced across the courtyard and disappeared down the hill to the left. A big round cooking pot followed, spinning crazily on its edge. Shutters banged. Clothes were swept off the line and hurled away. Thatch was torn from the roofs in front of us. Crack, crack, down went the banana trees with their loads of unripe fruit. The goat pen toppled over and rolled down the hill behind. Tiles flew from the roof above our heads. And down below, our new porter's hut bobbled and shuddered and shook in the wind.

It was all over in less than ten minutes. The howling gradually faded away, and we were left in utter stillness. Our porter came up, trembling with fright. He had been hanging on to the top bamboo support of his hut, both feet off the ground, to keep his dwelling from being swept entirely away.

Then came the rain. It rained all evening and all night. Inside the house Sukh Maya and her mother prepared the meal. Mud ran everywhere in rivulets. Darkness fell. Finally we were called in to eat. That night we slept on the porch, propping our umbrellas over us to keep off the rain leaking through the damaged roof.

In the morning the air was clear, but everywhere remained the signs of the evening's havoc. Today no water came from the pipe: The spring above had collapsed, and the pipe had filled with mud. Bir Bahadur showed up to see us off and told us of the heavy damage at his end of the village. He himself had lost some baby goats and most of his chickens. Worse, the roof of the cowshed where we had slept had blown completely off, and much of the grain stored there had been destroyed.

Before we could leave, a crowd of patients gathered to be examined. We hired a second porter, and then Bir Bahadur prayed for the Lord's blessing on our journey and for the healing of the sick people in the village. After that, with many smiles and good wishes all around, we set out on our journey.

After two hours of walking, we crossed into the next *panchayat,* and there, quite by chance, we found the *pradhan panch* in a teashop. We had hoped to meet with as many of these *panchayat* leaders as possible during our survey, though we knew the chance of bumping into a *pradhan panch* just by walking through his *panchayat* was about one in fifty, if that. But this kind of coincidental meeting was to be repeated over and over as the days passed. It was as if people we hoped to meet had been simply put in our path.

A little farther on a man came running up behind us, shouting for us to stop. After catching his breath, he said he'd been hoping to meet me for many years now and finally the chance had come. When I asked him what for, he said that eleven years ago I had done a vasectomy on him and that ever since then one leg had been shorter than the other. This was a complication of vasectomy I hadn't heard of! The man was persistent. We finally figured out he was having cramps in one leg—unrelated to the vasectomy, of course—which made the leg feel shorter. He went off unconvinced, though we measured his legs right there on the trail and proved they were of equal length.

A little later we met an old Muslim patient whom we had treated for many years, rather unsuccessfully, for asthma. His attacks were so severe, in fact, that he used to arrive at the hospital as blue as a bluefish and barely able to breathe. Today he looked remarkably chipper, and we asked him how he was getting along. He said that two years ago he had had a dream in which two angels dressed in white appeared and told him to boil up the bark of two kinds of trees and then drink the liquid. He had done so and had been well ever since. Did we want to know the remedy?

So much for modern medicine. He did add, however, that we had cured his son a few years back by putting a tube in his chest and draining off two liters of fluid. The son had been one of Cynthia's tuberculosis patients.

Up 2000 feet and down the other side was a government health post, one of twenty or so that we hoped to visit on our survey. The way led past a school, where we were instantly mobbed by a hundred children asking us English vocabulary words. We left with several children in tow, who relentlessly plied us for words all the way up the mountain. Cynthia was too tired to answer—it must have been 110° F in the shade—so the task of humoring them fell to me. We discovered, however, that their main object was not to improve their vocabulary but to take us to see their sick relatives, for which purpose they had been let out of school. We had not intended to spend time on this survey seeing patients, or we'd have been all day doing nothing but that. But we couldn't refuse even if it did mean walking half an hour out of the way.

"Why don't you people go to your health post?" we asked. And the answer was always the same: no medicine, no doctor, no faith.

When we finally reached the health post, we found it as the people had said. There was no health assistant in charge. The auxiliary health worker was off in Kathmandu trying to get reassigned. The assistant nurse-midwife had been transferred to the government hospital in Pokhara. We found, however, a junior clerk on duty to keep the place open and a sweeper to keep the place clean and to treat the patients who came, who weren't many because there was no medicine. We were to find a similar situation in almost half of the health posts we visited. The government's health care was free, but for many that meant no care at all.

After seeing the health post and the dozen patients who materialized on our arrival, we returned partway along the same path by which we had come, only to find that many people, having heard we'd been by, were now out on the trail waiting to tell us their medical problems or call us to their homes to examine the sick. As a result, we didn't reach our evening destination until well after dark. There we had the usual Nepali meal, squatting on the dirt floor in the fetal position, shoveling the food in with our hands as fast as we could before the great plate of rice got too cold to be palatable, our eyes smarting from the thick smoke of the cooking fire. Squatting there with us was a little tuberculous child who managed during the course of our meal to cough up four ounces of phlegm, which was gobbled up by a rooster. The child, it could truly be said, was coughing his lungs out.

It was too hot that night to sleep in the teashop, so we went back along the trail a few hundred yards and slept on a partially covered platform we had seen on the way into town. We hoped it wouldn't rain, as there was hardly a roof on the thing, but at least it was cool. Anyway, better to be soaked than to itch.

Before dawn the next morning, a stocky farmer stomped up onto our platform, setting the planks beneath us to dancing up and down like a row of diving boards. He was followed by his son, whom he had brought for us to examine. The son had an inflamed eye, which he was rubbing incessantly.

We fumbled around for our flashlights. Cynthia looked at the eye first. "It's an allergy," she said groggily. "He needs anti-allergy medicine."

"No he doesn't," I said. "All he needs is to stop rubbing his eye with that dirty hand."

"He's rubbing his eye because it itches," said Cynthia. "From his allergy," she added, in case I might have missed the connection. "As long as it keeps itching, he'll keep rubbing."

"As long as he keeps rubbing, it'll keep itching," I retorted.

"Don't forget that I'm the pediatrician. I know more about children than you do."

"Yes, but I know more about eyes. Besides, who ever heard of having an allergy in only one eye?"

"It happens all the time," said Cynthia carelessly. I was about to say something when I noticed the boy was now rubbing both eyes. "There, you see?" said Cynthia. Logical consistency was no impediment to her. She could play it either way.

"The trouble with you surgeons," she went on, "is that if something doesn't need cutting, you don't think it needs treating."

"Eyewash," I said. "You medical people have pills for every problem, and half the time they don't even work."

A compromise was finally reached: The boy would get his medicine, and he would also stop rubbing. Cynthia wrote the name of the medicine on a slip of paper and gave it to the father. Father and son trounced off—and our day had begun.

Before leaving town, we met with the *pradhan panch* of that panchayat, an old friend and former patient from whom I had removed several hundred small kidney stones three years before. He was at home, not far off our trail, and was eager—as were most *pradhan panches* we met—to start a health program in his *panchayat*. Stirring up such interest was, indeed, one of the main purposes of our trip.

We stopped for morning rice in a little one-room teashop at the edge of a little eight-house village set at the crossing of two major trails. There was the usual hour's wait for the meal to be prepared, so we used the time to talk to people we knew and to examine patients. The shop was typical: cramped, dark, everything coated with a mixture of mud, soot, and dust, with chickens running to and fro, stepping on the freshly washed plates laid out on the dirt floor. The first time a chicken ran across our plates, we politely asked the proprietress to rinse the plates with boiling water. It was an idiotic request. Boiled water is too precious in Nepal to waste on such frivolities. But she was obliging. She sprinkled a few drops of water on each plate, smeared it around with her dirty hand, and then doled out the food.

This morning the chickens were more of a nuisance than usual. They were mostly young ones, fluttering about like giant flies, attacking our food and making off with a beakful the moment we weren't looking. The only solution was to eat fast and hope the acid in our stomachs was sufficient to kill off the germs we were ingesting along with the food.

In addition to the antics of the chickens, children in various states of undress and dirtiness wandered in and out; students on their way to school stopped by to watch us eat for a few minutes before sauntering off again; and finally, customers trickled steadily in to chat or to purchase cigarettes, matches, biscuits, or batteries from the narrow, blackened shelves. The meal itself was the usual fare: a great mound of rice, a small bowl of lentils, and a tiny dish of spiced vegetables. In the village, that's it—morning and night, day in, day out.

And so our journey went. The days were full from dawn to dark, walking uphill and down, meeting with *panchayat* officials, visiting health posts and medical shops, seeing patients old and new, and then at night trying to get some sleep under usually adverse circumstances. And then there were the tea stops. It's odd that one should crave hot sweet tea on such hot sticky days, but crave it we did. On the trails of Nepal, tea is the staff of life. And for three cents a glass, I don't know of a better buy anywhere.

On the sixth day we stopped at a village boasting two resident practitioners: one a "compounder," who vaguely practiced modern medicine, and the other a *kabiraj,* who practiced herbal medicine. I was in the first man's shop when a young woman with a breast abscess came in, whom he had been treating with penicillin injections. She wasn't getting better and obviously needed the abscess lanced. I asked the compounder if he could drain abscesses, and he assured me he could, though what he was going to use for anesthesia I hadn't a clue. The compounder gave the woman another shot of penicillin and then went inside to find a knife. The woman stepped out.

I then went over to see the herbal doctor, and there in his shop I saw the woman with the breast abscess, whom he also had been treating—with herbal medicine. The woman's husband was there, too, thoroughly drunk, as well as outraged that these two doctors had been ripping him off when all his wife needed was to have the pus drained out.

Then the compounder showed up, looking for his patient, whereupon a lively altercation arose. Each practitioner in self-defense quoted and misquoted me liberally, while the husband seemed bent on using my presence to discredit them both. The argument soon attracted the greater part of the village. The two practitioners heatedly defended their knowledge, experience, and integrity and insisted they had wanted to drain the pus all along. And to prove it, they each offered to stick a knife into the woman's breast right there on the spot.

"The devil you will," roared the drunk husband, and the crowd nodded and murmured yes or no, depending on whose side they were on. The practitioners had their following, and the husband had his. Soon all the villagers were shouting and raising their fists, at which point we left, having contributed enough to the uproar already. In the end, the husband took his wife to the Amp Pipal Hospital.

Chisopani, our stop for the night, was home to five young Christian men. Four of them had permanent jobs in different parts of Nepal and came home only two or three times a year. They all had heard of Christianity through the church at Amp Pipal, and before the four had moved away, they used to come regularly to the church services, a two-hour walk up Liglig Mountain. Imagine our surprise, then, to find four of the five young men at home the very day we arrived there. Our visit had not been expected, there was no special holiday; the whole thing was unplanned. Our time together passed profitably and culminated the next day in a two-hour worship service to which twenty villagers came. The second-story porch on which the service was held had no railings, and we feared lest a Eutychus doze off and fall to the ground below. But no one fell or even dozed. After seeing about thirty patients who had gathered during the service, including a former Caesarian-section patient who now had hookworm anemia and was blaming the operation, we took our leave, much encouraged in spirit, and headed westward into the late-afternoon sun.

Not far out of town we met the *pradhan panch*. He had been hoping to see us, he said, to discuss plans for a new clinic he wanted to start in his *panchayat*. How much would the mission be willing to help? he wanted to know. How much was the *panchayat* willing to do on its own, we asked. After parrying back and forth, we left it that he should try to shake loose some money that he claimed the district *panchayat* had promised him for building a clinic—but which we later found out hadn't been promised at all. Shaking money loose in Nepal is a little like panning for gold in your bathtub: All that's left, in the end, is the stain.

As we walked along with perhaps half an hour of daylight left, we noticed someone coming toward us who looked familiar. When we drew closer, we saw to our astonishment that he was the fifth Christian of the village we had just left. He was headmaster of a school two days away and was coming home for the weekend to help his mother organize the rice planting. We could not but marvel at this chance meeting, yet it was all too brief; we parted ways half glad, half frustrated.

Our destination for that night was the house of a former patient with whom we had become good friends over the years. He was a big blustery fellow who had first walked into my office and complained that one of his teeth ached. When I asked him why, in that case, he was walking bent over double, he replied that on the way to the hospital his belly had begun aching, too; and lo and behold, come to examine him, his appendix had ruptured! We fixed his appendix and then pulled out his tooth, and as a reward for our efforts we received a standing invitation to come to his house.

Just outside our friend's village we chanced to pick up with a tall, lanky fellow who told us that six years ago he had been all over Nepal and northern India trying to get cured of a serious illness and had finally landed at Amp Pipal Hospital, where I had given him fifteen cents' worth of medicine, and ever since he had been perfectly well. He asked us to come to his house for the night.

"We really shouldn't," I said. "We plan to spend the night with a man we've known for a long time, and he'll be offended if we don't stay with him."

"Who's that?" the lanky man asked.

"Oj Raj."

"Oh, he won't mind a bit if you stay at my house. He's my uncle. Besides, he lives another hour beyond the village. You can't make it now anyway."

So we followed the lanky man to his house and soon found ourselves seated on thick carpets, sipping spiced tea in front of the biggest Nepali house we had ever seen. When the man's younger brother came out, I immediately recognized him as the person who had called to me on a main street in Kathmandu ten days earlier to ask my advice about a bone infection in his wrist. The advice had saved him a fat medical fee and a many days' wait in Kathmandu. I had never expected to see him again, much less to be spending the night at his house.

We were fed a rich man's fare that evening, and after talking about religion and politics for the better part of three hours, we went to sleep on soft mattresses out on an airy verandah, the only drawback to which were the holes in the roof that came to light during a midnight rainstorm. In the morning Cynthia and I examined the entire family—fifteen in all, including aunts and grandmothers, nephews and nieces—all of whom were infected with hookworms. The reason was not far to seek: Their "latrine" was a small grassy strip near a stream out in back of the house, and it was a good trick, especially at night, to find a spot where no one had gone in the past twenty-four hours. Which leads one to ponder: What does it profit a man to have a great house if his family is eaten by worms for lack of a toilet?

The normal hour's walk to Oj Raj's house took three hours. We were assailed on all sides by patients thanking us for treating their old illnesses or trying to get help for their new ones. We were already two days behind schedule, but there was no way we could proceed any faster. People chased after us on the trail, ran out of their houses to call us, ambushed us at almost every corner. We met Oj Raj halfway to his house. He had planned a trip for that day, but because of the rain in the night he hadn't gone. He escorted us the rest of the way to his house, where he killed a chicken in our honor and fed us another enormous meal. Twenty more patients came to be examined, and it was afternoon by the time we were finally able to leave. Back in town we stopped to see the government health post, only to find sixty more patients waiting for us to examine them. Almost everyone had either worms or amoeba, and in very short order the two local medical halls had run out of medicine. We left at five o'clock, with a three-hour journey ahead of us. At least it was cooler walking in the evening.

As we neared our destination, a scattering of Nepalis trying to get home before dark joined our little party. One I recognized as a man I had thrown out of the outpatient clinic two years earlier for creating a disturbance—he claimed he had lost his turn—but this evening he was cheerful and friendly, recalling the incident with evident pride. He invited us to his house for the night. Another man, whose son we had treated for typhoid, also invited us to his house. A third man whose bladder stone I had removed some years before invited us, too. We said no to these men because we were hoping to spend the night with a Christian who we had heard lived in the area. Oh yes, Babar Gurung, they all knew him; he was a big man in town, owned a clock shop, a radio shop, a photo shop, and a medical hall, and was the town's chief doctor as well. He would be happy to see us, they were all sure.

Babar was home and greeted us exuberantly—the more so when he found out we were Amp Pipal doctors, which fact he immediately announced to the several dozen people milling about his establishment. And an establishment it was. Babar's various enterprises were housed in different buildings: the medical hall here, the clock shop there, with several residences interposed for Babar's extended family, which included a brother just retired from a Gurkha regiment who had the physique and bearing of an Olympic judo champion. Babar, in contrast, was Nepal's answer to Bing Crosby: airy, personable, expansive, perpetually in motion, and possessing a lilting, mellifluous, nonstop voice.

While the women prepared the meal in the kitchen, men and guests sat in the courtyard in lively discourse, interrupted only once by the nearby slaughter of a goat elected to provide balance to our diets that evening. The meat was a grand affair, the goat superb, the company amiable, the mood jolly, helped along by a little brown jug that passed to and fro and never seemed to grow empty. Such are the Gurungs of Nepal.

Babar Gurung was honored that we had come. With pride and pleasure he showed us to his special guest room in the back of the clock shop, a cozy cubicle with one small window. It was the hottest and muggiest night of our trip. There was no movement of air inside or out. The bed, too, was a problem; it was only three feet wide—for both of us. Nepalis sleep together on narrow little mats like sardines on a cracker, but Cynthia and

I have never gotten the knack. And then the itching began. I couldn't scratch without waking Cynthia. I couldn't move without waking Cynthia; we were both sunk down together in a deep depression in the midst of a suffocating mattress we might have appreciated in January but hardly in June.

I wondered, too, if, along with clocks, radios, and cameras, Babar wasn't into bugs, perhaps hatching them in his guest room. In any case, the insect life provided only a mild diversion to the chief attraction of the evening: a grand wall clock of large proportions, obviously the pride of the clock part of the establishment. The clock, with a wall all to itself, hung in the clock shop, which was connected to our room by a small doorway without any door. The clock was in fine fettle, and finer still were its Big Ben chimes, which burst upon the premises with the resonance of kettle drums precisely on the quarter-hour. Exhaustion, in time, might have overcome the effects of bugs and prickly heat, but it could not overcome the anticipation of the next chime.

After suffering the clock for three hours, I gingerly got out of bed, found my flashlight, and tiptoed across the clock shop toward the clock. It was a pendulum clock, with a big golden pendulum swinging ponderously back and forth behind a glass panel. All that was needed was to open up the panel, touch the pendulum, and the clock would be stopped, with no one the wiser. Then I saw a man sleeping beneath the clock; it was Babar's brother, the judo champion. The brother stirred. I quickly switched off my light and waited. Then slowly, I groped my way to the wall, steering clear of the brother's bed. I felt for the clock. It was wrapped in plastic, front and sides, to keep out the dust. Leaning dangerously over the brother's bed, I carefully reached all around, feeling for an opening in the plastic. There was none.

At that moment the clock struck three.

After the echoes and reverberations had subsided, I listened for the heavy breathing of the figure below me. All was well. It was clear that the clock would have to come down. With utmost care I reached up to disengage it from the wall. I sensed I was taking a terrible chance: It would be just my luck to have the clock come crashing down, crushing the brother's skull or shoulder and then bouncing onto the floor to disintegrate into a thousand pieces—no doubt with gong ringing. Then the dogs would be aroused, the family alerted, the populace awakened, and into the shop would pour the outraged citizenry of Bhirti Bazaar, clubs at the ready, to apprehend the wretched scoundrel who had tried to make off with the pride and glory of the only clock shop in all of Lamjung District.

The reader will no doubt be relieved to know that nothing of the sort happened. The clock was successfully removed, the brother continued sleeping, and the pendulum, confused by the new centers of gravity to which it was being subjected, stopped when I set the clock on the counter. I tiptoed quietly away and was promptly off to sleep. Two hours later the household came alive. Day was breaking, patients were gathering, and the brother and one of Babar's sons were fussing with the clock on the counter trying to get it going again, each thinking the other had taken it down. I was tempted to tell them just to give the pendulum a little push and all would be well—except they'd be on Afghanistan Central Time—but recalling how arsonists often get caught watching their own fires, I discreetly turned the other way. The next time I looked, the plastic was off, the casing was opened, and brother and son were immersed in the works. I truly hope they were able to get it going again without breaking it. I so much wanted to tell them that just a wee little push on the pendulum . . .

Babar was full of energy that morning, getting everyone tea, rounding up patients for us to see, and attending to visitors and customers that streamed into his various shops. He was obviously highly respected, and by the standards of a Nepali village, his accomplishments were impressive. Not only was he the one man in the district who repaired clocks and radios and ran a photo studio, but he was also an accomplished medical practitioner—and a self-taught one at that. He set fractures, delivered babies, gave enemas, and treated all sorts of illnesses, and did so, as far as we could judge, with surprising competence.

And he was compassionate toward the poor. Many were the patients he sent to the Amp Pipal Hospital with money out of his own pocket.

After tea, we met together with Babar, his brother, their wives, our porters, and a couple of villagers for a small worship service. It was a useful time, for though Babar was a believer of vibrant faith, his understanding of Christian doctrine was imprecise. He had thought, for example, after reading the four Gospels, that Jesus had been born and had died four separate times. Babar's brother wanted to know what was wrong with Ram and Krishna—weren't they incarnations too? Yet the brother freely acknowledged that the lives of the Hindu incarnations were far from exemplary. If this was so, how then were they to show the way to a holy God?

"They can't," said Babar simply.

After the meeting we went to Babar's medical hall, where fifty patients had lined up to see us. When it looked as if the patients were going to continue all day, we watched for a lull in the line and then snuck out the back of the clinic, leaving Babar to see whoever came afterward. Those we had seen first were quite ill, but as the morning wore on and the complaints grew more trivial, we realized that people were just coming to have us lay hands on them and that Babar could treat them as well as we. Besides, we had many miles of trail to cover that day.

The succeeding days found us entering the higher foothills, where the nights were cooler, though the way was harder. The area was inhabited mainly by tribal people, few of whom were familiar with the Amp Pipal Hospital. One afternoon as we walked along, we were hailed into a tiny teashop set alone on a long high ridge. "You're from Amp Pipal, aren't you?" asked the teashop owner by way of greeting.

When we said yes, he went on: "I was sure you were. We've been to your hospital. Please come in and accept our hospitality."

We hesitated. We had just had tea an hour before, and furthermore, we felt a little uncomfortable about accepting the generosity of a man so obviously poor and needy. He couldn't have had many customers in a day, and what kind of living was he going to make anyway selling tea at three cents a cup in that remote and desolate place? Certainly it wasn't right not to pay for our tea.

"Please come in," the man said again. "At Amp Pipal you have served us. Now this is our chance to serve you."

His wife and two sons were in the shop, and they greeted us with broad smiles as if we were old friends. The wife sent the younger son out to fill the water jug and then retired to the mud stove in the corner and busied herself with lighting the fire.

"Get those books down," the father said to his other son, a lad of about fifteen. The boy took two booklets down from a top shelf; they were a gospel of Luke and another small booklet of Bible verses.

"He reads to us from these every day," the man said, looking proudly at his son. "They are wonderful books. Do you have any more like them?"

It so happened we did, and thus we were able to give them something after all in return for the tea and biscuits they served us. It was a happy exchange. As we departed, we thought about the countless patients who filed every day through the Amp Pipal outpatient department and for whom we had seldom the time to do more than lay a hand on their belly. But here were four, anyway, who had received something more than a paper packet of worm medicine. In the coming weeks we would learn of many others like them.

The trail led along the ridge for a while and then crossed a long expanse of terraced fields, plowed and ready for rice planting. We slogged through mud, sloshed through irrigation ditches, and teetered along the soft edges of the paddies. It was impossible to make much time; indeed it was all one could do to keep from slipping.

In one particularly slick and narrow stretch of trail, we chanced to meet some water buffalos. Meeting water buffalos is a common enough occurrence on the trails of Nepal; in fact, it's rare to walk half an hour without coming across them, alone or in groups. Usually nothing comes of these encounters: The traveler steps aside, the beasts plod on, and the worst that occurs is a flap in the face from a swishing tail. This is not to imply, however, that an encounter with a water buffalo should be taken lightly: They do gore people, and that not infrequently, if the number of victims that show up yearly at Amp Pipal is any indication.

The most interesting place to meet a buffalo is on a rice terrace. It's no little trick to get by a buffalo on a foot-wide trail with knee-deep muck on the left and a seven-foot drop on the right, and still keep your sneakers clean. And, of course, it's rarely one buffalo: Usually there will be three or four, or eight or ten. Following the buffalos will be a little boy with a stick, who is ostensibly driving the buffalos to wherever they are going. Ideally, there will be a little boy in front of the buffalos, too.

Today there were four buffalos. The lead buffalo and I passed without incident, but when the creature saw Cynthia coming behind me, it got excited—perhaps because of her gaudy green and yellow umbrella—and started to run toward her. Cynthia promptly jumped down to the terrace below. The little boy leading the buffalos ran at the excited animal with threatening gestures, whereupon the beast swung around and headed back along the trail toward me. I jumped down into the next terrace. Then along came the rear boy, running up to stop the buffalo, yelling and waving his stick. It's very much like catching the runner between second and third, though in this case the runner is alarmed and confused, along with the infielders. The excitement is heightened when, as is usual, there is more than one base runner. And indeed by this time all four buffalos were hot in the action. One of them suddenly jumped down onto Cynthia's terrace. Cynthia jumped back up, only to meet another base runner and have to jump back down again. This sort of game can go on for some time, until all the runners are out and the side is retired.

After vying with the buffalos, we entered the most scenic part of our journey thus far. The trail again ran along the crest of a narrow ridge, offering panoramic views of deep valleys falling off to either side. Scattered on the green and brown terraced slopes were little thatch-roofed hamlets, golden orange in the late afternoon sun. The dwellings thinned out as we went along, however, and seemed to drop farther and farther below. Ahead was a large mountain, its whole left side forming a sheer cliff of 2,500 feet, as if cleaved off by some mighty stroke. We wondered whether our trail would lead below or above the cliff, especially since we seemed headed right for the middle of it. As we drew closer, we could make out a fault line running transversely across the cliff face and slightly upward; and indeed, this turned out to be our trail, wide enough in the daylight to pass safely if we paid attention to where we were stepping. Straight down to the left was a free fall of 1,500 feet, after which the ground splayed out into the valley another 2000 feet below.

Two miles ahead at the far end of the cliff was a tiny saddle, and perched on the saddle was a tiny village. Aglow with orange sunlight streaming in through a low-lying break in the clouds, the village looked like an illustration from a child's storybook. Just at the village, the cliff abruptly ended and was replaced by a sharp ridge that went loping off into the sunset. As we neared the village, we noted that it contained ten structures in all: two houses, two temples, five shacks, and a primary school. The crest of the saddle was just wide enough for a path, and the buildings hung off either side, supported by tall posts or sagging stone foundations. If one were careless and rolled off his back porch, it would be hundreds of feet down before he'd come to a stop. At a good gust of wind, one could imagine the whole village lifting off and flying away. And if it did, few people would note it: The nearest settlement was two miles down the trail.

In the center of the village was a water spout with a spigot three feet off the ground. That such an insignificant, out-of-the-way place should have piped running water was odd indeed, though that didn't keep Cynthia from taking a "shower" under it—much to the delight of the village's twenty children who gathered to watch her technique.

One of the two proper houses served as a hotel, and the proprietor happily offered us his "private room," a boarded-off end of the front porch that barely accommodated two narrow wooden beds. Ventilation was provided by the inch of space between each board slat. Our porters were given the back porch to sleep on, with its stunning drop off the edge.

While supper was being prepared, Cynthia and I sat outside and watched the black storm clouds gather in the lingering twilight. They were coming in low, settling over and around us, and soon it was completely dark. Thousands of fireflies cavorted in the void beneath us, giving the startling impression of a universe spun upside down, with stars below and clouds of land above, and the little village a floating island drifting somewhere in between.

Voices interrupted our reverie. Twenty men came stumbling and puffing up the steep path below us and filed into our hotel. How they thought they were going to fit, we didn't know—the place had only six beds, and we had taken four of them—but they were obviously intending to stay. They were *panchayat* officials from surrounding *panchayats* on their way home from a meeting in the district capital, half a day's walk to the north. They made no small commotion as they jockeyed for space and ordered tea and rice. Just sitting down, they filled every square foot of the little establishment. While they were sorting themselves out, we went into the kitchen to eat.

The cook's task was further complicated, of course, by the need to prepare supper for the twenty new arrivals. Yet she remained undaunted. How a woman cooks at all in this country amazes me. Her kitchen is invariably cramped, hot, smoky, and dark. Her stove is a low, hollowed-out mound of mud with two openings to put the pots on and a third in which to stick the firewood; or it may be merely a shallow pit in which stands a metal tripod. In either case she has to cook at least three dishes at once, and how she manages to end up with everything ready and hot and never move once from where she is squatting is a mystery to me, and something that American kitchen designers ought to look into.

It takes a long time, of course—an hour and a half to prepare a meal from scratch, and triple that time for twenty-four guests. And all the while she squats on the mud floor, hot, suffocating, eye-stinging smoke all around, moving pots and kettles here and there, picking off various ingredients from nearby blackened shelves, stirring, ladling, mixing, and at the same time seeing that everyone's plates are heaped full with seconds and thirds. And her task is made even more difficult by the constant stream of visitors to the kitchen: a big shaggy dog covered with mange; chickens fluttering in and out, raising dust; children squatting down near the stove, coughing, spitting, and demanding to be fed.

Usually we eat squatting, but tonight we had the luxury of a bench to sit on and another bench to eat on. Our "table" was a board set on two biscuit tins, a perfectly adequate table until it was knocked down by a retarded man who had trouble controlling his limbs and who was in and out of the kitchen eight times during our meal. Others, too, were losing control of their limbs from too much liquor, and they also passed through the narrow kitchen to pay their drunken respects to the cook and ask how the food was coming. Altogether it was a lively meal.

It got me to thinking about the virtues of a mud floor. First of all, a mud floor is cool in summer and warm in winter. Second, it's absorbent. Puddles from leaky roofs can disappear in no time. Chicken droppings desiccate in seconds. The elimination of little children are similarly accommodated, and those elements that remain are quickly eaten by the dog. And the whole thing can be resurfaced at no cost. A fresh batch of red mud and cow dung, and presto, you have a new floor as neat and tidy as you could wish for. It's laid on every morning in every Nepali household. And I defy you to beat it for either efficiency or economy.

The hotel was lit by several tiny alcohol lamps, half-candle-power each, and thus we could sit unobserved in relative darkness and listen to the animated tales of the other guests as they recounted the latest scandals they had heard in the district capital. By eleven o'clock they showed no sign of stopping, so Cynthia went to bed and I went out to enjoy a spectacular display of lightning that went on until midnight; and then the rain came.

And come it did, accompanied by great blasts of wind that

blew the rain into our room as if no boards were there at all. The roof leaked too, in small streams, so out came our plastic, and when that wasn't wide enough, our umbrellas. The rain stopped in an hour and the *panchayat* people did too, so we were finally able to drift off to sleep. But I dozed only fitfully; I had the sensation that water was continuing to drip on me. As my bed was a wooden platform raised only two inches off the mud-puddly floor, I figured that water could easily enough run onto me, though I couldn't tell from where. I finally got out my flashlight and discovered a twelve-inch worm slithering across my chest. I gently eased him off, discouraged a few more from coming my way, tightened the sleeping bag around my neck, and hoped for the best. The rain had brought the creatures out; there were hundreds of them everywhere.

By four o'clock the twenty *panchayat* officials were up, snorting, blowing, and hawking. They were clearing out their systems for the day, the louder and longer the better. Throat clearing and spitting rituals over, they all had tea and were off to their homes, leaving the place in quiet and solitude once more.

The night's storm had cleared the skies, and now for the first time on our trip we could see the snow-clad mountains, 26,000-foot Manaslu and Himalchuli, amazingly close at hand. Immediately in front of us the land plunged 4000 feet into the gorge below; and on the other side, rising tier after tier, low hills, then higher hills, turning to rocky jagged ridges; and then finally the snow line, above which the mighty peaks soared effortlessly into the sky.

The sun came up behind the mountains, wiping away shadows and creating new ones. Clouds floated motionless below us and above us, thin wisps, white and gray, pink and silver. And as the hillsides below were swept with sunlight, they turned to brilliant emerald, layer upon layer, rolling richly down before us.

There was no water in the village tap today: In the night a landslide had carried part of the pipe away.

That morning, the eleventh day of our trek, we set out for the capital of the Lamjung District, taking care as always to avoid walking through the village toilet situated along either side of the trail on the way out of town. But a little way from the village all was clean and pure once more, and we enjoyed a pleasant walk through the thickly forested mountainside until we came on the ancient Lamjung capital located on a promontory overlooking the modern capital 3000 feet below. There on the edge of a precipice stood the four-hundred-year-old historic castle, which had been the citadel of the former kings of Lamjung. The setting was stark and dramatic: above, the ancient red-brick fortress with its stone roof and faded gnarled woodwork; and far below, the tiny tin-roofed houses of the present district capital strung out along the great valley of the Marsyandi River.

Anticipating the need to meet with various officials in the capital, I kept my eye out for a place to bathe and tidy up. We saw several springs on the way down, but they were always crowded with women washing their clothes, their children, or themselves.

Finally, not too far from town, I spied a lovely tap just over a stone wall at the edge of a cornfield. No one was in sight. I stripped down to my underwear and hastily began to bathe. Some boys appeared and wanted to cool off in the water, and when I asked them to wait, they sat and snickered on the wall. A young girl came to fill her water jug, and then another. A woman with a big load came and wanted a drink. Another brought some soiled clothes to wash. A queue formed, as if for circus tickets. I escaped into the cornfield with the job poorly done, but it didn't matter. Ten minutes down the trail I was as hot and sweaty as ever. The whole effort hardly seemed worth it.

Our day in the district capital was remarkably intense. We met several hundred people—government officials, *pradhan panches,* former patients and their relatives. We saw nearly everyone we had hoped to see and many whom we hadn't expected to see. We met with the Chief District Officer (CDO), a gruff, beefy, unshaven fellow, new to the district and obviously unhappy to have been assigned to such a backwater as Lamjung. We met with one *pradhan panch* after another, usually out in the middle of the street where we would be quickly surrounded by other interested people as well. Delegations of people came up and asked for medical help in their *panchayats*. The *pradhan panch* we had met several days back—the one who was trying to shake loose money for his clinic—collared me and took me off to see the president of the district *panchayat*, who, in contrast to the CDO, looked like the upwardly mobile young man who rides business class in ads for Singapore Airlines. And so it went for a solid ten hours.

To add to the carnival atmosphere, people kept calling to us out of their houses and shops to come and examine this patient or that. Crippled people showed us their limbs and asked if anything could be done. Former patients whom we had treated at Amp Pipal came up to greet us; some had had tuberculosis or meningitis; others had been operated on for cleft lips, cataracts, bear maulings, and bladder stones. One little boy who ran out to say hello had had a tiny stone lodged in the tip of his penis, blocking the passage of urine. His bladder had been bulging and under great pressure. After putting him to sleep, I had plucked out the stone and stepped back, and the little fellow had gone off like a loose hose, spraying the walls, windows, and the unwary spectators I had called in to watch the procedure. If only all illnesses were so simple—and so much fun!

In the midst of the melee I found time to visit the district prison, where an acquaintance was incarcerated on charges of murdering his pregnant girlfriend. It was a sordid business, whoever had done it: The girl's skull had been crushed with a large rock. The young man had heatedly denied any guilt; he was happily married, and besides, he had spent the night of the crime with a German tourist who would have been happy to testify on his behalf, except that the testimony of foreigners may not be admitted as evidence in Nepali courts, or so we were told. The young man's trial was coming up in two months.

Visiting the jail was a bit reckless, I suppose. I walked into the warden's office and asked respectfully, "I would like to see Tirtha Bhatta." Perhaps he thought I was Inspector of Prisons for the United Nations. He was on his guard.

"What do you want with him?"

"I have something to say to him."

"Say it to me."

"No, I'd really prefer to say it to him, if possible."

The warden eyed me suspiciously. In the two years he had been in charge, I was probably the first foreign visitor he had encountered. "Very well," he said at last. "But you can't see the prisoner alone. I'll come with you."

I had wanted to give Tirtha a gospel of John, but now I saw that I had better clear it first. "I'd like to give the prisoner a booklet," I ventured.

"Show it to me," said the warden, holding out his hand.

I got the booklet out of my bag and gave it to him. Then I sat for five minutes while he read through the first chapter. He read intently but betrayed no emotion. "Do you have any more like this?" he asked, nodding toward my bag.

I had with me a few small pamphlets entitled "Who Is He?" I offered him one. This was evidently more comprehensible, for his expression loosened as he read, and his eyes brightened.

"This is very good," he said. "I'd like to keep these booklets."

I suggested we give them first to the prisoner, then afterward he could read them if he liked. I wondered if he was getting ready to turn me in for distributing Christian literature, which was against the law.

He readily agreed to my suggestion, however, and getting up from his desk, he escorted me through the courtyard, through a tall iron gate, past guards with bayonets, and finally to the prisoner's compound, where I waited in front of more bars. The guards called for the prisoner.

Tirtha appeared in surprisingly good spirits and seemed glad to see me. With bayonets to right and left and the warden leaning forward to catch each word, I asked Tirtha if he had any message for his mother. He had no message, he said.

Rain began falling, and the warden and the soldiers retreated a little way off for cover. "Are you guilty?" I whispered to Tirtha, looking less for an answer than a reaction.

"No," he said out loud. "God knows I'm innocent. Even if

they judge me guilty, it doesn't matter as long as He knows the truth." He pointed to the rain.

The prisoner and I were getting soaked, and since I could see little chance for meaningful conversation, I merely said: "You do well to call upon God, for it is truly His judgment that matters most, and nothing you have done in your life will escape His judgment. But He is also willing to forgive—if you meet certain conditions. You can read about those conditions and about what God is prepared to do for you in these booklets." I handed the booklets through the bars.

The only person we never got to see was the District Medical Officer. He was off in Kathmandu, trying to get funds for running the fifteen-bed district hospital, funds that had been promised but had not been given. The hospital was a roomy and well-built structure, the gift of some foreign agency, but the business of operating it had been left to the government, and there matters stood. It had no staff and no equipment. "It will open next year," we were blithely assured by the health assistant on duty. We said we surely hoped so. The hospital would help take some of the load off Amp Pipal as well.

The next day, after a four-hour side trip upriver to visit another health post, we left the district capital and headed east in the direction of Amp Pipal. We had been walking an hour when it began to pour, so spying a teashop nearby, we headed for cover. The shop was all of eight feet by twelve feet, a typical little hut made of sticks and leaves with a leaf roof. The front was open, but happily the wind was blowing from the other direction. With our party of four, our luggage, some chickens, a couple of other people who had come in out of the rain, and a sick man who hadn't yet gotten through his medical history in the half-hour we'd been walking together—with all these, huddled together, the shop was crammed to capacity.

At one end of the shop the proprietress squatted, a wizened, hook-nosed, beady-eyed woman of eighty or so, who looked like she had come straight from the land of the Munchkins. There she hunched in front of her little one-kettle mud stove, peering at us intently as if wondering which of us she was going to eat first.

We ordered tea, which would be served up in turns since there were eight of us in the shop and only four glasses. These the old woman duly cleaned, using her fingers for wiping and water dripping off the roof for rinsing—which wouldn't have been bad except that's where the chickens roosted when it wasn't raining. One could see that she, too, had a high regard for dirt floors, for she treated hers like a Formica counter, placing on it cup, spoon, kettle lid, and tea strainer. She rubbed her itchy feet. She rubbed the stirring spoon. She stirred the tea. Visible foreign objects floating on the surface she picked out neatly, letting heavier objects settle to the bottom with the tea leaves. The tea was served.

In between the first and second servings, the old woman brought two goats in out of the rain. Two drenched wayfarers followed, crowding into the hut. Outside the teashop, people still walked on the trail, some with plastic over them, others with umbrellas. Porters with their loads, usually unprotected, hurried on their way; to stop for the rain was a loss of money for them, and they cared little if the cement or grain they carried got "slightly damp." The same was true, evidently, for a man with a large black business typewriter on his back: no plastic, no umbrella, not even a case—just typewriter bobbing through the rain on its way to the district capital to adorn some government office. And when it didn't work, people would shrug it off as incomprehensible, or to be expected, and think nothing more about it. Such are the difficulties of modernizing a gadgetless society.

As the rain showed no sign of letting up, Cynthia got out her Bible, and as we often did while resting or waiting for a storm to pass, we read to our porters. As usual, the others around listened with interest, even Miss Munchkin. And when the rain finally ceased, the other people in the teashop asked for booklets to take home with them. And if they themselves couldn't read, they had children who could. Indeed, the people here hunger for reading matter and will snap up anything they can get. And the Gospel would be at the top of the list if we could find a way to distribute it casually without stimulating the investigative juices of the authorities.

When we returned to the trail, the path led us along the site of a new motor road still under construction. The road had become a river of mud in the meantime, making our travel next to impossible. Coming on an uncompleted section on a steep hillside, we saw a hundred workers with picks and iron bars scratching and pecking at the earth. Mao was right when he said two thousand men could move a mountain in a year. It's on this principle that road building in Nepal is founded. The contractors, however, are not above using a little dynamite here and there, as an immense explosion just ahead of us amply demonstrated. A rush of rocks and boulders came tumbling down across our path. Men with shovels attacked the pile, and as we watched, we saw what the term "labor intensive" really means: two men to a shovel, one pushing, one pulling. Beyond the pile a detour led us sharply up a twisting mud-slick goat trail, near the top of which we were told to hurry, lest the dynamite go off again. What with rain, mud, and detours, the afternoon passed quickly with few miles to show for it, and darkness found us installed in a muggy little hotel along the river. We were by then fully five days behind schedule.

Our plan for the next day was simple: an hour's side trip to visit a health post, getting back in plenty of time to arrive at a friend's house ten miles down river. It would be one of our easiest days. We were on the trail at six o'clock the next morning, but the one hour the walk should have taken soon turned into three. It was a hot and humid climb, three miles long and 1,500 feet up, and Cynthia was dragging for the first time on the trip. We arrived at the village at nine and ate our morning rice at a nearby hotel. It was a pleasant place. They had used the floor broom to sweep the table, but such is to be expected in a land where the differentiation between floor and table is not well developed. The owner raised pigeons we soon learned; their nest sat on a shelf above our table. They passed the meal flying in and out, showering our plates with straw and feathers. Three "bombs" were dropped but the aim was poor and they missed the table altogether.

The *pradhan panch* walked in while we were eating, so we invited him to a glass of tea. As we chatted, the hotel filled with youngsters on their way to school. Word was out: Two doctors had come to town. Villagers, eager not to miss such an opportunity, pressed into the hotel, hastily dusting off their past and present illnesses for presentation. When there was scarcely room to raise hand to mouth, the *pradhan panch* drove them all out, telling the schoolchildren to be off to school and the others to drop by the health post, where the doctors would be happy to see them. We promptly said no we would not, that in villages with their own health posts we saw patients only "on referral." The distinction was lost on the crowd, of course, for the only person at work in the health post was a young assistant nurse-midwife who promptly referred to us everyone that showed up.

By the time we had finished eating and had walked over to the health post, there were fifty people in line. Inside, the waiting room was jammed with bodies. We pushed our way into the examining room, a confining space six feet wide and ten feet long, with a window at the far end opposite the door. Along one wall was an examining table, and along the other, a cupboard, a desk, and two chairs. We knew we couldn't escape seeing all these patients, so without wasting time, we got to work, Cynthia taking the children and I the adults. We stationed a worker at the door to admit the patients one by one, and we asked the *pradhan panch* to call the names and help keep order. But the worker was too spineless to keep even the children out, and the *pradhan panch* was a glad-handing politician who couldn't say no; so bedlam reigned, and every few minutes the examining room got so full of people that no one could move, and I had to clear them out myself.

By the end of an hour we had seen forty patients, and the line outside was as long as it was when we started. It was plain that the whole *panchayat* was coming to see the doctor. Those who couldn't get in at the door bypassed the line and jumped in the window. Teachers from the school came to be examined, and with teachers gone, the students came too. A crowd massed around the health post. It seemed as if the entire school of seven hundred students had been let out. Even at a minute a patient, we'd be lucky to finish by nightfall.

The exercise was growing more and more pointless. In the first place, the health post had no medicine, and the little medical hall in town had run out of stock by the twentieth patient. Second, other than worms, most of the people had nothing wrong with them. A few of the people were former patients from Amp Pipal whom we were happy to see, but the bulk of the people were just along for the ride.

Finally, having spent two and a half hours seeing over a hundred patients, I went outside and announced the closing of our impromptu clinic to all but the "very sick." At once two dozen people pushed up to me, pointing pitiably at eye, ear, and stomach, or wheezing and coughing noisily. Those that looked ill I pushed inside, bolting the door after them. Since Cynthia by this time had begun holding gynecology clinic in the examining room, I set up shop in the crowded waiting room. One man had an anal condition, so everyone inside had to face the wall while I examined him, his behind to the window so there'd be enough light. The only problem came from the giggling spectators looking in from outside.

When I had seen all my patients, I went out to inspect the medical hall, leaving Cynthia in the examining room to finish up her gynecology patients. People were still arriving to be examined, only now they were coming from outlying villages— word had spread. Some had even been carried. So once more I began seeing patients, this time under the pipal tree outside the health post. Just as I finished the last of them, my eye caught Cynthia leaping unprofessionally out of the examining-room window. As she ran around the side of the building, thirty women piled out the front, trying to head her off. We escaped down the path in the nick of time.

"What on earth did you do that for?" I asked when we were out of sight.

"They wouldn't let me out," Cynthia said. "They were all clamoring to be examined. I would have been there all day."

I looked back just once to see a man running after us. There was something in his expression that made me stop. It was the hotelkeeper. We had forgotten to pay for our breakfast.

It was two o'clock, and we had twelve miles to go. In spite of a few obligatory house calls, we got down to the main trail along the river in one hour. We soon met a couple carrying their nearly dead baby back home from a medical hall a couple of hours down the road. The child had been given some sort of potion, quite useless under the circumstances, since the child's main problem was dehydration from dysentery. As it had begun to rain again, Cynthia brought the child into a nearby teashop, where she asked the unbelieving proprietress for some sugar, salt, and water with which to make up some rehydration solution. Then she proceeded to feed the baby with a spoon. Although we were there only a short time, it was long enough to see a dying child restored to life. Several children owe their lives to Cynthia's being in the right place at the right time on that trip—and to a little water, sugar, and salt.

We reached our friend's town at six o'clock. He insisted that we spend the night at his family home, which was a short walk, he said, up the hillside above the town. The "short walk" turned out to be a two-hour, 1,800-foot climb in the rain, and most of it in darkness. The house—rather, three great houses that might have suited the needs of a medieval baron—sat eerily on a vast wooded mountainside overlooking the valley far below, now hidden beneath mist and cloud. Our friend's wife and mother greeted us graciously and then disappeared to prepare our supper, a labor requiring two hours since the family had already eaten and they had not anticipated our arrival.

In the morning we could look out and see just how far up we had come for our night's lodging, and we couldn't help noting also that our route would take us back down the same way and up the opposite side to the north. While waiting for breakfast, we inspected our friend's five hundred fruit trees, most of them prize tangerine trees whose fruit was sought after by merchants coming from as far away as Kathmandu. This year, however, not a single tangerine hung from the branches; the entire crop had been wiped out by a devastating hailstorm only two weeks before.

When we returned from our tour, Cynthia and I examined the family, all of whom suffered from worms. It was not hard to see why. A little child had just done his business in the courtyard, and his mother was washing him off among the dishes waiting to be rinsed. We couldn't restrain ourselves from admonishing our host concerning the unhygienic habits of his family. "You may be a man of progress when it comes to managing fruit trees," I said to him, "but you're certainly not when it comes to managing stool." He took the rebuke good-naturedly and replied that "our village women like to play in the *goo,* and it's hard to change their ways."

We left our friend's house two hours later than planned, dropped back down to the river, and then headed up the other side. Our trail led upward into high country we had never seen before. I was grumbling about being late, and Cynthia was saying, "Shush. Maybe God planned it that way and has someone in mind for us to meet." I couldn't deny it was possible: It had already happened many times.

We stopped for tea in a dip in a long ridge extending northward to the snows. We asked the name of the place, but the name meant nothing to us. Some teachers from a nearby school came out for their tea break. After chatting with them, we got up to leave, and as we walked out the door, there, standing in front of us, was an old and dear friend whom we hadn't seen in years.

He too was a teacher in this school; this was his home. He had been headmaster of a mission school years before, and we used to stay with him on our village clinic rounds. I remember well the evenings spent together singing hymns and reading from the Bible. And then he had moved, somewhere way off in Lamjung District, and we had lost track of him. Until today.

He still had his Bible and his hymnbook and his faith. But he had been alone so long that the flame had almost flickered out.

"If you share your faith, it will grow stronger," Cynthia said to him at the end of an hour and a half together. "And God will raise up others to join you, and you'll no longer be alone."

We wished that we could have spent more time with him, but there were other places to go, and we needed to see other people in other places, and we had only two days left to do it in. We departed, promising to come back as soon as we could.

Four hours farther up the trail we stopped for the night at a health post that sat on a high promontory, with sweeping vistas stretching out before us to the north and east. We could see Liglig Mountain two days off across the Chepe River, and if we'd had binoculars, we could have seen the hospital as well. Here we had a choice of routes, one of two long ridges to follow down to the river below. The two ridges represented two *panchayats,* and we had wanted to visit both, but now had run out of time. We chose the northerly ridge, where one of my former bear-maul patients lived.

After an hour on the trail, we looked back and saw two young men coming after us on the run. When they finally caught up with us, they were so out of breath they had to sit down and rest before they could speak. They were two teachers from the *panchayat* we had bypassed; I had removed the tonsils of one some years before, and Cynthia had treated the other for typhoid fever. They had come after us, they said, to ask for our help in starting a health program in their village, and since we were close, would we not consider including their village on our way back to Amp Pipal. At this point we were halfway to the northern *panchayat,* and to get to their village would require dropping down 2000 feet into an untraveled gorge and then climbing up the other side. We could see the entire route laid out below us; nobody could tell us this time that it was just a "short walk." After calculating how much time and energy we had left, we decided we could do it. We parted ways, agreeing to meet the young men at their village that night.

Very soon we began to feel we had made a wrong choice in taking the northern route home. This *panchayat* was a wild and desolate place, thinly populated, its trails narrow and infested with leeches. The few houses we passed seemed uninhabited except for snarling dogs; at this time of year people were out in their fields, often hours from home.

"What makes you think you're going to find your patient at home?" Cynthia asked. "No one's at home around here; there's no one even to ask where he lives." We did find a few people to ask, however, and we eventually made our way to the cluster of houses where my patient was said to live.

The place was deserted. In my mind I heard Cynthia saying, "You see?" When we passed the last house, I gave up hope; this had been a goose chase and I was the goose. Then I saw the little path leading around a knoll to a little house, and behold, as we had found every day of our trip, the person we had wanted to see was there waiting for us.

The reunion was heartwarming, perhaps more for me than for my former patient. In minutes the entire family had appeared, from where I don't know, and within twenty minutes half the village was there. It was always that way: It was hard to go anywhere in these hills without attracting a crowd.

Many family members had been sick since we had last met, and some even now were seriously ill. We asked Sher Bahadur, our porter, to pray for those who were sick, and when he had finished ten minutes later, he had prayed not only for the sick but also for the spiritual enlightenment of the entire village, throwing in a brief summary of God's plan of salvation as well. As I listened to the prayer of this uneducated village Christian, I thought of the words of James: "Has not God chosen those who are poor in the eyes of the world to be rich in faith?" I would as soon have this brother pray for my healing as any educated person I know.

The family pressed us to spend the night. But when they finally accepted that we couldn't stay, they brought out a great keg of yogurt and insisted on feeding us two large bowls each. We promised to return some day, and we departed with every intention of doing so. We left behind the last of our Christian booklets, though only one or two of the school-age youngsters could read.

Down, down, and up, up to the teachers' village; we made it

just before dark. After supper, Cynthia sat on our host's porch and talked about health for three hours with twenty village elders, who sat in rows in the courtyard. A small kerosene lamp set on the edge of the porch cast a pale wavering light over the features of the villagers. Cynthia excelled at this kind of meeting and soon had the elders actively discussing the community's health problems and suggesting solutions. Eventually they took over the discussion entirely, at which point I began to doze off; it was almost midnight. Cynthia gamely kept at it, and at one o'clock the newly stirred-up health enthusiasts shuffled off into the night, and we retired.

The pounding of the *diki* woke us at four: The daughter-in-law had begun husking the day's rice. Momentarily chagrined, we quickly realized that if we had slept any longer, we would have been mobbed by patients and delayed who knows how many hours. So we left at the first faint light, proceeding quickly and quietly through the village. Even so, half a dozen patients were out waiting for us on the path.

Hardly five minutes of that last day passed when we didn't meet someone we knew or wanted to see. We met one *pradhan panch* and four of his *panchayat* council members in a teashop where we stopped for tea. We passed a second *pradhan panch* on the trail. And we ran into a third *pradhan panch* where two trails crossed; had either of us been a minute off, we would not have met.

We saw scores of former patients, and in one village where we stopped to eat, it seemed as if I had operated on half the community at one time or another. A dozen people came up to show us this scar or that, and one old woman hobbled over and stuck out at me what looked like a tiny curled-up sausage link— which was all that was left of her tongue following an operation for cancer eight years before.

As we approached Amp Pipal that evening, we reflected with wonder that we had seen on our journey virtually every person we had hoped to see—and many, of course whom we hadn't thought to see at all. We had prayed before we started out that God would lead us, and the church at Amp Pipal had been praying too; but we never imagined we would be led quite so precisely, so unerringly. We had missed the doctor in the district capital, that was all. No, we had missed one other person, a Christian brother whose house we had visited on our fourth day out. If only we had seen him, too, we could have said our trip had been perfect.

With these thoughts in mind we reached the hospital. A voice in the dark called out, "Hello, Doctor"—and we recognized the Christian brother whom we had just been thinking about. He had been in Amp Pipal that day and had been hoping to see us before he left early next morning. A better ending we could not have wished for.

fifteen

Gorkha District

A FTER THREE HECTIC DAYS of rest in Amp Pipal, Cynthia, the porters, and I set out on the second leg of our journey. The first leg, we knew, would be hard to match. Rice planting had begun in full frenzy. The rain no longer came in isolated showers but poured relentlessly day after day, drenching the land. Our route would be more sparsely settled, and the distances between villages would be far greater. We would be climbing into the wild country to the north, at the very base of the snows. People in their right mind never traveled at this time of year—unless they happened to be two doctors out doing a survey.

The hospital was the scene of much excitement the day before we left: Sixteen people had been bitten by two rabid dogs, and men were out with guns, searching for the animals without success. The next day, therefore, on our way out of Amp Pipal, we stopped in the bazaar briefly to see if the *pradhan panch* was in and to alert him to the danger of a full-scale rabies epidemic. To our surprise we found not only the *pradhan panch* but all nine *panchayat* council members gathered in a teashop: They were electing their *upa pradhan panch* (deputy mayor). Thus we were able to alert the whole council at one sitting. After a useful meeting, we proceeded on our way, late as usual. With this kind of beginning it looked as if our second trip was going to be a replay of the first.

The first day brought us up into the high country north of Amp Pipal. It rained all day, but there'd be no more sitting out the rain in teashops this trip: We had too much ground to cover. Besides, there weren't going to be that many teashops to sit in.

As we climbed higher into the clouds, we entered that eerie, misty world of the Himalayan monsoon. Now and again the clouds would break, revealing still other clouds floating far below, giving us the unreal sense of being much higher than we were. Once, looking back, we glimpsed the black tip of Liglig Mountain ten miles off, jutting through the mass of white. A moment later the clouds swallowed it up. In the midst of these clouds, with no other land in sight, one feels remote, detached. Even near at hand the mist can be so thick that objects thirty feet away remain completely hidden.

Yet the monsoon season has a beauty of its own. True, you can't see the shining snowy peaks, the high rocky ridges, the far foothills—or the near foothills for that matter. But the silhouette of a tree floating in the mist twenty feet off can be a pretty sight. And not only trees float by, but giant eruptions of bamboo break through the mist, shooting up like fireworks; and strange rock formations and overhanging cliffs appear suspended in the grayness, as if attached to nothing.

After climbing through fog for over two hours, we came up on a solitary, one-room mud hut with "Hotel Siranchok" written in English on its door. Smoke rose from the thatched roof, signaling the presence of hot tea and a warm fire within. It was the cleanest establishment we had seen in the hills, attributable, no doubt, to the owner's having recently taken a two-week health course at Amp Pipal. The tea sped us on our way, and after two more hours of climbing, we arrived at the home of an Irish schoolteacher named Margaret McComb, one of the grand old missionaries of the Gorkha hills. She lived in a house belonging to the local *pradhan panch,* whose wife had had two huge ovarian cysts, teratomas, the largest I had ever seen. The wife was fond of regaling one and all with a vivid account of what had been pulled from her belly: "two great yellow bags filled with cheese, hair, bones, and teeth." A pathologist couldn't have said it more accurately.

The next morning we were invited to the home of one of the

few baptized Christians in the entire region north of Amp Pipal. The man was a Gurung whose wife had been treated by Cynthia for tuberculosis. The wife had stopped coming for treatment prematurely, as many of our patients do, and the disease had recurred. She came again, and stopped again. When she came a third time, almost dead, Cynthia told her that she was not entitled to the expensive "second-line" drugs that would now be necessary to cure her; these drugs, of which we had but a limited supply, were reserved for patients who had proved to be faithful in their treatment. The woman had been repeatedly warned but had not heeded; now she had lost her chance.

For some reason—she's not sure why—Cynthia decided to treat the wife anyway. "It's not that you deserve it," Cynthia said to her. "But in showing you mercy, I'm giving you an illustration of how God deals mercifully with every person who turns to Him in faith." The message may have overshot the wife, but it hit the husband, and over the course of his wife's treatment he received the Gospel and became a follower of Jesus. The wife eventually recovered, after weeks on the edge of death, and here, two years later, she was busily preparing a meal for the doctor who had saved her life.

They served us the finest meal they could provide, with extra dishes lavishly spiced. When we arrived, the husband was chasing after a fat and energetic hen that was destined to become the main course. The entire morning passed in cooking, talking, eating, and in the end, praying. We left at noon, our tongues tingling, and our stomachs stuffed with food.

We were behind schedule as usual. On this second trip we weren't going to be able to run five days over as we had on the first trip, and I must confess to having been fidgety about the time. Today we had many miles to travel. We were headed for the next *panchayat,* where we hoped to meet the *pradhan panch;* after that we were to move on to yet another village for the night.

We took a shortcut, so we thought, 1,500 feet down and 1,500 up in the broiling sun (it had rained all morning), but when we reached the other side, we discovered the *pradhan panch's* house was another 1000 feet up the ridge: We had been given wrong directions. So leaving Cynthia and the two porters to wait where they were, I climbed up to the *pradhan panch's* house, only to find that he had left an hour earlier and wouldn't be back till evening. Our infallible timing was off. This was Nepal as usual: nobody home.

Back on the main trail a Gurung tribesman carrying a rifle and a birdcage caught up with us. He had been out hunting, and he showed us his hunting bird, whose call, he said, enticed other birds for miles around into range of his gun. Very clever, though that day he had bagged nothing. Khushiman, which means "happy heart," was a warm and jolly fellow, and he invited us to spend the night at his house two hours away.

"My father was very sick a few years back," he told Cynthia, "and you treated him, and he got well. Then a year after that he had too much to drink and got sick again. My brother was here then and said, 'Take him to Kathmandu.' So we did; but he got worse. My father said to us, 'If you had taken me to Amp Pipal, I'd have been well by now.' So we took him back to Amp Pipal."

"What happened?" we asked.

"He died on the way." It was the only time all day we saw him look sober, and it was only for a moment. The rest of the time he bubbled on about this thing or that until we reached his village, just as the sun was setting.

It wasn't a village, really, but a cluster of six houses stuck off by itself; the houses all belonged to Khushiman and his brothers. For Cynthia and me, who were used to staying with Nepalis more prosperous and educated, this was a chance to see how the "real" hill people lived. Not that Khushiman was poor, but one would go far to find someone less sophisticated. He bounded up the steps to his porch, beaming at everyone, obviously pleased to be bringing along the first foreigners to set foot in the village, and two doctors at that. For a day's catch, we were better than birds in a bag.

Khushiman parked us on a mat on the porch and went inside the house, whence, amid much clanging and banging, he called out to us: "Care for some *raksi?*"

We and our porters politely declined the homemade liquor, so Khushiman brought us tea instead, served in great medieval-looking brass chalices. Then he sent his daughter out to pick some corn and roast it for us for appetizers.

At that point Khushiman took the cover off the bird cage and hung it on a tree just off the porch. Instantly we were treated to an extraordinary demonstration of the bird's vocal prowess. I defy any zoologist to produce a similar-sized creature that can make more noise. To say its screech was shrill, piercing, rasping is to say nothing.

"It's call can carry five miles if the wind is right," said Khushiman, with a cheerful grin. I could believe it; I'd go for ten, with or without the wind.

By this time twenty children—grandsons, granddaughters, nieces, and nephews—had crowded onto the porch, all seeming to share in the infectious gaiety of our host. The children were treated with affection and respect rather than as nuisances, and when the piles of roasted corn came round, they got first pick.

Khushiman organized everything. Squatting there in his red felt topi, black vest, and white loincloth, he played perfectly the role of benign potentate, one moment giving instructions to his wife, next moment telling people where to sit, passing the corn around once more, or filling up our chalices with tea. In between duties, he would disappear into the house and fortify himself with a pull or two from the *raksi* jug.

Aside from the bird, who serenaded us unflaggingly, there was only one other jarring note to the scene on the porch: A wee child, seized with the urge, squatted next to me and proceeded to relieve himself. A large dog crept up, consumed the business as it was coming out, and licked the child's bottom clean. No fuss, no muss, and nobody noticed but me.

Smoke pouring from the door signaled that the cooking of our supper was under way. A lull in the conversation prompted Cynthia to take out her tape recorder and begin playing some of the Gurung language tapes she had brought along. A hush fell on the porch. The youngsters had never heard their own language on tape or radio before, and they listened with fascination. Khushiman was listening, too, after a fashion. Dandling an infant on his knee, he was rocking dreamily to and fro, his face a study in supreme contentment.

At ten o'clock an enormous meal was served. Many of the children had gone back to their own houses, but a dozen people remained for supper on Khushiman's porch. By eleven, all had eaten. Khushiman ordered a second bed brought out on the porch—one was already there—and a search was made for extra pillows and bedding. The whole family bustled about in this pursuit, eager to attend to every detail of their guests' comfort.

When all was ready, Khushiman brought his hunting bird from outside, covered the cage, and hung it on a peg over my pillow: It was the bird's customary sleeping place. Then the family squatted in a semicircle on the porch and waited for us to go to bed. The faint light of an alcohol lamp played on their faces. We lay down in our clothes and pretended to sleep. The family watched on with unblinking eyes—motionless, shadowy forms. Were they going to remain all night in that position? There was movement in the cage overhead. I didn't feel free to shift the bed, much less the cage, with all the family sitting there; and besides, I was supposed to be asleep. Finally after half an hour, the family left, and Cynthia and I undressed and got in bed. I didn't forget, however, to make a slight adjustment in the location of my head.

Even then sleep did not come easily. Dogs growled and fought in the courtyard. At 2:30, the daughter was up working the *diki*. At 3:30 the wife began sweeping the porch. And at 4:00 the delicate endings of my auditory nerves were cauterized by a raucous scream from above my head. It was a sign to get up.

We left an hour later with smiles all around, having examined half the inhabitants of the village, many of whom had serious medical problems. Our porters were having problems too, it turned out: They both had bellyaches—from last evening's corn, they claimed, which had been overripe and underroasted. Overeaten would be closer to it.

We ate our morning rice at the house of an old acquaintance who lived in the next *panchayat,* and while we were there, the *pradhan panch* dropped in. He too was an old friend: I had removed three ovarian cysts from his wife, he reminded me; and though it seemed one too many to me, he was sure it was three.

Our path then took us by one of the old mission-built schools, long since handed over to the government. School was out for rice planting, and the place was empty except for a naked young woman who came out to see who we were. She was a "crazy" person, we were told, who lived in the school when the students weren't there, and who had been "that way" for five or six years. Such is the treatment of mental illness in rural Nepal.

For the rest of that day and far into the night, we met with old friends, former patients, and several people who at one time or another had expressed an interest in the Gospel. We saw them in their fields and on the trail, and we saw them after dark in the village where we stayed the night. It was a busy and rewarding time.

Next morning we had planned to leave early, though we hadn't planned to leave quite at four o'clock. A Brahmin woman had arrived early to be examined, hoping to be first in line, which she was. Plunking herself down next to our mats, she practiced her list of complaints on our hostess in the tones of a news commentator. Four times Cynthia asked her to be quiet and to let us sleep a little more, but she might as well have asked a radio to turn itself off. We finally got up, laid hands on the radio and a few others who had come in the meantime, and took our leave. If we had slept any later, we would have had trouble leaving at all.

That morning Cynthia and I had planned to split up; she and the two porters were to make a leisurely ascent of a ridge to the east, at the top of which I was to meet them for rice. Meanwhile, I was to detour to the west to visit a newly established health post, of whose existence I had only just learned.

Getting to the health post involved dropping down 1,800 feet to the Chepe River and climbing back up the other side; I had gotten directions the evening before. But the trail quickly faded out, and I was soon slipping down rice paddies and crashing through cornfields, with no one in sight to ask the way. I got down to the river all right but found it was high from the rain in the night. After several false attempts, I found a place I could cross and got over safely. I started up a little trail, but it seemed to be leading in the wrong direction. Just then, fortunately, I met a woman in a rice paddy and asked, "Is this the way to Majhebari?"

"*Ho* (yes)," she said, the way they always do, not wanting to disappoint you, and off I went, three miles out of my way and 1000 feet too high before I got steered back down again to the place I was aiming for.

"How did you get across the river?" they wanted to know when I finally reached the health post.

"I walked." They stared at me, as if unable to make up their minds whether I was really that dumb or only appeared to be.

When I was ready to leave, an arthritic old man, a former patient, insisted on escorting me back down to the river and even provided me with a strong pole with which to cross over. My arrival may have been out of their hands, but they had no intention of leaving my departure to chance. I was glad for the pole: This time across, I was much more aware of the current's power.

Breakfast was waiting at the top of the ridge 3000 feet up, and by the time I sat down to it, my drinking water and energy had been long since exhausted. Cynthia had spent the time profitably talking with *panchayat* officials and old friends, in addition to inspecting another health post that was located there. By early afternoon we were ready to move on, down the other side of the ridge to the Daraundi River, where we would spend the night. The journey was uneventful except for the last 1000-foot drop into the river gorge, which turned out to be the slickest and steepest trail we had yet been on, red clay, almost straight down without switchbacks. The trail was little used, and one could see why. If it had rained at all that afternoon, we couldn't have made it. As it was, we spent much of the time on our seats.

At the bottom we found an inviting stream, and sending our porters ahead to arrange for our night's lodging, we enjoyed the luxury of a bath and change of clothes, the first in four days.

Even as we were getting out of the water, a great storm rolled in, with darkness quickly following. By the time we got down to the river it was pitch black and pouring rain, and we had lost our way twice and were covered with mud. Our bath was but a pleasant memory.

In the morning we set out for Barpak. Cynthia hadn't wanted to go to Barpak. The walking was treacherous, the journey tiring, the season awful. Besides that, most of the people we knew had moved elsewhere, we'd heard. What was the point in killing ourselves if we had nothing to do there? In particular, we had been told that the little church had disbanded and was no longer meeting. Its leaders were gone. We'd be lucky to find one Christian left.

Perhaps for the sake of that one Christian we went. Also, once we were in Barpak, we could visit another village where a few of Cynthia's former patients lived. And still farther north we could visit an isolated government health post where a recent dysentery epidemic had wiped out twenty-nine lives. So we went.

The trail led for an hour along the Daraundi River. Here the river twisted through a deep narrow gorge, the roar of its water reverberating off the canyon walls on either side. Lush rain forest filled each nook and gully, and out from the cliffs great trees reached into the mist at peculiar angles, defying gravity. The path crept northward, first through a wood, then across sand and rocks thrown up by the river, later along a one-way ledge. Twice the trail crossed the river on Nepal's famous swaying bridges with their rotting wooden planks. And then up out of the gorge the trail rose, up the steep, winding rocky staircase that ascends 3,500 feet to Barpak.

It was drizzling as we began to climb. Puffs of cloud glided by, lazily brushing the upper reaches of the canyon walls. Trees of all shapes and sizes clung to the cliffsides; grotesque, gnarled trunks shot out horizontally and then turned upward at right angles. Great Himalayan mountain ash and *Langtang* pines were interspersed with bizarre fern trees with huge frond-like leaves. Black-faced, white-maned, long-tailed langurs gamboled through the forest, following us along on either side and chattering excitedly. The leeches were out too, and soon the telltale splotches of blood began appearing on our pant legs. And everywhere, the wild orchids bloomed—disdainfully called "monkey flowers" by the Nepalis but appealing greatly to Cynthia's fancy, nonetheless.

"Oh, isn't that a beauty?" said Cynthia, pointing out an exquisite specimen growing halfway up a nearby tree. She had addressed the question to Sher Bahadur, one of our porters. Sher Bahadur amiably agreed that it was even as she said.

"There are two there: Maybe you'd like to take one home, too." Sher Bahadur thought that would be lovely, and seeing where his duty lay, he obligingly climbed the tree and fetched down the two plants along with a quantity of moss, dirt, and roots to insure their survival.

"What are you going to do with that?" I wanted to know.

"What do you think? I'm taking it home. Besides, one of them is for Sher Bahadur."

"What makes you think he wants an old jungle flower?"

"He said so himself. I'm sure he appreciates beauty." Sher Bahadur's expression was inscrutable.

"I'd like to know how much he's going to appreciate carrying an extra five pounds of mud and wilted weeds up and down these hills and all over for the next eight days."

"I'm sure he doesn't mind," said Cynthia, demurely but firmly.

"Well, I mind," I answered.

"Oh, that's the trouble with you—all work. Nothing but work, work, work. Can't we have a little human interest on this trip—some feeling, some beauty?"

Beauty? Sher Bahadur was tying up the mud and moss in a plastic bag, and the melancholy flowers protruding from the top looked as if they were gasping for breath.

Just then a party of Gurung girls trooped by, and Sher Bahadur, ever gallant, quickly plucked the blossom from his plant and offered it to the prettiest of the group. With much blushing and giggling the girls passed on, and we resumed our journey, botanical acquisition tied in place and bobbing up and down upon Sher's back.

Listening to the brusque, stubby dialect of these northern tribal girls, we appreciated all the more the natural beauty and vividness of the Nepali language, the official language of the country. Rich in "sounding" words, mainly adverbs with no exact translation, the hearer can almost experience the action taking place without even knowing what the person is saying. The snake slithers *surukka* through the grass; the soup slips *salakka* down our throats. *Jurukka* we jump, and *phatakka* we fall. And when our intestines gurgle, they go *bulukh-bulukh, gulung-gulung*.

The language has a host of tiny one-syllable words—*nai's, ni's, na's,* and *ta's*—that have no intrinsic meaning of their own but can change the meaning of an entire sentence, often drastically. It's not surprising we misunderstand so much of what Nepalis say. It was all for missing a *na* or a *ni* that Cynthia was so sure Sher Bahadur wanted to carry orchids home on his back—which, incidentally, he carried without a murmur for the next eight days. The orchids weren't murmuring either: They were dead.

The rest of the morning we climbed in dense cloud. We only knew we were approaching Barpak by the more and more frequent piles of excrement lining either side of the path. And then, suddenly, we were there, the crude stone buildings looming up at us out of the fog—Barpak, with its twelve hundred houses stuck out on a narrow shelf of land two-thirds of the way up a 10,000-foot ridge.

We asked directions to the house of the one Christian we knew, Dhani Ram, an ex-Gurkha soldier who had served with distinction in World War II. He had first heard the Gospel in Britain and then again at Amp Pipal—once as Helen's patient, another time when he brought his daughter to be treated for burns, and a third time when he had a "water worm" removed from his nose. During that visit he had been baptized by a visiting Nepali pastor. Dhani Ram was now the leader of the Barpak church—if you could call it a church.

We found Dhani Ram at home. He greeted us warmly and invited us in. He explained that his son had become ill that day or he would have been out in his fields miles away, for it was the millet-planting season in the high country. After we had examined his son, we sat and drank tea and talked about the condition of the Christians in Barpak.

It was true what we had heard: The Christians had scattered for fear of the police, and the few Christians who remained hadn't met together in months. Some weeks back three hundred men had come at night to Dhani Ram's house and had threatened to drag him out and beat him unless he recanted his faith. He stayed inside and the men went away, but the memory lingered.

As Dhani Ram told us about the other believers in town, we could see his fires beginning to be stoked. "We must call them for a meeting," he said, pressing his palms together. "How about tomorrow morning early—at seven o'clock? We could go around this afternoon and invite them—if they're at home." The fire suddenly dampened: He had forgotten that everyone would be in the fields.

Maybe a few would still be at home, we suggested. In the end we decided to make the rounds of their houses; perhaps we'd find someone with whom we could leave word of the meeting. Yet that could be dangerous, too, if the word spread too far: Dhani Ram wasn't eager to have the police showing up—or three hundred villagers.

A drearier scene can scareclly be imagined than a walk through Barpak in the rain. Filthy narrow streets run between grim stone walls, behind which houses crowd shoulder to shoulder in long rows, suddenly ending, with nothing beyond but gray void and swirling mist. Though it's the biggest town in Gorkha District, Barpak has no high school, no medical facilities, no amenities of any kind such as are found in villages a twentieth its size. We did discover one sign of progress: a newly established tree nursery, from which 90,000 seedlings had been transplanted to the barren slopes surrounding the town. We came across a second sign of progress too, one perhaps of even greater significance: a new four-person public outhouse with automatic flush. A stream ran beneath the outhouse and carried everything off through the center of town. The four cubicles were on the conservative side, just right for children and adults without elbows. But it was clean, I had to admit; perhaps it had never been used.

As we had expected, the town was deserted; no one was on the streets. But before the day was over, we had met every one of the sixteen people Dhani Ram had hoped to invite to the meeting next morning. All except one had been at home, and that one we met coming in from the fields. Whether they all would show up in the morning was another matter. The field work they had neglected today would call all the more urgently tomorrow. And there were the police to consider.

The coals grew dim in the fire pit at Dhani Ram's house that night as we listened to tales of far-off military theaters, of battling Germans in the campaign for Italy, of fighting Communist insurgents in the jungles of Malaya. And at the end, as always, out came the war trophies: eight shiny medals with their multicolored ribbons. These were only replicas, said our host; the originals were on display in a military museum in Britain.

The replicas looked impressive enough, and we were led once more through the eight campaigns signified by the multicolored ribbons and the eight heroic acts that had won each shining medal. And the best was saved for last: The Cross of Saint—I forgot who—presented by Queen Elizabeth herself, for killing four men in one day. He showed us the photograph of the presentation, lovingly embedded in layers of tissue paper. I drew the lantern closer. When I looked up, there were tears in the old soldier's eyes.

As we sat there on the mud floor of Dhani Ram's blackened kitchen, these events seemed worlds away, fancies of the imagination, no more real than tales of Star Wars.

Or was it the other way around? The unreal part was being in Barpak.

"Do you know where I got my first wound?" Dhani Ram went on, after a silence of several minutes. There had been no mention of wounds all evening. "Right here in Barpak."

"Oh?"

"That's right. And do you know who gave it to me?"

We had no idea.

"*You* did," he said, turning to me with a playful grin, wrinkles showing up all over his face.

I hadn't a clue what he was talking about.

"Don't you remember the vasectomy camp you held here nine years ago—the first one we ever had in Barpak? I was the very first person to step forward. I led all the others."

I didn't reply at once. I had this absurd vision of Dhani Ram leading a charge of his fellow townsmen against an invading force and ending up with scalpel wounds of the scrotum. "Oh yes, I remember the camp well," I said. Dhani Ram was pleased, and the wrinkles spread across his face once more.

At six in the morning the people began gathering, and by seven o'clock all who'd been invited had arrived for the meeting. They had come one by one by various paths, passing unnoticed through the obscuring fog. We sat together on a second-story porch, with Dhani Ram as leader. We had only one hymnbook in the group, but we sang snatches of songs anyway, partly from memory, partly from whim, the energy of the singing being in no way dependent on the singers' knowledge of the tune or the words. Several people took turns reading from the Bible, selecting passages that related to their situation: passages exhorting them to be of good courage, to stand together, to oppose the forces of darkness that hemmed them in like the oppressing fog outside. Soon they were picking up the themes themselves. One man said it took only a tiny candle to overcome the darkness in an entire room and that they were that candle. Another man said that the reason they were weak and frightened was that they didn't meet together, and he suggested they start meeting twice a week.

"That's right," a third man said. "The police can carry us off one by one easily enough, but what are they going to do with seventeen of us at once?"

"They won't do anything," another man chimed in.

One of the men, a former *pradhan panch* who had lost his position partly because of his Christian beliefs, began to speak.

He described Barpak as a city of darkness, and it was their calling and duty to rise up and with God's help transform it into a city of light. He said that they as a church needed to grow, not only in courage but also in numbers. Surely there were others who were ready to turn to God, and it was their job to find them, to bring them in, to prepare them for the struggle ahead. It would not be easy. They could expect persecution—far worse than they had experienced before. The Devil wasn't going to sit still with Christians pounding at his gate!

At the end of the speech we almost thought they might rush out and begin attacking the Enemy's stronghold without even waiting for the benediction. But they didn't. They prayed, with earnestness and fervor. And at the end Sher Bahadur, our porter, prayed.

From the beginning, Sher Bahadur had taken an active part in the meeting, feeling himself to be in a real sense an ambassador from the church in Duradada to the church in Barpak. In the course of his prayer he said how he had heard that there was no longer any church at Barpak, that the believers had scattered. He had come with no expectations. But now all that had changed. He thanked God that here, indeed, was a church, and that it was very much alive. And on behalf of the Duradada Christians he prayed for God's blessing and power to fall upon the brothers and sisters in Barpak. When he was done, the meeting ended. It had lasted two and a half hours.

We lightened Sher Bahadur's load by fifteen pounds that morning as we passed around the literature we had brought, and when we took our leave of that little congregation, it would have been hard to tell whose hearts had been more uplifted, theirs or ours.

If Barpak was from another world, we were soon to arrive in a place that was even more so. Another 3000 feet up a zigzaggy stone stairway and down the other side lay Laprak, a village straight out of *Grimm's Fairy Tales*. And the otherworldliness of the place was no doubt enhanced by its lying at the other end of six hours of solid fog in which we could see nothing but the trail extending a few yards ahead.

fifteen

One comes on Laprak suddenly, even without the mist. Around a little bend—and there it is, five hundred houses jammed and jumbled together on a sloping ledge jutting from an otherwise endless length of steep mountainside. The ledge drops off abruptly into an awesome chasm 3000 feet down, and the lower houses of the village give the unsettling impression that they are ready at any moment to slide off the edge into the void beneath.

This town would have made the worst slums of Dickens' London look like the Emerald City. The awkward stone houses were piled every which way, and the irregular winding alleys between them are so narrow, you had to walk sideways to avoid brushing the walls. The walls themselves were seldom straight: some slanted in, some slanted out, some slanted in both directions as if the builder had been of two minds. Sometimes a whole house slanted this way or that and looked about to collapse. The roofs were made of wooden slats held down by large stones. There were no windows. Foul reeking buffalo pens extended off cluttered porches. We wondered where in this town we were going to sleep.

Even in the pouring rain the smell of sewage hung in the air. The paths were muddy rivulets of filth, washing away the waste of the town. We passed the main village spring: We would have been hesitant to wash our feet in its water much less drink it. Even our porters began to complain, suggesting we move on to the next town for the night. They didn't know the next town was five hours away.

If Laprak was novel to us, we were equally novel to its inhabitants. Foreigners seldom reached this far. We immediately attracted a crowd of children of all ages and degrees of dirtiness, some carrying younger brothers and sisters on their backs. They clamored around us, pushing and shoving to get closer, chattering away in their local language until one of them would spy the withered orchids with their dangling seed pots swinging solemnly back and forth, and suddenly the crowd would grow silent, respectful, as if awed by this testimony to the fleetingness of life.

We had come to Laprak to see three people in particular. One was a former patient of Cynthia's, a twenty-year-old woman named Ran Maya, who had been so desperately sick that Cynthia had given up hope five separate times during her hospital stay. The fifth time, with the mother's permission, Cynthia had removed the animistic charm from around Ran Maya's neck, and from that day on the young woman had begun to recover. Ran Maya spoke no Nepali, so Cynthia communicated with her through her mother. Together they stayed three months in the hospital, at the end of which time the daughter had been carried home to Laprak, a four-day journey, by one of the Christians from the Duradada church. Then a year and a half later, fully recovered, Ran Maya heard that Cynthia was leaving on furlough and walked four days to Amp Pipal to say good-bye to her and bring her a gift of eggs, potatoes, and two live chickens carried in a basket on her back.

The second person we hoped to see was a *panchayat* council member named Nanda Lal, whose daughter Cynthia had treated for tuberculosis. The third person was a schoolteacher named Bishnu, whom Cynthia had heard about through a mutual friend.

We asked directions to the houses of the three people, but no one understood our questions, or if they did, they didn't know the answers. We were halfway into the village before we finally found an adult who was able to point out where they lived. But the council member and the schoolteacher were not at home, so we continued on to Ran Maya's house, at the very lowest end of the village.

We arrived with our entourage of forty children at a tiny, squalid one-room dwelling, and there on the porch we found Ran Maya, nursing a new baby. It had been over two years since she had made that last trip to Amp Pipal, and she looked at Cynthia as if she were seeing an apparition. Then came those quiet and beautiful moments, first of recognition, then of uncertainty, then finally of realization that indeed it was Cynthia, and that she had come. Then Ran Maya, laying aside her baby, got up and went to Cynthia and embraced her.

fifteen

When Cynthia asked about Ran's mother, Ran told her she was in the house deathly ill. When we went inside, we found the mother lying on a straw mat in front of the fire pit, too sick even to change position, a breathing corpse. Cynthia knelt down beside the mat and examined her.

"There's nothing more to do," Cynthia said. "She's too far gone."

"We can pray," suggested Sher Bahadur, who had come inside, along with most of the children and a number of curious adults.

"Would you like us to pray for her?" Cynthia asked, looking first at Ran Maya and then at her father. We never prayed aloud for a patient without first asking for the family's permission.

They agreed, and both Cynthia and Sher Bahadur laid their hands on the sick woman and began to pray, first one and then the other. The fifty people in the room pushed forward, straining to hear. When the prayers were finished, we went outside, and there waiting for us were Nanda Lal, the council member, and the schoolteacher, Bishnu. They had heard we were at Ran Maya's house and had come looking for us. Nanda Lal immediately invited us to stay with him for the night, which we were happy to do. In the meantime, Bishnu asked us to her house for tea.

Bishnu, it turned out, was eager to talk about our religion and had many questions. When I asked her where she had gotten her interest in Christianity, she promptly said, "From Dr. Cynthia."

"How's that?" Cynthia asked. "We have never met."

"That's true," replied Bishnu. "But you once sent Ran Maya a letter in Nepali telling her something about your God. Since she can't read, she brought the letter to me, and I read it to her and became interested in what you wrote."

"What did I write?" said Cynthia, unable to recall exactly.

"You wrote that God had saved Ran Maya's body but that He could also save her soul and forgive her sins. When I read that, I wanted to learn about this God myself."

Cynthia promised to meet with Bishnu again later that night at Nanda Lal's house. But for now a crowd of people had gathered outside the door, asking us to come to their homes to examine the sick. So for the next two hours we visited a score of houses, accompanied wherever we went by children, adults, dogs, and goats. The people we saw were seriously ill; they couldn't have gotten up to come to us. We saw patients with tuberculous joints, tuberculous spines, bacterial meningitis, and fulminating typhoid fever. One man had his entire genitalia replaced by a massive fungating cancer, beyond hope of cure. And so it went, up and down the narrow twisting alleys, around the backs of houses, through pools of muck, and at the end the scene was always the same: the blind, the lame, the dying, in their dismal corners, without hope, too far from help.

That night Nanda Lal fed us abundantly from his meager store of rice. Laprak is an impoverished village, and its *panchayat* leaders share in its poverty. Not only that, the rice had been carried up four days from the south; and knowing what that involved, we could hardly enjoy it. It was potatoes we should have eaten; they were the staple here. Rice was as dear as caviar.

Yet this was the striking characteristic of these people: Desperately poor, desperately backward, they were among the most gracious and generous people we had ever met. Not a patient we saw but that the family didn't offer us food to take with us—they had no money. We would have had to hire another porter had we accepted it all. Ran Maya's father brought us a sack each of soybeans and popcorn. Nanda Lal, not content to stuff us with rice, loaded us up with eggs and potatoes for the next day—and the day after. People brought cauliflower and cucumbers, onions and eggplants, and we had done hardly anything for them. It would seem the poorer the person, the less calculating the generosity. The rich Brahmins to the south had never treated us so lavishly.

We talked with our friends late into the night. After a short but sound sleep, we woke in the morning to find a line of patients waiting to see us. We gave out our supply of medicines right and left: medicines for worms, amoeba, typhoid, for eyes, ears, and skin. And we gave out our books and pamphlets, including Laprak's first Bibles. At nine o'clock, after warm farewells, we left the town and our friends behind.

"We're late again, as usual," I said to Cynthia as we headed out into the third straight day of rain. "But fortunately we don't know anybody in this next village, and nobody knows us. We can see the health post in an hour and be at the Gandaki River by nightfall."

Indeed, we knew no one from the next village. I had been to Laprak twice before, but I had never gone beyond. It was fun to get into new territory for once. We made good time and got to the village at one o'clock. And while our porters were cooking up some of the food we had brought with us, Cynthia and I went up to survey the health post.

Three "peons" constituted its entire staff; there were no trained medical personnel. There was very little medicine, either, but the peons played doctor with what there was, "treating" up to a dozen patients a day. The one piece of equipment we found was a stethoscope lying in a drawer with a pack of playing cards, both ear pieces plugged with caterpillar cocoons. Indeed, stethoscopes can be a hazard in Nepal; I once had a spider crawl out of the tubing into my ear. Better caterpillars than spiders, anyway.

The major anomaly in the health post was a cupboard full of intravenous solution, fifty bottles of it, lugged up on the backs of porters at the time of the dysentery epidemic two months earlier. Reports of the epidemic had been so alarming that the assistant minister of health had flown out from Kathmandu in a helicopter to inspect the situation. The helicopter, unfortunately, wasn't able to land on the steep terrain and had to turn around and fly back. But at least he had made the effort. The year before a dysentery epidemic had wiped out over fifty lives in Laprak, but word apparently never got out.

While we were at the health post, we heard that the *pradhan panch* wanted to see us. This was odd because all the *pradhan panches* were supposed to be in the district capital that week for their annual wingding. As we walked to the teashop to meet him, we wondered what he wanted.

"Welcome to Gumda," he said with a broad smile. "I heard that you had arrived. I'm so happy you've come to our village." It seemed an overwarm welcome to offer two perfect strangers passing through town.

We thanked the *pradhan panch* for his welcome and said we were glad to be here. We told him that he had a beautiful town, which, after Laprak, was the emphatic truth.

We sat down on straw mats at the front of the teashop. The *pradhan panch* leaned forward, and looking closely at me, said: "Don't you recognize me?"

Those are always bad moments. I resorted to my usual ploy. "Ah, why yes . . . I think . . . I think perhaps I do. Where have I seen you before? At the hospital surely." I hadn't a clue. I couldn't recall ever seeing the man before.

He pulled up his shirt. There on his plump belly was a fine white line extending from his xiphoid to below his umbilicus. A few faint stitch marks were visible on either side. I looked at the scar. It was mine, all right; I have a special way of sliding past the belly button, and I can tell if it's mine in a jiffy.

Sher Bahadur sucked in his breath. "How can anyone survive after being cut open that far?" he asked no one in particular.

I couldn't remember ever meeting a patient from Gumda before—much less operating on one—and the *pradhan panch* at that. Gumda, I had thought, was beyond our reach.

"What is your name?" I asked the *pradhan panch,* as if that was going to help any.

It didn't.

"What illness did you have?" I tried again.

The man was obviously disappointed. "My stomach was blocked," he said, "and you opened it up. That was five years ago. I weighed forty kilos then. I hadn't eaten in months. You gave me forty intravenous bottles, and said that in another week I would have been dead. It was true. Now I weigh eighty kilos."

No wonder I hadn't recognized him. I felt better. He hadn't been *pradhan panch* then either, he said. Straining hard, I began to think perhaps maybe I did remember him after all.

He told us he was grateful to the doctors at Amp Pipal for

having saved his life. We accepted his gratitude but said we had not healed him, it had been God's work. We treated; God healed. The man said he had heard something about God at the hospital and was eager to learn more. Did we have anything he could read? Sher Bahadur had already begun opening the pack.

We talked as we ate our meal, and afterward the *pradhan panch* asked if we would examine some patients. We could hardly refuse, especially since the health post had no medical worker. For the next hour and a half we examined the thirty patients who had gathered, and then we made a few house calls. We finished at four o'clock, with just enough time remaining to reach our next destination by dark. We said we would try to return some day and spend more time, and the *pradhan panch* said he hoped we could do so. With that, we set out for our next stop, the Bhudi Gandaki River.

Ahead of us was a descent of nearly 5000 feet. The first part of the trail led along alpine meadowland, offering from time to time grand prospects of the river gorge before us. High above and all around rose an immense cragged wall of somber gray, extending upward into the clouds, while in front of it the piled-up land tumbled wildly down into the great black chasm of the river. The descent began abruptly, becoming steeper as we went. A man we met showed us a shortcut down to the river: He said we would not make it the long way around before dark. Our porters decided to take it. They knew of a little "hotel" at the bottom, and they were eager to reach it.

The shortcut dropped off into some corn terraces, a tiny mud track twisting back and forth along the rows and in and out between the stalks. At the beginning the terraces were four rows wide, but before long they had narrowed to two rows, with eight-foot drops between. What a place to plant corn, we thought, so far from anyone's home, so steep; these people had to be desperate to plant such hillsides. Soon we were jumping down from terrace to terrace and had lost all semblance of a trail. Dusk had fallen. It was still 1,500 feet to the bottom, with the steepest part to come.

Our porters realized they had made a mistake. Somewhere

700 or 800 feet up, the real trail had gone off in another direction. Now we had reached a place where we could proceed no further. The cornfields had ended, and the ground ahead plunged straight off into the river gorge below.

As we wandered to the right and left, looking for a way down, we saw a tiny tent made out of straw matting. We had seen many similar structures during our journeys in the high country, but invariably they had been empty. They were used at certain times of the year as a shelter for shepherds grazing their animals. To our amazement, as we approached the tent, a man came out, equally amazed, I'm sure, to see us at that hour. He readily agreed to show us the way down the cliff; if we hurried, we could get down the dangerous part before it was completely dark. After that, we could use our flashlights the rest of the way.

It was a path a mountain goat might have found congenial. Slick with evening dew, it was in many places only six inches wide, with sheer drop-offs of hundreds of feet. Our porters got down surprisingly well, and our guide held on to Cynthia as she inched her way across the difficult sections. In half an hour we were over the worst of it, and our guide returned up the path to his tent, ten rupees (sixty cents) the richer for his trouble. (In Nepal even God's angels need money.) We descended the rest of the way by flashlight, and when we finally reached the main trail running along the river, we found the hotel we had hoped to stay at only twenty yards off. The next nearest hotel in either direction was two hours away.

The hotel was a quaint establishment set on the edge of a narrow ribbon of land that fell off precipitously into the river below. It was built of bamboo strips lashed loosely together, and its see-through walls, like vertical venetian blinds, invited fresh currents of air to flutter in and carry away the stale humidity of the evening. The place was tidy too, and the mud floor was as clean as a mud floor can be, especially in the dark.

Our proprietress was a pretty, young Gurung woman, who at first tried to dissuade us from staying. A band of robbers was abroad, she explained, fourteen in all, who would likely be attracted by two foreigners—though surely no robber had been around to witness our unorthodox descent. Only last month, she said, three Japanese trekkers had been robbed of all they owned right in her hotel, and she didn't want it to happen again. We started to scoff at the danger, but then remembered the Italian trekker who had been shot to death by robbers just below the Amp Pipal Hospital only two months earlier. Before then, such acts of violence toward foreigners had never occurred in the placid hills of Gorkha District.

After serving us a few rounds of tea, however, our hostess began to warm up, and the prospect of flirting for the evening with two handsome Tamangs soon dispelled her fear of robbers. She fixed us a meal, and after we had eaten, we settled down for the night and were soon asleep.

Well, not quite. The "no-see-ums"—little bugs that crawl into your pores—were out that night, and none of us slept more than an hour. In any event, the robbers didn't turn up; if they had, we'd have been wide awake and ready for them.

One of Nepal's major rivers, the mighty Gandaki, flows southward from the Tibetan border, collecting along the way the melt-off of a dozen glaciers and the waters of a thousand tributaries. Beginning north of the great mountains at almost 20,000 feet, the river cuts a tortuous course through the very heart of the Himalayas, gathering force and volume as it rushes down into the plains of India to spend its muddy energy in the blue waters of the Bay of Bengal.

After three days and nights of rain, the river had become a frenzied giant, white and brown, heaving itself up and running over on its mad race down the twisting canyon. For all the next day, the river was to be our traveling companion; together we had twenty-five miles to go. The day itself, even in the first gray light, promised to be hot and muggy, and the sun at seven o'clock made good the promise. We might have appreciated the sun back up at the higher altitudes; down in this steamy river valley it was the last thing we wanted. But we needn't have fretted: At nine o'clock it started to rain, and it poured for the rest of the day.

All day the gorge of the Gandaki River was a roaring carnival of shimmering, flashing, catapulting waterworks. Looking up and down the gorge at any point, one could see twenty waterfalls cascading down the 2000-foot cliffs, some mere threads of silver, others great noisy cataracts pummeling the rocks beneath. The falls came in every size and shape. Some falls we crossed partway up on long logs, the water rushing beneath, filling the air with sound and spray. One huge torrent shot out from the cliffside at right angles, like water out of a diversion tunnel. And in one spectacular panorama, we stood and counted over fifty separate waterfalls, all, as of one mind, pouring themselves into the great swollen river at their feet.

At midmorning we came on a poorly dressed couple carrying two sick children in their arms. When we asked if they had gone for treatment, they said they had tried, but the bridge had just been washed away and they couldn't get across the river to the health post. They were on their way home again.

It took them a few moments to realize they had met someone better than a health post. The children were seriously ill. Fortunately, Cynthia had with her the necessary medicine—which the health post probably would not have had. Without it, the children would surely have succumbed.

In a village a little further on we found other sick people in a similar quandary: no health post. So Cynthia held an impromptu clinic on the front porch of a teashop, and within a short time she had used up our remaining supply of medicine. For the rest she wrote "prescriptions" on little scraps of paper, to be filled at the nearest medical hall ten hours downriver.

Half an hour later we came to the washed-out bridge. It had consisted of a gigantic log, flattened on the top and laid across a narrow point in the channel through which the entire volume of the river hurtled with explosive fury. The water had simply risen too high and had swept the log away as though it had been a matchstick. About 100 feet below the narrows, in fact, we saw the log caught in an eddy, circling slowly round and round, unable to get back into the main current of the river. And across the way, high above the opposite cliffs, we could make out the tiny tin-roofed health post, a little fleck of silver on the gray-green slopes. This was one health post we wouldn't have to visit.

After fifteen hours of slipping and slogging through mud and sand, up and down the cliffs rising abruptly from the water's edge, we reached our destination for the night, a stifling bazaar town stretched out along a bank above the river. We checked into the only hotel in town, had our meal, and went to bed. Cynthia had a private cubicle to herself, while I slept with the porters. The rooms, as usual, were free. Village hotels charge only for meals, which at seven rupees (forty cents) for all you can eat isn't a bad deal. Of course, you do without amenities like running water and outhouses and beds and mattresses. Usually all that's provided is a straw mat. But other things come with the room too. This night a large rat walked onto my sleeping bag, assessed the situation, looked me briefly in the eye, and walked off with my sock, no doubt mistaking it for Limburger cheese. I left the other for him as well.

In the morning Cynthia got up and couldn't walk. Her feet were cracked and blistered from the wet sand that had accumulated in her shoes the day before. We decided to split up for the last four days of the trip, Cynthia hobbling back by a direct route to Amp Pipal, and thence to Kathmandu, while I circled off to visit three more health posts and the government hospital in Gorkha.

The walking that day and for the rest of the trip would prove no less harassing to Cynthia than what had gone before; for in this season in Nepal, the trails turn to irrigation ditches and sloshy stream beds, while the sky above assaults the traveler with its alternating regimen of rain and solar hot flashes. But in spite of discomforts, Cynthia had a satisfying journey back to Kathmandu, stopping many times along the way to visit friends. By the time she got to Kathmandu her feet were healed.

For me, the next day provided the unexpected pleasure of crossing back over the Daraundi River on one of Nepal's *twings*. One could say the trip would not have been complete without it. The *twing* in question was of recent construction, replacing a bridge that had collapsed the year before. But when I got down to the river, I found it was out of action. It was a newfangled, steel-cable *twing,* and in place of the old-fashioned wooden seat that used to slide along a rope, this one had a snappy (if rusted) steel cart suspended from two wheels that ran along the cable overhead. Here, even into the hinterlands of Nepal, the industrial age had penetrated! But a little piece of progress divorced from all the rest brings decidedly mixed blessings: Witness this *twing.* The old ropes used to rot, true enough, but at least the villagers could pull them tight. This steel cable, however, couldn't be pulled tight no matter what they did, so they had left it sagging across the river.

The cart was propelled by an operator who stood in the cart and pulled on the cable, hand over hand. This was quite easy going down the sag but a different matter going up. When the cart was not in use, it was tied to one of the cable posts on either side of the river. The reason the *twing* was out of action on this particular day was all too obvious: There was the cart, hanging desolately from the middle of the cable, ten feet above the churning, foaming water, and no way to retrieve it.

This was a bit of a nuisance, frankly, for it was already late in the afternoon, there was no place on my side to spend the night, and the next nearest bridge was four hours downriver. While I was standing here, however, a young lad came up and asked if I wanted to cross. When I nodded, he said, "Wait right here," and promptly went off, found a long pole, stripped down to his underwear, and proceeded into the water toward the cart. Then for the next hour, with a supporting cast of cart, cable, and river, our young hero was the protagonist of a tense drama, none the less engaging for its small audience. The pole barely reached the cart, the cart showed little interest in moving up the cable, and for the hero, one misstep meant a free trip to the Indian Ocean. Four times the cart almost reached the shore but then rolled back down again into the middle. By this time a small crowd had gathered on both sides of the river, and when finally the cart was secured to its post, a cheer went up in honor of the intrepid boy who had risked his life to put the *twing* back in business. The fellow's motive was plain enough: He was going to ferry the passengers and collect the fees—one rupee each.

I got into the cart and off we sailed, the two little wheels whistling over our heads. Indeed, the *twing* would be a fine idea for Knott's Berry Farm should people ever tire of Montezuma's Revenge. When we reached the middle, the cart slowed to a stop. Then the young lad stood up and began to pull on the cable, fairly effectively at first, but then as the cable got steeper, more and more slowly. Several times I thought he had lost his grip and that we would soon be spinning backward down the cable. But he held on.

We reached a point at which both of us together could pull no further. Six feet below and about three feet upstream was a large rock rising out of the river, from which other rocks led safely to shore. The lad said that he would hold on and all I had to do was jump onto the rock and I'd be home free. But would I pay him his one rupee before I jumped. I paid and climbed out over the railing of the cart. I was a bit encumbered with backpack, shoulder bag, canteen, and umbrella, but it was a big rock, quite impossible to miss. But then something happened that I hadn't anticipated. As I swung my weight over the rail, the little cart swung the other way and dumped me right out—something to do with actions having equal and opposite reactions—and cursing Newton all the way down, I landed in three feet of water just next to The Rock. All that resulted, happily, was a wrenched groin, a shin scraped down to the periosteum, and a good dousing. I thought I might have heard a cheer too, but it was hard to tell above the roar of the river.

My final stop two days later was the government hospital in Gorkha, six hours east of Amp Pipal. I reached town at four o'clock and went straight to the hospital, hoping to catch the doctor before he got off duty. Well, I discovered he was generally off duty at one o'clock and that was after starting at ten. Not bad hours. He was in his quarters on the hospital compound in a state of great excitement. A mad dog had been spotted on the compound a few minutes before and had come right onto his porch where his children were playing. He hadn't seen the dog himself, but he was in a panic nonetheless, because he had read in an article recently that a mad dog can give people rabies just by licking their skin.

When I arrived, the doctor was in the process of bathing his children from head to toe in disinfectant solution, and as soon as that was done, he started splashing the solution all over his porch as if he were swabbing down the deck of a ship. All the while he was shouting instructions at various hospital gatemen and sweepers to track down the dog and gather any information about it they could. Everyone who came by was sharply questioned about where the dog went, what it did, whom it touched, and so forth. When the uproar had subsided and these essential matters had been attended to, the doctor greeted me courteously and proceeded to ask me all I knew about rabies. Apparently the scare was legitimate: Two local people had died of rabies in the past week, and stories were circulating of other deaths as well. Add to this the furor in Amp Pipal the day before Cynthia and I had left for the survey, and it became a district-wide problem of serious proportions.

An hour later as I was walking back through town, I encountered the dog on the main street. A dozen little kids, whooping and hollering, were chasing it pell-mell this way and that, throwing rocks and sticks at it, and even attempting to kick it; in response the dog would periodically turn and attack his assailants, teeth bared, foaming and snarling. Meanwhile, the adults of the town stood safely in their doorways exclaiming "La, la! Oo, oo! Ah, ah!" and doing absolutely nothing to save their children from being bitten. I went to visit a few other people, and an hour later the dog was still being chased all over town; by this time several other dogs, along with a much greater number of children, had joined in the fray. Half a dozen times I met that wretched dog, and each time it was looking madder and foamier than before. The government doctor, for his part, should have been up and doing something about it, but no doubt he hesitated to step out in the same street with the dog for fear of tracking its saliva back into his house.

But then, in the doctor's defense, who of us has ever tried to kill a mad dog? Without a gun. It's a tricky business, and one, I'm sure, we'd much prefer to leave to others.

At about seven-thirty in the evening I went to Gorkha's large "tourist" hotel, which actually charges for the room, not just the meal. The hotel was mostly empty, so I had my choice of rooms. I chose one on the non-sunny side, where it would be cool and quiet. It was a bit of a luxury, a private room, but since I was exhausted from our travels of the past weeks, I felt I deserved a good night's rest without rats crawling over me or insects playing hide-and-seek in my pores. The room cost two dollars and fifty cents. I had a nice meal for a dollar; the price included four eggs I had ordered to restore my depleted cholesterol levels. At nine o'clock I went to bed.

I was just about asleep when I remembered I hadn't asked the hotel clerk to wake me in the morning; the one daily bus for Kathmandu left at seven-thirty, and I didn't care to oversleep. But I didn't feel like getting up just then either, so I asked God to wake me instead. Then I began to worry if He would do it; I usually relied on an alarm clock. I thought I heard Him say: "Never fear," so taking the thought for the deed, I went off to sleep.

Well, not really. Some junior officials from the Ministry of Cottage Industries were also staying at the hotel and were enjoying some well-earned relaxation after their official day's work. As Nepal's best brew flowed in, great raucous songs flowed out; and though I was three walls removed and had Mack's Finest Pillow-Soft Ear Plugs plugged tight in my ears, I could hear every word they were singing as if they were right in my room. Just before midnight they passed into the third stage of anesthesia, and the hotel was quiet once more.

Half an hour later I was awakened by an extraordinary altercation outside my window. About three yards off was a wooden shack that belonged, I presumed, to one of the hotel workers, and the row was coming from inside it. A man was arguing with a woman, and neither was getting the upper hand. I was loath to shut the window because of the heat, so I merely waited patiently for them to stop, figuring they couldn't go on at that intensity for long without losing their voices or murdering each other. Just as I predicted, they stopped after an hour.

Then it began to rain. Along with the rain came the wind, and by the time I awoke, I was soaked from coccyx to cranium. I closed the window, put my pillow where my feet had been, and tried to sleep. But I continued getting wet: A stream of water pouring down from inside the window casing onto the window-sill was splashing on me. I got up and moved the bed. Finally I dozed off.

At three o'clock I was awakened by a new noise. The rain had stopped, but the wind had picked up, a regular gale, and it was rattling the tin roofing of the little shack from which the altercation had proceeded earlier. After a particularly violent bout of clanking, I went to the window, shined my flashlight, and saw that one of the tin sheets of the roof had blown to the ground. I could see the others too, vaguely held down by rocks, flapping up and down in the wind. One by one, over the next hour and a half, the remaining five sheets blew off the shack, after which the wind, having no further reason for blowing, died away, leaving all in peace once more. It was time to get up. Rosy-fingered dawn had appeared in the east.

I paid my $2.50, thanked the proprietor, and walked up to the bus stop. As I walked, I thought I heard someone say: "Don't forget to thank Me, too, for waking you up."

And thus, with a yawn, the survey came to an end. In five weeks we had trekked almost three hundred miles, visited twenty health posts and thirty medical halls, met two thousand former patients and examined eight hundred new ones, talked with twenty-two *pradhan panches* and dozens of other officials, and met all but one of the seventy Nepali believers we had hoped to see—all this without previous arrangement and during the worst possible time of the year. It couldn't have been planned better had we tried—at least the daylight parts. As I waited for the bus to leave, I felt a deep sense of awe and gratitude and fulfillment.

It also felt good, for a change, to be on a bus. Even the Pashupati Super Deluxe Express.

A Change of Scene

sixteen

Living It Up in Kathmandu

I N 1985, CYNTHIA AND I began new work: Cynthia became medical officer of a large community-health program in the district south of Kathmandu, while I settled down to write a New Testament commentary in Nepali, a project that would take two years. Both of these assignments meant a move to Kathmandu.

Kathmandu was not the same city we had known fifteen years earlier, when we had first arrived for language school and orientation. The quaint mud and brick town of former times had been overrun by concrete buildings, exhaust fumes, dust, and noise. Greater Kathmandu had become a crowded bustling Asian city with a population of almost a million. It was a far cry from the sleepy little village of Amp Pipal.

We noticed other changes in Kathmandu. English medium primary schools had become the rage among middle-class Nepalis, and dozens of these schools had sprouted all over the city, with enticing names like Little Angels School, Precious Hearts School, and Future Stars School. One school was called Little GEMS, which stood for Graded English Medium School. More than once, passing by one of these schools, I have heard the children singing in English "Three Blind Mice" or "Old MacDonald Had a Farm," an unexpected touch of my childhood right in Kathmandu. Another touch was the sight of Santa Claus riding down one of Kathmandu's main streets—on an elephant.

But some things had not changed, such as the pomp and ceremony accorded royalty. A road crew at work was a likely sign that the king or queen would soon be passing by. A further

224

indication of an impending royal passage were the ubiquitous bright red arches spanning the city streets. These arches were forever being erected and dismantled, and by noting their placement one could chart the comings and goings of the royal family. The greatest profusion of arches, however, went up for the visit of Queen Elizabeth and Prince Philip. Every business and organization from the Nepal National Bank to the Nanglo Bakery was determined to put up an arch of its own. One of the proudest was a fine red arch on which was emblazoned in gold letters: "Rara Noodles Welcomes the Queen of England." They are pretty good noodles, too.

Our first task in Kathmandu was to find a place to live. This meant riding off on my bicycle each day to check out all the houses within a fifteen-minute bike ride of Cynthia's office. Up and down the streets and alleys I would go, and when I saw people out in their yards, I would ask them if they knew of any nearby houses for rent. One man responded by looking slowly around as if noticing his neighborhood for the first time and saying he didn't know of any, at which point I spotted a "To Let" sign on the very next house, the owner of which was out of town and wouldn't be back for a week. It was not an efficient method of house-hunting, but there was no other. After a week of nonstop searching, I had found only two suitable houses that fit our budget and were ready for occupancy. We chose one, but on the eve of moving in, we discovered that the landlord's daughter had previously rented the house to someone else. So we rushed back to the second house, which was still available, and took it.

I was secretly happy that the first house had fallen through, because I liked the second one much better. The neighborhood seemed quieter, and that was important for my writing project. A few open fields surrounding the house lent a rural atmosphere. And the house was brand-new, which meant everything would be functioning properly. The only disadvantage to the house was that it wouldn't be completed for another two weeks, and we needed to move in a week.

In this way we were introduced to the peculiarities of

Kathmandu's construction business. Our landlady, who lived on the first floor of the two-story house, had a keen eye for saving a rupee wherever she could. She had hired the cheapest workmen and used the cheapest material, and as a result she had built a penny-wise, pound-foolish house, the consequences of which she had figured to pass on to her tenants. No two lines ran parallel anywhere in the house. The hall, for example, was half a foot wider at one end than at the other. The carpenters evidently suffered from a loss of vertical and horizontal orientation, especially when it came to the door and window frames. Sometimes a single frame would start out in one direction and end in another. Bolts missed their latches by as much as an inch. Most novel of all, the carpenters had used unseasoned wood (it was cheaper), and two years afterward the geometric patterns were still changing, enhanced by the addition of curves and twists.

The painters must have had visual problems of their own. Cynthia was put off by the clashing multi-colored paint scheme, which she said was nauseating, but which I rather liked. One thing we did agree on was that the rent was higher than the flat deserved; but then the landlady had us over a barrel and knew it.

We were delayed in moving in for two days because the driver of the truck carrying our household goods was caught in a roadblock and had his license confiscated because of a faulty taillight. At first we were amazed at this unusual interest in traffic safety on the part of the Kathmandu police, but the next day in *The Rising Nepal* we learned the cause: It was National Traffic Safety Week. One of the main objects, the article said, was to control the bus "logjams," the great fight to get in or out of the buses at every stop. The article helpfully explained that "the front door is to be used by disembarking passengers, while embarking passengers are to use the front [*sic*] door." The policy continues to this day, as anyone living in Kathmandu will readily affirm.

We began moving into our new flat in the midst of the terminal exertions of the carpenters, plasterers, plumbers, and painters. Part of the carpenters' efforts seemed directed at demolishing the work of the other workmen. They were hard on the windows as well, breaking three panes in the course of their banging; these the landlady refused to replace because "they were only linear cracks." Planning and coordination were not part of the proceedings. Nothing was done in the right order. In Kathmandu workers get paid by the day rather than the hour; even if they work only an hour, they get paid a full day's wage. For this reason, workmen are never called to do just an hour's work; they come for the entire day. Thus each category of worker has to get all his work done on the day he comes, or else it never gets done at all. So the painters paint and then the plasterers plaster, and then the carpenters come—and the whole cycle is set in motion again.

The two painters were decent fellows who chain-smoked, and decorated all the floors with drips and drops at no extra charge. The chief painter's left eye was badly crossed, explaining why they had trouble with borders, sort of like the Russians and Chinese, and it was always hard to tell which side had won, the red or the yellow. They were also partially color-blind, which showed up when they were called back to repaint areas that had been replastered by the plasterers. They touched up the kitchen yellow with living-room pink, and dabbed on different shades of green in the bedroom; and if Cynthia was troubled by the preliminary coat of paint, you can be sure that she was more so on seeing the perfected work. I consoled Cynthia by reminding her that these irregularities of her new house were merely some of life's "givens"—like mosquitoes and leprosy—that one had best accept with good humor.

My own humor wasn't always up to the demands placed on it. The pink blotches on the kitchen walls got to me after a while, so I found some matching yellow paint and managed to eradicate the pink. Cynthia compounded the challenge by spilling half a bowl of cake batter on one wall of the kitchen, a trick in itself when you think of it, especially as the design she created covered an area a yard square. No matter how many times I painted over that design, it still showed through. It seemed that the paint, which is called "distemper" paint (distempered would be closer), didn't mix with the oil in the cake batter, and no matter how much paint went on, the oil cut right through it.

We even had trouble matching the white paint. The doors and window frames were all painted with Jensen & Dribbleston Limited's finest fast-drying, smooth-flowing, high-gloss synthetic white. I had actually saved one of the empty cans of this paint as a sample in case I had to do any patching myself and needed more paint. It was a good thing, because after a few weeks the unseasoned wood of the doors and windows began to tack and shift and no longer fit into their frames, all of this necessitating much sanding and filing away of Jensen & Dribbleston white enamel. So off I went with my empty paint can and bought the identical paint in the same-sized can. I wasn't going to risk getting a different shade of white from a different company.

But when I applied the paint to the fifty or so denuded areas I had created, it turned out to be different from the glistening white the painters had used; it was a new shade altogether, more like Old Pearl. With a second coat it had turned to Battleship Gray. I chucked the paint out after that, leaving the woodwork looking as though it had been torpedoed with tapioca pudding, a fitting memorial to the quality of Jensen & Dribbleston paint. In fact, down by the Bagmati Bridge on the way into Kathmandu, Jensen & Dribbleston Limited has a large billboard that says, "Whenever you think of color, think of us." Indeed I shall.

We had less of a time with the plumbers. In Amp Pipal our main plumbing problem had been straightforward: a repeatedly plugged septic-tank line that backed up into the bathroom when you least expected it. Here in Kathmandu the plumbing problems were more subtle: kinked pipes, leaky fixtures, flushers that didn't flush, and drains that didn't drain (because they were plugged with plaster from the plasterers). Once these matters were fixed, the plumbing worked pretty well.

Plumbing, however, implies the presence of water. Without water, plumbing is peripheral. One thing the landlady didn't tell us when we rented her flat was that the water dried up between

February and June. She had built her water storage tank above-ground instead of beneath (it had been cheaper that way), so whenever the pressure in the water main dropped, our water stopped. But ever an improviser, our landlady hauled out the drum that the distempered paint had been mixed in and hired a boy to fill it with water each evening. This distempered the water, and us along with it, but after a few days the taste of the paint was diluted away. It was not nearly so bad as the time the water department put ten times the proper dose of disinfectant in the city water supply; for a month everything tasted of potash.

The last job remaining was to connect the electric light fixtures and wall sockets. For this project, the landlady hired two surly, unkempt Indian electricians who couldn't have been over eighteen and who spoke almost no Nepali. The moment I saw them, I grew apprehensive. Just the way they sauntered up and blew their noses on the front stoop in the Asian fashion bespoke trouble to come. The two electricians had brought the electrical fixtures with them in a gunnysack, somehow managing to dent a third of them on the way.

The chief electrician's name was Bhim, so I named his partner Bham. They walked into the bedroom and said they would begin there. I noticed their hands were filthy and suggested they wash them before they got fingerprints all over the walls. They said it would not be necessary. Bhim had with him a large electric drill with one bit, three-eighths inch, big enough to hang our refrigerator on the wall had we wanted to. The drill was a menace. Bhim handled it as if it were a machine gun. He never bothered to aim it, but rather, teetering on a stool with drill spinning, he would lunge at the wall in the general vicinity of the free wires where the fixture was to go. Wh-r-r-r went the drill, filling the room with plaster and brick powder. After Bhim had driven the drill in up to the hilt, it would be Bham's turn to pound a sleeve into the drill hole and then chop it off flush with a chisel and sledgehammer. Yes, sledgehammer. These guys meant business. No wall was too tough for them. I mildly suggested that Bham saw the sleeves off in advance so he wouldn't have to chisel the walls, and to my surprise, he took my suggestion. But when he used our new wooden chairs as a sawhorse, I told him to go back to his first method. The chisel behaved as if it hadn't seen a sharpening stone in a decade, but when I offered mine, he took offense, so I dropped the matter.

I have never in my life come across two workmen with less respect for property and less care for the quality of their work. Walls were gouged, scraped, scratched, and fingerprinted. The fingerprinting was enhanced by the red-brick powder that poured forth from the drill holes. Drilling holes in the ceiling was even more fun, for the powder got in Bhim's eyes, making his aim wilder than ever; but, I'm happy to say, he got the ceiling every time.

We were given a respite in the middle of the afternoon when Bhim crossed two hot wires and blew the fuse for the whole house, upstairs and downstairs, much to the chagrin of the landlady. The fuse could be replaced only by the Municipal Electricity Department, and when they would come, no one knew. So Bhim and Bham retired for the day since they needed current to run their drill. They returned the next morning and finished the job, and our ordeal was ended.

Not quite. About three weeks later one of Kathmandu's spring winds blew up and began blowing through the cracks in the doors where the wood panels had shrunk and warped. The breeze inside was strong enough to blow one of Bhim and Bham's light fixtures right out of its screw holes. Two nights later the light fixture over Cynthia's desk fell out, even without a wind. Five more lights lost their moorings in the next two weeks.

In Kathmandu even the most routine undertakings have a way of turning into capital productions. We hadn't been settled into our house and into our new work very long before I received a request from the Zondervan Publishing House for some biographical material and a photograph of myself to use on a book jacket. Figuring they wouldn't appreciate an eight-year-old passport photo taken by the Krishna Foto Concern and having no other to send them, I decided to go downtown and have my picture taken at a proper photo studio. Surely Zondervan deserved that much. I also decided to get my hair cut at a proper barber shop on the same trip; Cynthia had been cutting my hair for the past fifteen years, but I figured this time I needed a professional job.

Getting into downtown Kathmandu from our house wasn't a trifling matter. To begin with, it was a thirty-minute bicycle ride. I had bought a secondhand bike from a friend at a good price, though he had not informed me that the seat would bite me in the *gluteus maximus* whenever I leaned to the right. We had about four minutes of bumpy dirt road to negotiate before hitting pavement, and I never did manage to get over that stretch without getting bit at least once.

Another problem with the bike was that the front tire held air for only three days. I had a pump, but the washer was shot, and I hadn't been able to find a new washer the right size. So whenever I went out anywhere, I had to walk the bike fifteen minutes down to the neighborhood bike shop to get the tire pumped up.

So it was on the day of the photograph. I had just gotten the tire pumped up at the shop when I noticed a little rinky-dink photo studio right across the street. I felt a sudden urge to go in there and have my picture taken and spare myself the thirty-minute bicycle ride downtown. I went over and looked at some of the proprietor's sample snapshots and wondered if he might have been staff photographer for a penitentiary. The "studio" contained two lights, a wooden stool, and an ancient camera. Deciding that Zondervan deserved better, I got on my bicycle and headed downtown. Besides, I hadn't yet had my haircut.

I was halfway to town, riding along minding my own business, when a Volkswagen passed me on the right and then suddenly cut left in front of me. The car's rear bumper caught my front wheel and sent me flying through the air. I landed on my shoulder fifteen feet down the road, ruining my best shirt, which I had put on for the occasion. A large crowd materialized. The driver was apologetic, especially when a policeman showed up, and he insisted on driving me to a hospital. I told him I was fine, that I was a doctor and knew all about these things and not to worry. The bicycle was bent up, but with the help of some onlookers, we straightened it out, and I was on my way again after no more than a twenty-minute delay.

After that, however, I found it difficult to steer. My right arm seemed weak, and ten minutes later my right shoulder began to hurt. I knew then that something was wrong, but it was too late to turn back; I was almost at my destination.

I spent half an hour searching for a suitable barbershop and finally found a promising one that offered haircuts for ten rupees (fifty cents). I went in, sat in the chair, and the barber went to work. He seemed to know his business, but I couldn't help noticing a peculiar twitch in his movements. Then I spotted the cause: The barber's nose was running. I had not seen such a runny nose in twenty-four years in the medical profession. He would take a few swipes with his scissors and then wipe his nose with his other hand and put it back on my head. No handkerchief needed. I distracted myself for the rest of the haircut by tallying up the number of swipes he got in between wipes. It averaged out at seven. It was as slick a haircut as one could ask for.

I rode over to the Daas Photo Studio. Daas had been the best studio in town when we were in language school fifteen years earlier, and after all this trouble, I was going to get the best. The studio was no longer where I remembered it, so I rode around for twenty minutes, asking where it had moved to, but no one seemed to know. Finally I stopped at a photo-supply shop and was told that Daas Photo Studio had gone out of business twelve years earlier. I was directed to a new and modern studio in the photo-studio section of town.

The people there were happy to oblige me, but just as my turn came up, the electricity went off in that part of the city. I waited an hour. I asked how much longer they thought it would be before the power came on, so they sent a boy out to inquire. Fifteen minutes later he came back saying only two more hours. Having learned in Nepal to double such estimates, I decided I couldn't wait. My shoulder was getting worse, and I feared if I waited, I might be unable to ride my bike home. I resolved to go back to the little studio I had seen when I first started out.

Having already invested six hours in this photo project, I was determined to get it over with that same day. I arrived back at the little studio at four o'clock and found myself in luck. Everything was working. We had some difficulty hiding the ripped and blackened portions of my shirt, but we managed. Zondervan will never be the wiser.

I concluded that I had either dislocated my acromio-clavicular joint or broken the end of my clavicle. In either case, no treatment was needed. Indeed, I was getting on fine until about three weeks later when I went out to throw a stone at the landlady's dog, that had been barking an hour under my window. My shoulder went "crunch," the missile went wide, and it was another six months before I could throw a stone again with any accuracy.

While Bhim, Bham, and Company had been terrorizing the insides of the house, I hadn't noticed the outside noises; but after they left, the real nature of the neighborhood began to manifest itself. For instance, the landlady's dog, Tiger, so sleepy and docile in the heat of the day, assumed a different character as soon as the sun dipped behind the mountains in the late afternoon, and I don't think he slept again until the night fog had burned off at ten o'clock the next morning. He was the biggest dog in our part of town. Before we arrived, he had staked a claim to the ledge above our bedroom window, from which he could survey the entire property and ward off all intruding dogs, cats, owls, and bats. Tiger had the best bark in the neighborhood, and his howl was even better. I would have named him Wolf, but as there are no wolves in Nepal, the landlady probably didn't think of it.

Tiger was not the only dog in our neighborhood. The owner of the house behind us also had a dog named Tiger. Then across the street lived Yapper, Yelper, Howler, and Woofer. The whole ensemble came to life after dark, ostensibly to guard people's houses but in reality to troop around and make a general nuisance of themselves. It was a nightmare in mating season when the dogs were in full heat and howl, after which one could look forward in due course to the arrival of little Yappers and Yelpers to add to the nightly chorus.

The dogs, however, played only a supporting role in the cacophony that enriched life in suburban Kathmandu. The day began with the roosters at between three and four o'clock in the morning. One of these roosters lived under our bedroom window until we ate it for supper one day; it had belonged to our landlady. Then at dawn reveille would sound from the army barracks three houses away. Then came the singing holy men, who would stand outside our door or window and sing until we either paid them or rushed out as if to throttle them. Next came the wandering mendicants, who carried little drums with them to let people know they had arrived. They shook these drums nonstop for half an hour if they suspected we were at home and ignoring them. Most consistent of all, however, was our neighbor across the street, a hulk of a man with a barrel belly and a ringing voice, who chanted his prayers for twenty minutes each morning out on his patio so that all the neighborhood could hear. Then, when Pavarotti was done, it would be news time on Radio Nepal, and half a dozen radios would crackle into action on all sides. In fact, our neighborhood was so well supplied with radios that we seldom missed more than a minute of Radio Nepal's daily programming from early morning to midnight; someone's radio was always on duty.

By eight o'clock the day would be in full swing. Royal Nepal Airlines' flight to Delhi would clear our house and roar off to the west, followed by the twenty-five other flights that would take off over our house that day. Trucks came up our dirt road, bringing sand and bricks for the new houses that were going up across the street and in the vacant lot behind us. Then came the merchants: the rag man, the old bottle man, the mango sellers, the cabbage sellers, the basket vendors, all shouting out their wares every few steps as they walked along.

Some days were enhanced by special effects. It is the custom in Kathmandu for particularly religious and well-off families to hire priests to conduct special services of varying lengths. The families place loudspeakers on their rooftops to amplify the chanting and singing. The larger the loudspeaker and the higher the volume, the more merit accrues to the person putting on the service. These services last one, three, five, seven, or nine days, depending on how much people are ready to pay for such things, and hence they are called "one-ers," "three-ers," "fivers," "seven-ers," and "niners." The service continues without interruption except for four hours of respite between two and six o'clock in the morning, when everyone in the neighborhood goes to sleep. One never knows in advance how many days a service will last. One of the tensest moments comes at the end of the first twenty-four hours of one of these affairs, when you wait to see if the loudspeakers will continue. An even worse moment comes at the end of three days, and a still worse one at the end of five.

Perhaps you're wondering why I didn't just shut the windows. Well, first of all, during the hot season we needed air, as anyone who has lived directly under a flat cement roof with no air conditioning will tell you. Second, shutting the window didn't help anyway. Our landlady had bought the very cheapest glass: It didn't block sound waves, it merely passed them on. In fact, some frequencies—small barking dogs and sopranos on Radio Nepal—actually pick up volume as they pass through our window panes.

However, all these disturbances were nothing compared to those that arose from the big house standing right outside my study window. When we had moved into our apartment, the house had stood silent and vacant—but not for long. I had comfortably settled into the work of writing the commentary when two large trucks loaded with tables and sewing machines arrived at the big house. Forty Indian tailors, none of whom spoke a word of Nepali, had come to set up a garment factory. They all lived, ate, and slept right in the big house. It wasn't just their machines that produced noise; their radios and midnight video parties produced even more.

Every morning at three o'clock a van came to collect the previous day's work, and the driver invariably had to spend minutes honking his horn and banging on the front gate to arouse the stuporous gateman. I suspect all the tailors were deaf

because I never once heard them speak in a normal tone of voice.
Or maybe they were just in the habit of shouting in order to be
heard above the noise of their machines. That's the excuse they
gave me for turning up their radios full volume. It was futile to
plead with the manager for silence because he was louder than
anyone else. He spent most of the day yelling at his tailors, or
yelling into the phone as if he didn't trust the wires to carry his
voice.

We were thankful, at least, that the tailors weren't carpenters
or boiler makers, or—dreadful to contemplate—that the garment factory wasn't a boarding school. Thankful though we may
have been, it was a relief six months later when the tailors moved
out and silence once again descended on the big house. For
about one month.

We had been hearing the rumors for days, but then the awful
moment of truth arrived in the form of thirty rambunctious six-
year-olds. Yes, the big house had become a boarding school. It
was a high-class school, a special project of the queen to foster
appreciation of Hindu culture and religion. Every morning at
6:30 sharp the school day began with a half-hour of calisthenics
on the fifteen-by-twenty-foot patch of lawn that lay just over the
wall beneath my window. The exercises were conducted by a
true enthusiast, who barked out instructions as if he were
training a regiment of Gurkha soldiers instead of a class of first
graders. I asked the man one morning if his charges were hard of
hearing that he should have to shout so loudly; he shrugged and
said it was just his style and we should be thankful we no longer
needed an alarm clock to wake us up.

We lived with the school for eight months. Most tolerable
were the four hours of classroom study, during which the
students would recite the alphabet, the national anthem, and
many other songs and sayings. But the rest of the day was like a
perpetual recess. Even my earplugs couldn't dampen the sound
of those thirty taut pairs of vocal cords.

Then one day we watched as the children, followed by their
desks, chairs, and trunks, were carted off to another location
with better facilities. For several months the big house was silent,

the grass grew long, and the only noise we heard came from the windows banging in the wind. We knew it couldn't last: The owner was looking desperately for renters. And he found them—again a school, but this time worse: a combination day school and hostel. The hostel accommodated forty older children, who went out to other schools during the day. While they were out, 125 primary-age children arrived at ten o'clock for day school and left at four-thirty. There weren't enough classrooms to accommodate all of them at one time, so one group was always at recess.

I don't know what happened to this school because a few months after it moved in, we moved out. Cynthia had completed her assignment for the community-health project, and I had finished work on the commentary—six thousand handwritten pages of Nepali script. I left determined never to take another writing assignment in Kathmandu.

Toward the end of our stay in Kathmandu, former president Jimmy Carter and his wife, Rosalyn, came to Nepal on a trekking holiday. We didn't find out about it until the final week of their visit, and then only by chance. We had been invited, along with some other guests, to our landlady's house for supper, and one of the guests, an obese, rumply man who mainly ate peanuts and raw turnips the entire evening, happened to be a recently released political prisoner. He was the number-three man in the opposition Congress Party, which had, at the time, been more or less outlawed. He told us that he had just been released from prison because of Carter's visit. He said that following a series of terrorist bombings in Kathmandu several months earlier, 8,500 members of the opposition party had been arrested, but just in the past week 7,200 had been released. Such is the influence of former American presidents in Nepal.

With two thirds of its national budget coming from foreign aid programs, Nepal's government is very concerned about its image. Holding too many political prisoners could jeopardize that aid, especially aid coming from a human-rights-conscious donor like the United States. No doubt the Nepali government overestimated a former president's influence in the American sixteen

government, but they were taking no chances. This fact was not lost on Cynthia. If Carter on a private visit and without opening his mouth could effect the release of 7,200 political prisoners, what might he be able to do with a few well-placed words on behalf of the oppressed Christian minority in Nepal?

Two nights later we had dinner with another missionary couple, Al and Peggy Schlorholtz. Al and Peggy were great Carter fans, and they knew all about his visit. Peggy and Cynthia at once got onto the subject of arranging a meeting with Carter, while Al and I, good-naturedly letting our wives humor themselves with these airy-fairy ideas, turned our attention to more weighty matters.

The next day Cynthia continued to humor herself by calling the American ambassador's wife, whom Cynthia knew. Mrs. Ambassador kindly informed Cynthia of the Carters' schedule. They would be arriving back from their trek on Monday (it was then Friday). On Tuesday evening they would be attending a state reception, followed by a private dinner with the king and queen. Then on Wednesday they would be leaving the country. There would be no time to arrange a private visit for ordinary citizens like us. However, the American Club was giving the Carters a public reception; did Cynthia want an invitation to that?

Cynthia wasn't interested. She and Peggy had their minds set on arranging a private meeting between Carter and several of the Nepali church leaders so that they would have the opportunity to tell their story to Carter in person. If the meeting could be set up for Tuesday, then Carter would have a chance to speak with the king that very evening. What could be better?

But how would they get in touch with Mr. Carter? Mrs. Ambassador suggested that Cynthia write to the Carters at the Soaltee Hotel, stating her case, requesting a meeting, and leaving her phone number. The Schlorholtzes had a phone, so that would be possible. Cynthia's only problem was that she had previously scheduled a week's field trip, which she would have to cancel if she hoped to see the former president. Was it worth canceling a tediously prepared field trip for a one-percent chance of meeting with Carter? Cynthia decided it was.

Al at this point ceased being a bemused onlooker and began to take an active part in the arrangements. Since the director and the assistant director of our mission were out of town at the time, Al was acting director. So Al offered to write Carter the letter requesting the meeting. Because Al, an American, represented the largest Christian organization in Nepal, Carter was more likely to be open to the invitation.

Cynthia, Al, and Peggy personally delivered the letter to the Soaltee Hotel on Sunday; Carter would get it the next morning. Meanwhile, they needed to contact three key leaders of the Nepali church. It is no easy matter contacting people in Kathmandu, especially as few have phones or motorized transport. They spent all day Sunday trying to reach the three leaders; two were found, but one was out of town until Wednesday, too late for the prospective meeting.

Then came Monday, and Peggy spent the whole day waiting by her telephone for the hoped-for call from the Soaltee Hotel. Cynthia and I didn't have much hope, and after receiving no word by nine o'clock in the evening, we concluded that nothing was going to happen. Cynthia began berating herself for canceling her field trip for nothing and thus inconveniencing not only herself but dozens of villagers who had had to change their plans too. But then at 9:30, Al and Peggy showed up to say that they had heard from one of Carter's secret service men and that a half-hour meeting had been set up for the next day, Tuesday, at 2:30 sharp. We were elated. At the same time Al and Peggy brought word that the third Nepali church leader had returned to Kathmandu earlier than expected. Now all that remained was to contact the three leaders and tell them the meeting was on so that they could prepare their case for Mr. Carter.

Not all Nepali Christians were excited about the meeting with Carter. For years both national and expatriate Christians had been ambivalent about the issue of religious freedom in Nepal. On the one hand, we all recognized that churches grow strong under persecution, and the Nepali church was indeed doing just that. On the other hand, government restrictions were almost certainly limiting the spread of the Gospel. Some Christians, both Nepali and missionary, didn't want to rock the boat and make things worse than they were. But most of the Nepali believers had finally begun to feel that it was time to oppose the government's stance on religion, which in fact violated the Geneva Convention on religious freedom, to which Nepal itself was a signatory. I personally felt it was time to take a more active role in ending religious persecution in Nepal. At that very time there were over one hundred Nepali Christians facing court cases because of their faith. Most of these were expected to serve time in jail.

We had very little time to get ready. That night Al and Peggy drove to inform two of the three Nepali Christian leaders of the meeting. The next morning I rode my bike to find the third leader, who was the head of the Nepal Christian Fellowship. He lived in a humble dwelling in a crowded section of town—such a contrast to the five-star Soaltee Hotel. He had no coat and tie, he said, so he would have to come just as he was. I then joined the three Nepalis to check over the wording of the joint letter they planned to present to Carter at the beginning of their meeting.

There was still a lot to be done. The letter had to be typed. The two other leaders had to go home and get dressed. The third leader and I went off to buy gifts for the Carters: a Nepali Bible and some handmade dolls. Then he and I went to my house for a snack while Cynthia wrapped up the dolls. I thought I had best look presentable myself, but my eighteen-year-old dress shoes, which I hadn't worn in months, had three big holes in them and looked pretty bad. We had no polish, but then polish would have done little for those shoes and nothing at all for the holes. It turned out not to matter anyway: when we later met Carter, he was wearing hiking shoes.

With great effort we all arrived at the Soaltee Hotel at two o'clock. The three Nepalis each signed the typed letter, and then we all sat down in the hotel lobby to collect our thoughts and decide who was going to introduce whom.

The Soaltee Hotel is an awesome place by Nepali standards.

The hotel had recently added a whole new wing, which was as large as the original building. The old lobby had been redone and was now resplendent with chandeliers, full-length wall mirrors, ornamented columns, and great red-leather armchairs. Along one wall were two elevators, old-fashioned relics that had survived the renovations and looked strangely out of keeping with the rest of the decor. They held just four persons each.

At 2:25 the twelve of us, now including several other American missionaries who had joined us, walked over to the elevators; we were taking no chances on being late. We were all a bit excited, it's fair to say. One elevator came down; it was empty. We had some difficulty deciding who should take this first elevator; we all tried to outdo the other in courtesy. We were men and women, young and old, Nepali and American. It took exactly two minutes for us to select the first four to enter the elevator. Just as the door was closing, one of them shouted, "Which floor?"

"Fifth," I quickly said, happy that I had thought to ask the desk clerk earlier.

These two elevators must have been among the first batch of elevators sent out to Asia by the Otis Elevator Company. The doors took forever to open and close, as if they had to wait for signals from company headquarters in New York. The first elevator creaked upward. Soon the second elevator arrived. It was 2:29.

It took less time to select the next foursome, and soon these had entered the elevator. "Fifth floor," I reminded them, as the doors crept together.

The first elevator had picked up some passengers on its way down. After an age it finally arrived, and the remaining four of us started to get on. But at that moment a bellhop who had been standing nearby asked, "By the way, whom are you going to see?" He must have overheard our animated conversation.

"President Jimmy Carter," we said.

"Well, in that case," he replied, "you are in the wrong building. He's in the new part of the hotel. These elevators won't take you there." It was now 2:33.

sixteen

I had a vision of our party pursuing each other up and down these elevators for the next half-hour—one group going up one elevator, while the group they were looking for was coming down the other. So we sent just two people up to find the first eight, while Al and I waited in the lobby to catch the ones coming down. Finally at 2:37 we assembled once more and marched off to the other end of the building, where a modern elevator that accommodated twelve people at once awaited us. The ride was so smooth that one of our party, a veteran missionary of twenty-five years, remarked, "In this elevator you hardly know you're moving."

Indeed it was so. We were at the fifth floor in an instant. We walked down the corridor past the three secret service men and into the Carters' sitting room only ten minutes late and were welcomed graciously by Mrs. Carter. Then the former president came in, friendly and cheerful, and he immediately put everyone at ease by his informality. He read the letter the three Nepalis had prepared and at once began to ask them detailed questions about the persecution of Nepali Christians, recording their answers on a small tape recorder. Both the Carters manifested genuine concern and sympathy for their Nepali Christian brothers and sisters, and they were deeply touched by the stories they heard.

Then Mr. Carter said that he would be having dinner at the palace that evening, and he promised to discuss the matter of religious freedom with the king. He would, naturally, use no pressure or threats, but he planned to tell the king that the persecution of religious minorities was a matter of great importance to him. He told the Nepalis not to get their hopes up but that he would do his best.

Then the Nepalis presented their gifts, and photos were taken of Carter reading his new Nepali Bible, upside down. One of the secret service men nearly backed out the window trying to include us all in a group picture. Then we filed out of the room and down the corridor to the elevator. The Carters had given us forty minutes; the time had flown by.

As soon as we were on the elevator, we all began talking at

once. We were jubilant. The meeting couldn't have gone better. The Nepalis had spoken eloquently. Their letter had been particularly effective. We recalled each significant comment that had been made during the interview. We projected into the future the likely results of Carter's meeting with the king. We fantasized about reversals of government policy and revisions of the Nepali constitution. We congratulated the Nepalis, and they in turn thanked us for having invited them. We recounted the extraordinary way in which God had made this meeting possible on such short notice. We rehearsed the many details that He had worked out and the frustrations and hopelessness we had experienced in the beginning, followed by the exhilaration at the end. Then the elevator door opened.

As we piled out, someone said, "Hey, this isn't the lobby." Someone else said, "This is the fifth floor."

The veteran missionary who had been so impressed with the smoothness of the ride up said, "We've gone down to the lobby and come back up without knowing it."

Someone else thought that we hadn't gone anywhere, which was the truth of the matter. We had been standing on that elevator for five minutes and no one had thought to push the button.

A secret service man was standing in the hall, trying to get an elevator for the Carters, who were already twenty minutes late for their next appointment. Had he not opened our elevator door, who knows how long we might have stood there talking? He suggested that we push the "L" button, which we did, with excellent results.

The next day *The Rising Nepal* was filled with pictures and accounts of the state reception for the Carters. On the following day the newspaper printed a long account of a press conference Carter had held the morning after the reception, just before his departure. Much of the article was taken up with Carter's statements in praise of Nepal's government, particularly in regard to human rights. (He was evidently referring to the release of the 7,200 political prisoners.) Radio Nepal and other Nepali periodicals confirmed this account. There was no mention of religious freedom or persecuted Christians. We were shattered. We felt betrayed. But then, three days later, someone showed us an article taken from the Calcutta *Statesman,* one of India's major newspapers. The last quarter of the article detailed Carter's press conference comments about the persecution of religious minorities in Nepal and how he hoped this would cease. He expressed his total opposition to any government policy that did not allow freedom of religious choice. He had come through for us after all, even in public! But because of press censorship, no one in Nepal knew about it.

In the months following the Carters' visit, we saw no discernible change in the government's attitude toward Christians. As the years passed, however, the predicament of Nepali Christians actually grew worse, and the church began to experience even greater persecution than it had before. But in spite of the dangers, the church continued its rapid growth. These Nepali believers had found in Christ something that their old religion and today's materialism could not offer—a new life—and they were prepared to suffer for it.

Revolution

"FREE PROF. MATHURA FROM JAIL!"
"STOP THE TORTURE OF PROF. MATHURA!"

These demands had been painted on the outside walls of the medical school in Kathmandu, along with other slogans, such as "Democracy or Death." The demands particularly interested us because Professor Mathura was the one who had invited Cynthia to teach in the medical school; he was to have been her boss. This was February 28, 1990, our first day back in Nepal for our fifth term, and we had taken a leisurely stroll to see the medical school campus. It was also our introduction to the Revolution, which is now history.

Within a few days the police had covered over the graffiti with whitewash, and the medical students were busy taking up a collection—to buy more paint.

In Nepal things rarely happen in typical fashion—including its revolutions. The essential framework was there, of course: an increasingly aroused populace rising up against an increasingly corrupt and oppressive government. But the quaint and colorful details were all hand-painted in Nepal.

I happened to be downtown two weeks after our arrival when word swept through the city that 50,000 protestors were marching toward the king's palace. I cycled over in that direction and was not surprised to see a troop of a hundred armed soldiers marching toward me. As I got closer, however, I discovered that the arms they were carrying were not machine guns, as I had supposed, but bagpipes. The Royal Company of Bagpipers was on parade—and 50,000 protestors were marching on the palace. Could General Ginger and the Army of Oz be far behind?

Day after day the crowds marched, demonstrated, blockaded roads, and burned tires, vehicles, and buildings. Flak-jacketed policemen patrolled the city, with reinforcements ferried here and there on cranes and dump trucks commandeered from the Department of Highways. Students held "pendowns"—that is, they put their pens down and refused to take notes in class—or they boycotted classes altogether. On days the students weren't striking, the teachers struck or held "chalkdowns." And in the evening, bands of revolutionaries and teenage delinquents spread through the city, ordering people to turn out their lights as a symbol of protest and threatening to throw stones through the windows of those who didn't.

The government, meantime, dug in its heels. There were sporadic shootings of demonstrators. Jails were jammed. On one day 800 university professors holding a protest meeting were arrested en masse. All news of the uprising was suppressed by the government-controlled press—or it was attributed to a "few criminal elements." The criminal elements turned out to include not only students and professors but also doctors, nurses, lawyers and airplane pilots, all of whom went on strike in succession.

Things finally came to a head on Friday, April 6, when the opposition parties called for a total nationwide strike. Men, women, and children took to the streets. Masses of people began pouring in from neighboring cities—Bhaktapur, Patan, Kirtipur—as if to relive earlier rivalries when these cities had been independent kingdoms. Surely someone in the crowd from Kirtipur recalled how Nepal's first king had spitefully cut off the noses of its citizens, and then gathered them into baskets and weighed them. The noses came to 146 pounds. That also is history.

By afternoon a crowd of 200,000 had converged on Durbar Marg, the wide boulevard leading to the king's palace. At the palace end stood ranks of policemen, armed this time with more than bagpipes. The crowd advanced. At its head was Cynthia's boss, Professor Mathura, just out of jail and wearing his long white doctor's coat. In a week he would be named the new Health Minister for his trouble.

In the middle of the boulevard stands a statue of King Mahendra, the present king's father. It was he who had outlawed opposition parties some thirty years before. The crowd began to pelt the statue with stones and bricks. This was too much for the police. They opened fire. By the time the commotion had settled, scores of demonstrators had been killed or wounded. One fatality was a British journalist, who was shot through the neck. No one is yet sure how many died that day because the police carted the bodies away. The official government count reported in the press next day was six dead.

That evening the king called in the army. Cynthia and I had gone out to catch the latest sidewalk gossip—the most reliable source of information available—but were quickly shooed back home: A twenty-four-hour "karfoo" had gone into effect, and anyone on the streets would be shot on sight.

At seven o'clock the next morning a sportily dressed young man with a battery-powered loudspeaker walked up our road, announcing that shops would be open for one hour. He was accompanied by four heavily armed soldiers, one of whom blew a whistle whenever the loudspeaker man paused for breath. At the sound of the whistle people poured out of their houses and raced for the shops. Within two minutes every one of the fifty shops in our area was besieged by ten to twenty agitated customers, each intent, it would seem, on buying out the shop altogether. And hundreds of other would-be patrons continued to flow out onto the main street from every alley and pathway.

In the midst of the bedlam, another group of soldiers with whistles came by, announcing that the hour was up and the shops were to close immediately. That provoked a logistical crisis, as hundreds of customers tried all at once to pay for the goods they had collected. How it all ended I'm not sure, but Cynthia got out with four bags of cornflakes, some tea, sugar, candles, and—what saved the day—two boxes of Brittania chocolate creme cookies.

Life under the curfew continued two days. Tourists were trapped in Kathmandu because the airport had closed down. Nepalis suffered, too. A young village woman carrying a load of grass in violation of the curfew was accosted by some soldiers near us. She panicked and ran, whereupon they mindlessly shot and killed her. Another man merely stuck his head out the window and was promptly shot in the eye. A child in our neighborhood fell off a roof onto its head. The parents, fearing the soldiers, kept the child at home, where it died a day later.

On the second day of the curfew, during the hour-long siege of the shops, a flurry of rumors swept the city, picking up additions and variations as it went.

"There's been shooting at the palace."

"The chief general has been shot and has been flown to Bangkok for treatment."

"No, it's the king who has been shot!"

"The queen has shot the king!"

And so the rumors flew. Then the whistle blew, the rumors ended, and the crowds headed for home.

What happened at the palace that day is not known, but at 11:00 P.M. Radio Nepal extended its usual programming to broadcast an important announcement from the palace. The king, the announcement went, had agreed to dissolve the rubber-stamp parliament, to dismiss his ministers, and to nullify the existing constitution. He also agreed to appoint an interim government made up of leaders of the opposition parties. It was a total capitulation. The last thing the announcement said was that the curfew was being lifted as of that moment.

Despite the lateness of the hour, no one, it seems, had gone to bed. The city erupted. People sang and danced on the rooftops. They ran out into the streets, where six were promptly killed by soldiers who had not yet heard the announcement. And throughout the night jubilation continued, together with preparations for a giant victory rally the next day.

In the morning the streets of Kathmandu began to fill with celebrants. From every hamlet and town they came, bringing with them copious supplies of bright red powder that they joyfully threw on each other and on anyone else who came in range. And they carried flags, flags large and small, of paper and cloth. Everyone carried a flag, from tiny children to aged grandparents. Cows and bulls had flags tied around their necks. People even attached flags to the hands of King Mahendra's statue on Durbar Marg, flags of the same parties he had outlawed thirty years earlier. The people must have been up all night making flags.

The flags, despite the variety of size and construction, were either the Congress Party's red-and-white-striped flag with its four stars (though many flags had fewer than four, signifying the night had been too short to sew them all on), or the red hammer and sickle of the united Communist parties. It was surely a sign of changing times to see large groups of Communists holding aloft their flag and chanting "Demo-crassy! Demo-crassy!" as they marched toward the center of town.

That afternoon Kathmandu witnessed the greatest gathering it had ever known. Three hundred thousand people paraded through the streets on their way to the Tundikhel, the huge open park in the center of the city. They not only walked, they also rode on jeeps, buses, and trucks. Trucks that only the day before had carried soldiers to their posts were today piled high with red-faced, flag-waving freedom fighters shouting, "We have won! We have won!"

But more was won than a political victory that day. Freedom of conscience and of religion also shared in the victory. The notion that Nepal's kings are Hindu gods may play well among the illiterate hill people, but among the rising educated classes it is scoffed at. The new political parties have promised to safeguard basic human rights and liberties. The leader of the majority Congress Party that has now been swept into power has pledged the rapid release of the thirty or more jailed Nepali Christians and the dismissal of the two hundred cases still pending against other believers. No longer will Christian literature be considered contraband. No longer will it be necessary to take all-night drives over the mountains to the

Indian border to bring back Bibles that have been tediously carried into the country in small parcels.

Victory day took place on Monday, April 9. The following Sunday was Easter, the greatest victory day in history. On Easter morning over 500 Nepali Christians marched through Kathmandu carrying flags with crosses and Scripture verses, singing as they went, and stopping from time to time to pray for the city and for the land. And three weeks later the Nepal Christian Fellowship rented the largest auditorium in Nepal and invited the Supreme Leader of the ascendant Congress Party to address an overflow crowd of 1700 Nepali Christians. The leader pointed out that of the four stars on the Congress Party flag the fourth star stood for religious freedom.

Indeed this is now God's day of opportunity in Nepal. The land is hungry for His word. The earthly foundations have been shaken; the oppression has begun to lift. Pray with us that the new leadership will rapidly deliver on its promises. Pray with us for the thousands of Nicodemuses who now need to come out of the darkness of fear and into the light of God's love. Pray with us that the church will grow as never before.

Afterword

And They Went

T HE CHURCH IN NEPAL will continue to thrive and grow even if Western missionaries have to leave. But that doesn't mean that the need for Western missionaries is over. The church's task of bringing Christ's light and love to the far corners of Nepal is so great and there are yet so few nationals equipped to do it at this point that the church will need help for many years to come. Expatriates and nationals are partners in this task. It is not a matter of Westerners helping out in the "Nepali" church, as if the church were owned and operated exclusively by Nepalis and we were called in merely to assist here and there. The church is bigger than that. We are talking, after all, about the church of Jesus Christ, a branch of which is now established in Nepal. All Christians in Nepal, both nationals and foreigners, are equally members of that church.

Of course, missionaries seek to encourage national leadership. National leadership is necessarily more permanent; missionaries may have to leave. Nationals know their people better and can usually relate to them more easily and witness to them more effectively. Yet expatriate Christians need to remember that it is their church too, and that they are equally responsible for its well-being.

Carried a step further, the church in Nepal is intimately joined with the church in the West, and Western Christians need to feel a shared responsibility for the church in Nepal, just as Nepali Christians need to feel a responsibility for the church in the West. One day the church in the West is going to be getting help from Nepali Christians, just as it is already beginning to receive help from other Third World churches. Both Third World churches and Third World missions are growing phenomenally, and in a few years their numbers will surpass those of the West. But for the present, most of the help still needs to be directed the other way. The young and persecuted church in Nepal needs the help of the affluent Western church.

On a worldwide scale, the imbalance between the church in the West and the church in the developing world is enormous. For example, over ninety percent of full-time Christian workers work in the West, whereas over ninety percent of the *need,* both physical and spiritual, is outside the West. And that doesn't count the majority of Christians, who are not in full-time Christian work.

Christ's church is worldwide; it knows no national boundary. Today some of Christ's people are hungry and persecuted. Others, such as Christians in India and Nepal, are surrounded by millions who have never heard the Gospel and whom they cannot reach without our help. Masses of people in the developing world live in abject poverty and face starvation daily. Yet we in the West are often more concerned with church politics, church buildings, and with enjoying the blessings God has so far bestowed upon us.

By far the greatest need around the world is spiritual. Spiritual needs are greater than physical needs to the same extent that eternity is greater than our earthly lifetime. And the need keeps growing. The world now includes more non-Christians than when the apostle Paul was alive or when William Carey sailed for India two hundred years ago.

The church is growing rapidly, but world population is growing more rapidly. Today over two billion people have never heard the Gospel, and what's more, the great majority of today's missionary force isn't even working among them. Reaching these "unreached people" is the most urgent task of the worldwide church. These unreached people are divided into thousands of distinct cultural subgroupings called "people groups." In India, for example, out of a total of 3000 people groups, only a few hundred have been effectively reached with the Gospel. Where are workers who will reach out to the remaining hundreds of groups who have no established church or witness among them? A proportionally similar situation exists in Nepal. Out of perhaps 200 people groups, we estimate that no more than 30 have been reached, if that.

We need to remind ourselves that the primary *purpose* of the church is evangelization, or, in the broad sense, missions. Every other activity in the church—worship, preaching, education, music, fellowship—should result in making us better witnesses, better missionaries. If the activities of the church do not do this, then they are not serving their fundamental purpose. The church is not primarily a hothouse for the nurturing of Christians; it is a training ground for preparing and sending missionaries, whether they are full-time or part-time, whether they work at home or abroad. Let the church recapture its missionary vision, and in particular, let it impart that vision to its young people. As Francis Xavier wrote back from India in the sixteenth century: "Tell the students to give up their small ambitions and come eastward to preach the Gospel of Christ."

The Great Commission is for all Christians, not just a few. Jesus said to His followers: "Go and make disciples of all nations, . . . teaching them to obey everything I have commanded you." We are the new disciples, and included in the "everything" we must obey is the command to "go." It is a command given by Jesus to every Christian; and as we contemplate where to go, whether to "Jerusalem" or to "Judea and Samaria" or "to the ends of the earth," our first thought should be to go where the need is greatest. If you see ten men struggling to carry a log, and nine are at one end and only one is at the other, you know at once what end of the log to go to if you want to help. Foreign missions is the one-man end of that log.

Ultimately, fulfilling the Great Commission depends more than anything else on one thing: the obedience of Christians. Jesus said; "If you love me, you will obey what I command." If we obey, the world will be reached in this generation. If we don't, it won't. It's as simple as that. Yes, it's essential to wait on the Holy Spirit; we can't do a thing in missions without Him. But if we are unwilling to obey Jesus, we will wait for the Holy Spirit in vain. Again, prayer is absolutely vital; it leads to spiritual revival; it releases God's power. But it does little good to pray if we are not willing to obey. Prayers must be doers. The same disciples whom Jesus instructed to pray for workers in Matthew 9 He then sent out as missionaries in chapter 10. God can only work through those who are obedient. People wait around for a missionary call. It's been given. It's been written. The missionary call isn't some sort of voice—it's a verse: Go, be My witnesses to the ends of the earth.

One of the greatest missionaries to India in the 1800s was Dr. Alexander Duff, a Scot. At the end of a long career in India, Duff returned to Scotland to die. But before he died, he was invited to speak to the General Assembly of the Presbyterian Church of Scotland. In the middle of his address, he fainted and was carried off the platform to an adjoining room. A doctor who was present examined him at once and told him that if he tried to continue speaking that day it would be at the risk of his life.

Over the protests of the doctor and the moderator of the assembly, the old white-haired missionary struggled to his feet and headed for the platform. With the doctor supporting him on one side and the moderator on the other, Alexander Duff climbed the steps to the pulpit. And as he did so, the entire assembly rose to their feet to pay him tribute. Then he said to the assembly: "When Queen Victoria calls for volunteers for India, hundreds of young men spring to the colors. But when King Jesus calls, no one responds." He paused; there was silence. Then he spoke again. "Is it true," he asked, "that the fathers and mothers of Scotland have no more sons to give for India?" Again he paused. Still there was silence. Then he said, "Very well, old though I am, I will go back to India. I shall lie down on the banks of the Ganges and die. Thereby I can let the peoples of

India know that there is at least one man in Scotland who loves them enough to give his life for them."

Then there was a stirring throughout that assembly, and men began to stand up, one after another, dozens of them, shouting out, "I'll go. I'll go. I'll go."

And they went.